D0141555

THE POLITICAL ECONOMY OF UNEVEN DEVELOPMENT

—— **ASIA AND THE PACIFIC** ——

series editor: Mark Selden

This new series explores the most dynamic and contested region of the world, including contributions on political, economic, cultural, and social change in modern and contemporary Asia and the Pacific.

ASIA'S ENVIRONMENTAL MOVEMENTS
Comparative Perspectives
edited by Yok-shiu F. Lee and Alvin Y. so

CENSORING HISTORY
Perspectives on Nationalism and War in the Twentieth Century
edited by Laura Hein and Mark Selden

CHINA'S WORKERS UNDER ASSAULT
Anita Chan

THE CONTENTIOUS CHINESE
Elizabeth J. Perry

THE POLITICAL ECONOMY OF UNEVEN DEVELOPMENT
The Case of China
Wang Shaoguang and Hu Angang

THEATER AND SOCIETY
An Anthology of Contemporary Chinese Drama
edited by Haiping Yan

NEW GHOSTS, OLD GHOSTS
Prisons and Labor Reform Camps in China
James D. Seymour and Richard Anderson

WOMEN IN REPUBLICAN CHINA
A Sourcebook
edited by Lan Hua and Vanessa Fong

Asia
and
the
Pacific

THE POLITICAL ECONOMY OF UNEVEN DEVELOPMENT

THE CASE OF CHINA

WANG SHAOGUANG
AND
HU ANGANG

AN EAST GATE BOOK

M.E.Sharpe
Armonk, New York
London, England

An East Gate Book

Copyright © 1999 by M. E. Sharpe, Inc.

All rights reserved. No part of this book may be reproduced in any form
without written permission from the publisher, M. E. Sharpe, Inc.,
80 Business Park Drive, Armonk, New York 10504.

Library of Congress Cataloging-in-Publication Data

Wang, Shaoguang, 1954–
The political economy of uneven development: : the case of China / by Shaoguang Wang
and Angang Hu.
p.   cm.—(Asia and the Pacific)
Included bibliographical references and index.
0-7656-0203-2 (cloth : alk. paper)
0-7656-0204-0 (paperback : alk. paper)
1. China—Economic conditions—Regional disparities. 2. China—Economic conditions—1976– . 3. China—Economic policy—1976– . I. Hu, Ankang. II. Title.
III. Series: Asia and the Pacific (Armonk, N.Y.)
HC427.92.W3843   1999
338.951—dc21   99-11412
CIP

Printed in the United States of America

The paper used in this publication meets the minimum requirements of
American National Standard for Information Sciences—
Permanence of Paper for Printed Library Materials,
ANSI Z 39.48–1984.

BM (c)   10   9   8   7   6   5   4   3   2   1
BM (p)   10   9   8   7   6   5   4   3   2   1

WIDENER UNIVERSITY
WOLFGRAM
LIBRARY
CHESTER, PA

Contents

Acknowledgments   vii
Figures and Tables   ix

Chapter 1: Introduction   3
  The Issue   3
  Debate   5
  The Significance of the Issue   7
  The Structure of the Book   11

Chapter 2: Theoretical Framework   21
  The Convergence Hypothesis   21
  The Inverted U-Curve Hypothesis   28
  Our Hypothesis   35

Chapter 3: Changes in Regional Disparity Since 1978   41
  Measurement   41
  Regional Disparity in 1978 and 1994   47
  Trends in Regional Disparity between 1978 and 1994   50
  Intraprovincial Inequality: Guizhou and Guangdong   60
  Minority Nationality Areas   63
  China in Comparative Perspective   67
  Subjective Regional Disparities   69

Chapter 4 : Multidimensional Facets of Regional Disparity   78
  Resource Endowment   81
  Economic Structure   92

Human Well-Being 107
Summary 128

**Chapter 5: The Economic Causes of Uneven
Regional Development** 143
The Proximate Sources of Output Growth 144
The Sources of Capital Accumulation 154
Summary 164

**Chapter 6 : The Political Causes of Uneven
Regional Development** 169
The Analytical Framework 169
Mao's China 171
The Policy Preference in the Reform Era 174
Central Extractive Capacity in the Reform Era 183
Growing Regional Disparities in Resource Distribution 191
Summary 193

Chapter 7: Confronting Inequality in China 199
Challenges 199
Rising Inequality Is Not Inevitable 203
Policy Goals 207
Three Important Relationships 209
Six Essential Actions 212
Summary 216

Appendices 221

Appendix 3.1 The Data 223
Appendix 5.1 The Method of Growth Accounting 228
Appendix 5.2 Estimating Provincial Capital Stocks 232
Appendix 5.3 Estimating Factor Shares 236

Bibliography 239
Index 255

Acknowledgments

This volume is partially based on a book published in China titled *Regional Disparity in China* (Shenyang: Liaoning People's Press, 1995). Although the original study has been almost completely rewritten for publication by M.E. Sharpe, we are indebted to our co-author of the Chinese edition, Dr. Xiaoguang Kang, who was too busy to be directly involved in writing the present book.

The current project started in late 1996. Over the past three years, many people and institutions have provided valuable support, advice, and practical assistance, without which this book would not have been possible.

We gratefully acknowledge the financial support from a number of institutions, including National Sciences Foundation of China, Ford Foundation, South China Program of the Chinese University of Hong Kong, Council on East Asian Studies of Yale University, and Washington Center for China Studies.

We would also like to acknowledge with deep appreciation the assistance of Qing Han and Shoulie Chen for data processing, and Anne Simone Kleinman and Mary Comerford for editorial support.

Thanks are also due to those colleagues who participated in seminars held in China, Hong Kong, and the United States, at which earlier versions of various chapters were presented. We are especially indebted to Professor Mark Selden, general editor of the series Asia and the Pacific, for his guidance and detailed comments on earlier drafts of this book. We have tried to incorporate as many suggestions and comments into the book as possible. Any remaining errors are, of course, our responsibility alone.

Shaoguang Wang
New Haven, Connecticut

Angang Hu
Beijing, China

Figures and Tables

Figures

2.1   Theoretical Relationship between
       State Preference and State Capacity   37
3.1   Per Capita GDP as % of National Average,
       1978 and 1994   51
3.2   Growth Rate vs. Initial Per Capita GDP, 1978–94   54
3.3   Growth Rate vs. Initial Per Capita GDP, 1978–85   54
3.4   Growth Rate vs. Initial Per Capita GDP, 1985–94   55
3.5   Growth Rate vs. Initial Per Capita GDP, 1990–94   55
3.6   CV Measured in Current Price and Constant Price   57
3.7   Changes in CV_w, With and Without BTS, 1978–94   57
3.8   Standard Deviation of Per Capita GDP
       (BTS included), 1978–94   59
3.9   Standard Deviation of Per Capita GDP
       (BTS excluded), 1978–94   59
3.10   Per Capita GDP as % of National Average in
       30 Autonomous Prefectures, 1994   65
3.11   Measures of Subjective Regional Disparities   70
3.12   What is the Worst-Possible Consequence That
       May Be Brought about by Excessively Large
       Regional Disparities?   72
4.1   Density of Transport Networks in Provinces, 1994   91
4.2   Industrial Structure in Provinces, 1994   96

4.3	Value of Fixed Assets in All Industrial Enterprises at Township Level and Above, 1995	102
4.4	Industrial Output by State Sector, 1994	104
4.5	Level of Urbanization, 1994	109
4.6	Per Capita Disposable Income in Urban and Rural Areas, 1994	111
4.7	Per Capita Consumption in Urban and Rural Areas, 1994	114
4.8	Geographical Location and Rural Poverty	118
4.9	Determinant of Mean Years of Schooling, 1995	121
4.10	Resource Endowment and Per Capita GDP, 1994	134
4.11	Economic Structure and Per Capita GDP, 1994	135
4.12	Private and Public Consumption and Per Capita GDP, 1994	136
5.1	Local Savings and Local Domestic Investment, 1985–95	155
5.2	Savings Rate and Per Capita GDP, 1978–95	156
5.3	Share of Centrally and Locally Channeled Foreign Investment, 1983–95	157
5.4	Provincial Shares of Accumulated Foreign Investment, 1983–95	158
6.1	Dispersion of Provincial Per Capita National Income, 1953–77	173
6.2	Central Capacity and Regional Disparities, 1953–77	174
6.3	Changes in Regional Disparity, 1978–94	179
6.4	Decline of Tax Effort in Provinces, 1978–95	184
6.5	State Capacity and Budgetary Investment, 1981–95	185
6.6	Sources of Fixed Investment Funds	185
6.7	Decline of Central Investment Control, 1981–95	187
6.8	Level of Development and Tax Burden	188
6.9	Dispersion of Provincial Budgetary and Extrabudgetary Expenditures	191
A5.1.1	Average Growth Rates of Provincial GDP and Per Capita GDP	231

Tables

3.1	Provincial Per Capita GDP, 1978 and 1994	48

3.2	Provincial Per Capita GDP as % of National Average, 1978 and 1994	49
3.3	Annual Growth Rate of Real Per Capita GDP, 1978–94	52
3.4	Guizhou and Guangdong, 1994	61
3.5	Classification of Counties by Per Capita GDP, in Guizhou and Guangdong, 1994	62
3.6	Regional Disparities in Guizhou and Guangdong, 1994	63
3.7	Minority-Concentrated Counties in Poverty, 1992	66
3.8	International Comparison of Regional Disparities in Per Capita GDP or Per Capita Income	68
4.1	Geographical Profiles of Provinces, 1994	83
4.2	Capital and Labor Force in Provinces, 1994	87
4.3	Structure of Production and Structure of Employment, 1994	94
4.4	Rural Industrialization, 1994	97
4.5	Distribution of Rural Labor Force, 1994	100
4.6	Openness of Provinces, 1994	107
4.7	Access to Information, 1994	115
4.8	Rural Poverty, 1993	117
4.9	Education, 1995	120
4.10	Selected Indicators of Technological Capability, 1994	123
4.11	Selected Indicators of Health, 1994	126
4.12	Multidimensional Facets of Regional Disparity, 1994	130
4.13	Selected Human Development Indicators: China and the World	133
4.14	Impacts of Budgetary and Extrabudgetary Expenditures on Social Indicators	139
5.1	Growth Indices of GDP and Production Factors, 1978–95	148
5.2	Average Annual Growth Rates of Output and Inputs (%), 1978–95	149
5.3	Sources of Growth (%)	150
5.4	Relative Contributions to Output Growth	151
5.5	Indices of Preferential Policy	160
5.6	Explaining Foreign Investment Flows	161
5.7	Provincial Average Net Export/GDP (%)	163
6.1	State Investment in Capital Construction by Periods	176

6.2	Preferential Policies by Types of Zones	180
6.3	Selected Fiscal Indices of China, 1978–96	186
6.4	Provincial Fiscal Surplus/GDP, 1978–93 (%)	190
6.5	Financial Markets in the Chinese Provinces	194
A5.2.1	Non-State Share of National Income, 1978	234

THE POLITICAL
ECONOMY OF
UNEVEN
DEVELOPMENT

1

Introduction

The Issue

Covering 9.6 million square kilometers, China is the third-largest country in the world. Given its gigantic size, there have always been significant regional variations in geographical conditions, resource endowments, the sectoral distribution of economic activity, and the level of socioeconomic development.

When the Chinese Communists came to power in 1949, they inherited an extremely lopsided economy. Industrial activities were to a large extent concentrated in Manchuria and a few major coastal cities. Although the coastal provinces accounted for only 11.34 percent of the land, they were the source of 77.6 percent of total industrial output. The rest of the country, meanwhile, produced only 22.4 percent of total industrial output. In particular, West China lagged far behind. Only 8 percent of total industrial output originated in this region, though it accounted for over half of the territory.[1]

The new government made a strong commitment to achieving balanced distribution of productive capacity and income. The First Five-Year Plan of the People's Republic gave high priority to the development of new industrial bases in North, Northwest, and Central China. Among 694 industrial projects built during this period, most were located in the inland areas.[2] But Mao Zedong was not impressed. In his famous 1956 speech, "On Ten Major Relationships," he dwelled on the relations between the coast and the interior. In his view, it was both economically irrational and politically unacceptable to keep 70 percent of industry in the coastal areas, and leave the rest of the country more or less untouched by modernization. To speed up the industrialization of the interior, he suggested that more new industrial facilities be located there. Only by doing so, he believed, would industrial activity become more evenly distributed.[3]

Indeed, Mao's era was marked by an unprecedented spatial redeployment of productive capacity. Thanks to its strong extractive capacity,[4] the central government under Mao had firm control over the geographic distribution of resources. Investment policy in this period clearly favored peripheral and backward regions. While more-developed provinces and cities such as Shanghai experienced substantial outflows of revenues, less-developed provinces received enormous infusions of funds for infrastructure and industrial development.[5] Moreover, in the mid-1960s, out of security considerations, China began a campaign to construct the Third Front.[6] From late 1964 to 1971, dozens of large- and medium-sized industrial enterprises were moved from coastal provinces and areas bordering on the Soviet Union to inland provinces, and hundreds more were built on site. Altogether, between 1956 and 1978, more than two thousand large- and medium-sized enterprises were established in West and Central China. This investment policy powerfully boosted industrial growth in the traditionally less developed regions.[7] In 1965, for example, the ratio of output value of agriculture to light industry to heavy industry for Central China was 71 : 15 : 14. By the end of the Fourth Five-Year Plan period (1971–75), the ratio had become 44 : 22 : 34. During the same period, the ratio for West China changed from 69 : 16 : 15 to 40 : 23 : 37.[8]

In addition to financing investments in less-developed regions, fiscal transfers were also used to reduce regional inequality in income and in the provision of public goods and services. Such government transfers made it possible for consumption to be much more evenly distributed than output.[9] As a result, Mao's era witnessed a strong trend toward greater equality in per capita consumption.[10]

The price of the rapid development of backward areas appears to have been quite high, though. Many now believe that, in terms of national growth forgone, Mao's policies greatly compromised efficiency for equity.

In 1978, China changed its policy orientation, shifting the emphasis from equity to efficiency. The years since have marked a period of rapid economic growth and rising living standards unprecedented in modern Chinese history. Moreover, no province has been excluded from the growth club. Every one of China's thirty provinces has experienced substantial real growth in the post-1978 period.

While economic conditions have improved in all regions in absolute terms, however, performance has varied markedly among the regions in relative terms. It may be impossible for market-oriented reforms to result in even development. By replacing a "redistributive" state-socialist economy with a market economy and by encouraging specialization over autarky, such reforms are supposed to bring about price realignment, resource reallocation, and spatial restructuring, all of which are bound to produce income shifts across regions. The important question is whether China's reforms have ameliorated or aggravated existing regional inequalities. This is a subject of great interest to economists, sociologists, and political scientists both inside and outside the country, because studying regional development during the post-Mao era is important for evaluating the success of China's market transition.[11] The spatial ramifications of the reforms have also become a major issue of policy debate within China in recent years, as became manifest in the course of preparing the Ninth Five-Year Plan (1996–2000). Due to growing concern over the possible political consequences of the allegedly widening regional gaps, the plan reordered the nation's priorities. The reduction of regional disparities is one of the main targets of the plan period, but the debate still goes on.

Debate

The ongoing debate on China's regional development strategy is concerned with four major issues: (1) Has regional inequality widened or narrowed since China introduced its market-oriented reforms? (2) What are the key factors that have contributed to changes in regional disparity? (3) Are regional gaps in today's China tolerable or excessive? and (4) What, if anything, should the Chinese government do to narrow regional disparities? There is no consensus on any of these four issues.

Whether China has been on a path toward regional convergence or divergence sounds like a simple empirical question. But fact-finding is not as straightforward as some may assume. Different opinions exist among Chinese and Western observers. While some scholars identify a tendency toward convergence since the introduction of market-oriented reforms,[12] others find widening regional gaps.[13] Still others report mixed results.[14] Why is it so difficult to establish the facts? This problem arises because different researchers use different units of analysis, indicators, and methods of measurement. They cannot agree on what is the best way to assess changes in regional gaps.

The answer to the second question is closely related to the answer to the first question. While those who see a strong convergence tend to attribute the narrowing of regional gaps to market forces,[15] those who see a diverging trend tend to blame the widening of regional gaps on various policy and institutional changes introduced during the course of reforms. These factors include fiscal decentralization, regional bias in investment strategy, price distortions, changing industrial structure, the open-door policy, the growth of the non-state sector, and so on.[16]

The possible effect of regional disparities on national unity is the third main question which scholars and policy makers inside and outside China are vigorously debating.[17] Will regional disparities cause social and political instability? Some regard it as natural for a country, especially a large country, to experience some regional variations during the course of rapid economic growth. The current level of regional disparities may not be small, but neither is it a source of concern. Is now the right time to address the issue of regional gaps? Absolutely not, these scholars insist. In their view, China's main task at present is to develop its economy as fast as possible. Solving regional problems should not be made a national priority. Rather, China should wait until its developed regions become much more developed—so developed that they can afford to support less-developed regions.[18]

Others disagree. They believe that the current level of regional disparity is not only excessive but that poor regions are already involved in fierce conflicts with rich regions. If China were to wait, the contradictions between regions might eventually become too sharp to be resolved; if regional gaps are allowed to widen, catastrophic political consequences might ensue. Accordingly, they argue that China must make serious efforts to narrow the regional gaps and at a minimum prevent them from growing.[19]

But what should be done to reduce regional inequality? For those who believe in the tendency of market forces to automatically adjust, the government need only remove market rigidities. If factors of production—labor, capital, and so on—are allowed to move freely, they will move along the economic landscape to seek "opportunities" or higher returns. According to these scholars, labor tends to migrate toward richer economies, whereas capital tends to migrate in the opposite direction. Eventually, returns to factors, or income, will be equalized among regions, and spatial inequality will thereby disappear.[20]

Others, however, maintain that state intervention is required to reduce regional disparities. In their view, poor regions are poor because investment in infrastructure, basic public services, and human capital is deficient. Therefore, it is vitally important for these regions to receive external assistance in their efforts to improve their physical and social infrastructure. No institution except the central government is likely to have the incentive and capacity to do so.[21]

Differences in ideology and research methodology undoubtedly affect Western scholars' positions on these issues. For Chinese who are involved in the debate, however, there is one more determinant of their positions—namely, their conflicting interests. Even during the Mao era, regions were clearly aware of their distinctive local interests. Nevertheless, under a "redistributive" state-socialist economy where resources were allocated primarily by central planners, the space in which regions could maneuver was rather limited. In the post-Mao era, reforms have significantly weakened the redistributive role of the central government. Regions now have to compete to gain access to more resources. As a result, awareness of local interests has been greatly enhanced. It is obvious that any change in the regional economic development strategy would affect regions' interests in one way or another. Therefore, in the debate over regional issues, what appear to be methodological and theoretical differences may, in fact, reflect conflicts of divergent regional interests.[22]

The Significance of the Issue

Of course, China is not the only country to experience wide regional disparities. Uneven development is a universal phenomenon of all modern economies. Such large developing countries as India, Indonesia, Mexico, and Brazil are cases in point.[23] Even developed countries are no exception. Examples include Canada, Great Britain, France, Italy, and the United States.[24] Therefore, regional equity is at the core of scholarly research and policy debates not just in China, but in many other countries as well.

Regional inequality is of interest for a variety of reasons. First, the issue of regional disparity is an issue of economic growth. If all regions had grown at the same pace, there would be no income differences between regions in the first place. Even if regional gaps exist, the initial gaps will disappear in due course if the poor regions are able to grow faster than the rich ones and ultimately converge with them. Although some economic theories predict convergence, the empirical evidence has been a subject of debate. In any event, it is an undeniable fact that regional disparities persist in most countries. To find the root causes of regional disparities, we have to trace the long-term growth paths of different regions in the national economy and to understand the dynamics of regional growth. So the right question to ask is: Why have regional rates of growth varied, and what are the factors that make growth rates differ across regions?[25]

Regional disparity is, moreover, not merely an economic issue but an ethical issue. Unless the process of economic development is intrinsically an even one, the society is often confronted with a choice between ethically motivated efforts to establish socioeconomic parity and the economically more advantageous strategy of letting inequality increase so long as it makes the whole economy grow faster.[26] No one denies the importance of attaining a high overall growth rate, but the question of who benefits from rapid economic growth should not be ignored. Rapid growth in some regions is certainly beneficial to the local populations, but this does not guarantee that the welfare of the people in other regions would similarly be improved. Therefore, the assessment of a development strategy has to take a broader view so that the ethical dimension is taken into consideration.

Some economists tend to use Pareto optimality as the only criterion of judgment. Sometimes also called economic efficiency, Pareto optimality is defined as a social state in which no one's utility can be raised without reducing the utility of someone else. As Sen points out, however, "[a] state can be Pareto optimal with some people in extreme misery and others rolling in luxury, so long as the miserable cannot be made better off without cutting into the luxury of the rich."[27]

Other economists take the Pareto principle a step further, allowing economic efficiency to encompass not just *actual* Pareto improvement, but also *potential* Pareto improvement (Kaldor-Hicks improvement).[28] The latter refers to change in which some persons gain, others lose, but there are overall net gains in the sense that hypothetically the gainers could compensate the losers and still be better off. The problem is that the redistribution is only hypothetical. It need not happen.[29] Thus, Kaldor-Hicks improvement might entail growing inequality.

One possible alternative to the Pareto criterion is the Rawls criterion: Increased inequality is acceptable only if it benefits the poor, or more precisely, only if the welfare of the poor is improving. By this criterion, any change that improves the prospects of the poor is good, even if the gaps between the rich and poor are widening.[30] Obviously, this is a very weak form of equality. Another alternative is what Milanovic calls the Verkhovensky criterion. Verkhovensky improvement refers to a movement that allows the welfare of the poor to improve faster than the situation of their rich counterparts.[31] This will result in the narrowing of the income gaps between the rich and the poor.

In line with these three criteria, a society may choose one of the following three strategies of regional development: (1) encourage the whole economy to grow at the fastest possible rate regardless of the consequences on regional gaps; (2) refrain from intervening as long as poor regions are growing; and (3) assist poor regions to grow at rates higher than those of rich regions.

Both economic growth and fairness in the distribution of income are desirable. But, unfortunately, the two goals are often in conflict with each other. Growth maximization may worsen the problem of inequality, while the pursuit of regional equality may slow down national growth. A development strategy should not be concerned simply with the maximization of one objective at the expense of the other: it has to consider trade-offs between them. However, it is impossible to specify where the optimal point lies, for the issue involves ethical judgments.

The study of regional disparity makes it explicit that any development strategy is founded on the basis of a certain ethical principle. It is impossible to avoid value judgments on income distribution in studying regional development.[32]

Third, regional disparity is an issue of political significance, because regional economic disparities may have adverse effects on the political stability and unity of the nation. The relation between inequality and political instability is a close one.[33] There are countless instances in which real and perceived inequities give rise to political conflicts. Interregional inequality could be a source of political conflict just as inequalities between social groups are. Regions are not just geographic and economic entities, but also social and political ones. Residents of one region tend to care more about the welfare of their fellow residents than about that of inhabitants of other regions. As a result, there tends to be a widespread sense of grievance among the people living in regions where average incomes are either noticeably lower or are growing noticeably slower than in other regions of the country. They may regard an insufficiently sympathetic central government as being partly responsible for their plight.

Meanwhile, those living in more-developed regions are likely to perceive that their economies are the nation's backbone. If the central government intervenes to correct regional disparities in such a way that high-income regions subsidize poor regions, then people in the former regions are likely to believe that such fiscal transfers to low-growth regions are just a waste of money, because, in their view, trying to sustain inefficient economic activity is irrational. Thus, any attempt to redistribute resources across regions is likely to provoke resistance from the rich regions.

In other words, persistent regional disparities may not only frustrate people living in relatively impoverished regions, but also alienate those living in affluent regions. History suggests that when regional dispari-ties become excessive, catastrophic political consequences can occur. Especially when ethnic, religious, or linguistic differences are com-bined with economic disparities, the result can be an explosive situa-tion. Examples include the secessionist movements in the Punjab in India, Bougainville in Papua New Guinea, Quebec in Canada, Lom-bardy in Italy, Katanga in Zaire, Biafra in Nigeria, and Scotland, Wales, and Northern Ireland in Great Britain.[34] Indeed, one factor contributing to the disintegration of both the former Yugoslavia and the former Soviet Union was growing income gaps among their ethni-cally populated republics.[35]

In 1993, Mahbub ul Haq, the principal author of the United Nation's Development Programme's (UNDP) Human Development Report, warned that the widening of regional disparities was threatening the unity and stability of seventeen countries. In particular, his team pre-dicted that Rwanda was in danger of disintegration and that Chiapas in Mexico might soon become a trouble spot. Barely before the report came out, troubles occurred in both places. Haq later pointed out:

> Regional disparity is an especially powerful index because poverty it-self cannot interpret the disintegration of a country. But if the poor

people are concentrated in one region, they can easily be organized, just as the peasant uprising in the Chiapas region of Mexico. When we were studying Mexico, the data of the Chiapas region was already catching our attention. Although the Mexican government was not happy, we still predicted that the region might become a trouble spot. And it has proved that we are right.[36]

It should be noted that UNDP's Human Development Report for 1994 listed China as one of the countries where regional gaps had become excessively large. UNDP's advice to China was that "it will need to take care that existing regional disparities do not widen further. Thoughtful state intervention will be required to ensure a more equitable distribution of social services."[37] Given UNDP's good record in predicting cases of national disintegration elsewhere, its advice should not be taken lightly.

The political dimension of regional disparities has another side: While regional inequality may generate political problems, uneven economic development itself may result from unequal distribution of political power. Most studies of spatial disparities focus on such socioeconomic variables as income, employment, education, migration, and the like. The political aspect of regional development has been largely neglected in explaining regional inequalities. But power relations in space obviously have a direct bearing on the process of regional development. Regions with greater influence in central decision making, for instance, are often able to obtain more resources for their own development than regions that have much less political weight. Thus, a plan aimed at achieving balanced regional development has to disperse not only economic activities but also political power.[38]

For much of intellectual history, economics, politics, and ethics were seen as parts of an indivisible whole. As modern economics has evolved, however, the importance of ethical and political perspectives has substantially weakened.[39] Nevertheless, to gain a full understanding of a subject like regional disparity, analysts have to apply all three approaches.

The Structure of the Book

Much progress has been made in studying regional inequality. Economists, geographers, sociologists, demographers, and others have devised ways to measure regional gaps and have developed theories to explain changes in regional disparities.[40] Although primarily a case study of China, this book intends to contribute to this rich and growing literature.

The purpose of this book is to explore various key issues in the current debate over the spatial effects of reforms. Rather than dealing with the issue of regional disparity solely from an economic perspective, as most other recent works do, this project applies a political-economy approach. In addition to systematically examining the broad patterns of regional disparities, it investigates the economic and political factors that shape these patterns. Moreover, the book draws attention to the economic as well as political consequences of widening regional gaps. On the basis of theoretical and empirical analyses, it also offers policy suggestions for easing tensions caused by real and perceived regional gaps.

The next chapter begins with a critical review of two dominant hypotheses of regional economic development: the convergence hypothesis and the inverted U-curve hypothesis. The convergence hypothesis predicts a tendency for poor regions to grow more rapidly than rich ones. Regional disparity is seen as a temporary phenomenon that will disappear over time. Since convergence is supposed to be a "natural" tendency, there is no reason for state intervention to reduce regional inequality.

The inverted U-curve hypothesis, however, is less upbeat. This hypothesis is frequently associated with Gunnar Myrdal and Albert Hirschman.[41] Both view economic development as a seesaw process between leading and lagging regions. According to them, the process is affected by two opposite sets of forces, known as spread and backwash effects in Myrdal's theory, or trickling down and polarization effects in Hirschman's theory. If the latter effects are stronger than the former ones, significant divergence in growth rates and incomes among regions is expected. Only when the former effects outweigh the latter ones may more balanced regional growth occur. However, such a situation is not likely to occur before economic development reaches a fairly high level. As a result, the early stages of economic growth tend to be characterized by increasing regional disparities. Yet, this second hypothesis predicts that regional inequality will eventually decline at more mature stages of economic growth.

We criticize both hypotheses. It is our belief that market forces, left to themselves, tend to increase, rather than decrease, regional inequality. A natural tendency toward convergence does not exist. There is also no invariant relationship between the levels of national economic development and of regional inequality. Rather, it is the interaction of political and economic factors that influences the growth of less- and more-developed regions. Our explanation of uneven spatial growth centers on two variables: the government's willingness to direct the flow of production factors on behalf of less-developed regions, and its capacity to do so. When the government has no intention to reduce regional disparities in the country, regional gaps are unlikely to narrow. Even if the state desires to reduce regional disparities, regional gaps may still expand if the state lacks the capacity to carry out its objectives. Only when the state is both willing and able to intervene on behalf of poor regions may regional disparities decline. The state's ability to intervene is mainly constrained by its extractive capacity. Excessive fiscal decentralization may significantly weaken the state's extractive capacity and thereby exacerbate regional disparities. Chapter 2 elaborates our hypothesis.

Chapter 3 attempts to establish the empirical foundations for our engagement in the debate over China's regional development. As indicated above, researchers have come up with very different observations about regional development trends during the post-Mao era. These differences, in our view, reflect differences in research method. Measured regional disparities depend, to a large extent, on five key parameters: the dimensions of regional development, indicators, measurement method, price index, and the unit of analysis.

In Chapter 3, only the economic dimension of regional disparities is studied. Gross domestic product (GDP) per capita, measured at the 1978 constant price, is adopted as the summary indicator of the overall level of development and well-being of regions. Many believe that this variable can measure regional economic welfare in much the same way as national GDP per capita can be used to measure national economic welfare. But our view is that, no matter how good it may be, per capita GDP alone cannot fully reflect regional differences in human welfare. Therefore, numerous alternative indicators are used in Chapter 4 to reflect the multiplicity of regional disparities.

Most studies of regional disparity focus on relative gaps. As far as politics is concerned, however, absolute gaps may be more relevant. Therefore, we pay special attention to changes in absolute terms. In addition to objective indicators, relative and absolute, we also use subjective indicators. In our view, what often counts most in politics is probably the perceived gaps rather than real gaps, although they are undoubtedly somehow related. In order to gauge how large the perceived regional gaps are in China, we have conducted interviews with numerous regional officials.

The province is the unit of analysis in this study. Most recent studies divide China into three large geographic regions, East, Central, and West, rather than thirty provinces. In our view, however, as an economic, administrative, and political unit, the province is politically more relevant and revealing than the geographic region.

After these key parameters are chosen, Chapter 3 goes on to document the regional variations of development level in 1978 and 1994 and changes in regional disparities between 1978 and 1994. We find that, by 1994, regional disparities in both relative and absolute terms had grown to alarming levels. While overall relative dispersion narrowed between 1978 and 1990, it has shown an unmistakable upward trend in the 1990s. If China's three metropolises, Beijing, Tianjin, and Shanghai, are excluded, however, a more bleak picture emerges: Regional dispersion only decreased marginally in the initial years of reform, but the years following 1983 have seen a steady increase in relative dispersion. As far as absolute dispersion is concerned, it has been growing throughout the entire period.

The ethnic dimension of regional disparity must concern anyone interested in the political implications of development. Chapter 3 therefore examines the cases of China's thirty autonomous prefectures of minority nationality in the national context. Only in three of these prefectures was GDP per capita to be found higher than the national average. Overall, GDP per capita in the thirty prefectures was equivalent to less than 60 percent of the national average, making them among the poorest areas in the country.

Furthermore, to demonstrate that regional disparities exist not only between provinces but also within them, Chapter 3 examines two provinces—Guangdong (one of the richest provinces) and Guizhou (the poorest province)—in detail. Intraprovincial disparities were found to be much larger in the former than in the latter.

Chapter 3 then compares China with seventeen countries for which data are available. It concludes that regional inequality is greater in China than in most countries of the world. More importantly, regardless of how large the real regional gaps are and how China stands in comparative perspective, most of the people we interviewed felt that the regional gaps "had been widening" since 1978, and that the current level of regional disparities in China was "too high."

Regional inequality has many facets. While Chapter 3 focuses on a single indicator of regional inequality—per capita GDP, Chapter 4 turns its attention to other dimensions of regional disparities. The chapter explores regional variations in geographic conditions, resource endowment, infrastructure, demographic characteristics, labor force, economic structure, foreign trade, foreign investment, technology, the degree of urbanization, consumption, the provision of public goods and services, human development, and so on. This chapter demonstrates that the rich and poor provinces do not merely differ in GDP per capita. Rather, regional inequality manifests itself in almost every aspect of economic and social life. The chapter has two main findings. First, GDP per capita is strongly correlated with most of the socioeconomic variables examined. Second, regional inequality, as measured by social indicators, appears to be smaller than that measured by economic indicators.

Why have some provinces been able to grow at much faster rates than others? Chapter 5 sets out to address this issue. The technique of growth accounting is first used to identify the immediate economic sources of growth. Its main finding is that the acceleration in capital investment has been the most important engine of growth for all Chinese provinces. The chapter then goes on to probe why some regions are able to mobilize more capital resources than others. In China, a province's investment capital comes from three sources: local savings, capital inflow from (or capital outflow to) other provinces, and foreign savings. Savings rates are found to be systematically higher in rich provinces than in poor provinces. Coupled with higher per capita GDP, higher savings rates give rich provinces a decisive edge in mobilizing capital from inside. Foreign capital is also found to have favored the developed coastal provinces. As for interprovincial capital flows, the most conspicuous change during the reform era is their drastic decline. Whereas rich provinces exported substantial proportions of their local savings to poor provinces before reform, they now keep most of their local savings to themselves. As interprovincial flows of capital dwindle, poor provinces are forced to rely more upon their own local savings to finance local investment. The result is slower growth rates there than elsewhere.

One may ask why rich coastal provinces have found favor in foreign investors' eyes, and why the interprovincial movement of investment resources has stagnated during the reform era. Chapter 6 attempts to answer these questions. It tests the political-economy hypothesis outlined in Chapter 2. The central government's policy preference and its extractive capacity prove to be very good predictors of changes in regional inequality, for both are decisive factors that affect the direction of capital flows in China.

In the 1980s, the Chinese government was obsessed with the "trickle-down" philosophy. In order to achieve the highest-possible aggregate national growth, Beijing shifted its investment priority from the interior to the coast. In the meantime, it extended generous preferential policies to coastal provinces that enabled these areas to attract large inflows of foreign capital. To the extent that the central government was very well aware of the trade-off between aggregate growth and regional inequality, it could be said that the increasing regional disparities observed during this period were part of a deliberate scheme of the central government.

In the early 1990s, for reasons that will be discussed in Chapter 6, the Chinese government reoriented its regional preferences. It now hoped to mitigate tensions caused by growing regional disparities. By this time, however, central extractive capacity had declined to such a point that it could no longer play a major role in redistributing investment resources from economically prosperous regions to poor regions. Fiscal decentralization was to blame for the erosion of central extractive capacity. Under the decentralized regime, all the provinces, rich and poor, were forced to become financially more self-reliant. With high levels of local savings and large inflows of foreign capital, advanced regions could move forward at full speed. However, the shortage of investment resources dampened the growth potentials of backward regions. Thus, despite the central government's policy reorientation, regional gaps continued to expand. In this sense, fiscal decentralization has become a powerful institutional obstacle to the rectification of regional disparities.

Chapter 7 begins with a brief discussion of the economic and political consequences of excessive regional disparities. It then probes the policy implications of the empirical findings of the previous chapters. In our view, balanced development should serve as the general guideline for regional policy. It is wrong to give priority to either efficiency or equity. Rather, efforts should be made to achieve a balance between the two values. After selecting the policy goal, the next issue is what mechanism a country should rely on in resolving regional disparities. There are reasons to believe that the convergence expected by neoclassical economists may not occur even under conditions of free interregional trade and factor mobility. We argue that convergence is unlikely to occur unless the state is willing and able to help poor regions by influencing the interregional flows of factors throughout the economy. Policymakers thus should also strike a proper balance between market mechanisms and government intervention. Chapter 7 concludes with some specific policy recommendations for preventing China's regional gaps from growing any further.

Notes

1. Sheng Bin and Feng Lun, eds. *Report on Chinese National Conditions,* p. 666. In 1952, about 80 percent of iron and steel production was concentrated in the coastal areas, particularly Anshan (Liaoning province). Paradoxically, the iron and steel industry was largely absent in areas where iron ore resources were abundant, such as Inner Mongolia, the Southwest, and the Northwest. In the textile industry, 80 percent of the spindles and 90 percent of the looms were concentrated in major coastal cities, such as Shanghai, Tianjin, and Qingdao. The modern textile industry was almost nonexistent in the main cotton-producing areas. See Bo Yibo, *Reminiscences of Major Policy Decisions and Events,* vol. 1, p. 475.

2. Bo, *Reminiscences of Major Policy Decisions and Events,* p. 476.

3. Mao Zedong, *Selected Works,* vol. 5, p. 276.

4. China's rate of capital formation quickly increased from 5 percent in the 1930s to about 25 percent in the mid-1950s.

5. Nicholas R. Lardy, "Regional Growth and Income Distribution in China," p. 177.

6. The Third Front covered two geographic areas. One was called the Southwest Front, covering much of Yunnan, Guizhou, and Sichuan provinces, as well as the western parts of both Hunan and Hubei provinces. The other was called the Northwest Front, covering most of Shaanxi, Gansu, Ningxia, and Qinghai provinces, as well as the western parts of Henan and Shanxi provinces. The Third Front is also divided into a "Major Third Line" (*dasanxian*) and "Minor Third Line" (*xiaosanxian*). See Barry Naughton, "The Third Front," pp. 351–86.

7. Between 1953 and 1978, industrial output grew at an annual rate of 20.1 percent in Shaanxi, 16.3 percent in Qinghai, 15.0 percent in Inner Mongolia, 12.0 percent in Shanxi, 11.8 percent in Sichuan, and 11.2 percent in Guizhou. See the 1993 statistical yearbooks of these provinces.

8. Sheng Bin and Feng Lun, *Report on Chinese National Conditions,* p. 667. Despite considerable efforts on the part of the central government, however,

the differentials in per capita output between regions did not narrow during Mao's era. Per capita output can be measured either by per capita GDP (gross domestic product) or by per capita NMP (net material product). See Thomas P. Lyons, "Interprovincial Disparities in China," pp. 471–506; Kai-yuen Tsui, "China's Regional Inequality, 1952–1985," pp. 1–21; idem, "Decomposition of China's Regional Inequalities," pp. 600–27; Tianlun Jian, Jeffrey D. Sachs, and Andrew M. Warner, "Trends in Regional Inequality in China," pp. 1–21.

9. Lardy, "Regional Growth and Income Distribution"; Tsui, "China's Regional Inequality."

10. Lyons, "Interprovincial Disparities," pp. 479–80.

11. The study of regional disparities in China has aroused extensive concern among Chinese and foreign scholars. Examples are Yang Kaizhong, *Zhongguo quyu fazhan yanjiu;* Lu Dadao et al., *Zhongguo gongye buju de lilun yu shijian;* Yang Weimin, "Diqu jian shouru chaju biandong de shizheng fenxi," pp. 70–74; Wei Houkai, "Lun woguo quji shouru chayi de biandong geju"; Chen Wen et al., "Zhongguo jingji diqu chayi de tedian jiqi yanbian qushi," pp. 16–21; State Council Development Research Center Group, *Zhongguo quyu xietiao fazhan zhanlue;* Lin Yifu et al., *Zhongguo de qiji: fazhan zhanlue yu jingji gaige;* Victor C. Falkenheim, "Spatial Inequality in China's Modernization Program"; P. Aguignier, "Regional Disparities Since 1978"; David Denny, "Regional Economic Differences During the Decade of Reform"; Dali Yang, "Patterns of China's Regional Development Strategy," pp. 231–57; Chor Pang Lo, "The Geography of Rural Regional Inequality in Mainland China," pp. 446–86; Lyons, "Interprovincial Disparities in China," pp. 471–506; T. R. Lakshmanan and I. H. Chang, "Regional Disparities in China," pp. 97–103; Tsui, "China's Regional Inequality," pp. 1–21; Woo Tun-oy and Hsueh Tien-tung, *Regional Disparities in the Sectoral Structure of Labor Productivity 1985–1989;* Albert Keidel, "China: Regional Disparities"; and Zhao Xiaobin, "Spatial Disparities and Economic Development in China."

12. Jian, Sachs, and Warner, "Trends in Regional Inequality"; Xu Lin, "Gaige kaifang yilai woguo diqu jian jingji fazhan chaju de fenxi," pp. 18–39; Song Xueming, "Zhongguo quyu jingji fazhan jiqi shoulianxing," pp. 38–44.

13. Keidel, "China: Regional Disparities"; Hiroyuki Kato, "Regional Development in the Reform Period."

14. Lyons, "Interprovincial Disparities in China"; Zhao Xiaobin, "Spatial Disparities and Economic Development in China."

15. Jian, Sachs, and Warner, "Trends in Regional Inequality."

16. P. Aguignier, "Regional Disparities Since 1978"; Hiroyuki Kato, "Regional Development in the Reform Period"; C. Cindy Fan, "Regional Impacts of Foreign Trade in China," pp. 129–59; Loraine A. West and Christine P.W. Wong, "Fiscal Decentralization and Growing Regional Disparities in Rural China"; Diana Hwei-An Tsai, "Regional Inequality and Financial Decentralization in Mainland China," pp. 40–71; Chen Huai, "Zhongguo 80 niandai yilai quyu jingji fazhan zhanlue de huigu yu qianzhan," pp. 3–12; Lin Lin, "Dongxibu chaju kuoda wenti fenxi," pp. 46–53.

17. See chapters in David S. G. Goodman and Gerald Segal, eds., *China Deconstructs: Politics, Trade and Regionalism.* Also see Gerald Segal, "China Changes Shape"; Anne Simone Kleinman, "Across China."

18. Hou Yongzhi and Hu Changshun, "Dongzhongxibu de xietiao fazhan," pp. 13–29; Hu Dayuan, "Zhuangui jingji zhong de diqu chaju."

19. Hu Angang, Wang Shaoguang, and Kang Xiaoguang, *Zhongguo diqi chaju baogao;* Wei Houkai, "Woguo diqi fazhan chaju de xingcheng, yingxiang jiqi xietiao tujing," pp. 2–13.

20. Xu Lin, "Gaige kaifang yilai woguo diqu jian jingji fazhan chaju de fenxi"; Song Xueming, "Zhongguo quyu jingji fazhan jiqi shoulianxing."

21. Hu, Wang, and Kang, *Zhongguo diqi chaju baogao.*

22. We have collected nearly 100 research papers on regional disparities published in China. As expected, those by authors from poor provinces generally conclude that regional gaps are large and growing. And they all end up with a call for central intervention to narrow the gaps. For examples, see Lin Lin (Sichuan), "Dongxibu chaju kuoda wenti fenxi"; Dai Leping (Hunan), "Dui woguo dongzhongxibu quyu jingji fazhan wenti de sikao," pp. 20–28; Mao Huihui (Hunan), "Suoxiao dongxi chaju bixu jiada zhongxibu de touru lidu," pp. 6–8; He Weixian (Guizhou), "Woguo xibu diqu shixian liangge zhuanbian de nandian yu duice," pp. 51–54; Li Xiangqi (Shaanxi), "Guanyu jiakuai xibu gaige yu fazhan ruogan wenti de sikao," pp. 37–44.

23. Hal Hill, ed., *Unity and Diversity;* L. S. Bhat et al., eds., *Regional Inequalities in India;* Costis Hadjimichalis, *Uneven Development and Regionalism;* E. Moudoud, *Modernization.*

24. Stuart Holland, *The Regional Problem;* B. Higgins, "Economic Development and Regional Disparities"; A. Boltho, "European and United States Regional Differentials," pp. 105–15; Donald J. Savoie, *Regional Economic Development.*

25. To study growth, economists tend to focus on cross-country comparisons. In fact, comparisons of regions within a country may offer better-controlled experiments than comparisons of countries. As Robert J. Barro and Xavier Sala-i-Martin point out:

> Although differences in technology, preferences, and institutions do exist across regions, these differences are likely to be smaller than those across countries. Firms and households of different regions within a single country tend to have access to similar technologies and have roughly similar tastes and culture. Furthermore, the regions share a common central government and therefore have similar institutional setups and legal systems. [Robert J. Barro and Xavier Sala-i-Martin, *Economic Growth*, p. 382]

Besides, the relative cultural homogeneity may help somewhat to isolate the effects of culture on economic development. For these reasons, it is probably easier to identify the determinants of growth by studying regions within a country than across countries.

26. Arthur M. Okun, *Equality and Efficiency.*

27. Amartya Sen, *On Ethics and Economics,* pp. 32–33.

28. Nicholas Kaldor, "Welfare Propositions of Economics and Interpersonal Comparisons of Utility"; John R. Hicks, "The Foundations of Welfare Economics."

29. Robin W. Boadway, "The Role of Government in a Market Economy," pp. 25–31.

30. John Rawls, *A Theory of Justice,* pp. 150–61.

31. Verkhovensky is one of the heroes of Dostoevski's *The Possessed.* See

Branko Milanovic, "Patterns of Regional Growth in Yugoslavia, 1952–83," pp. 1–19.

32. Even among those who recognize the necessity of income redistribution, many maintain that only interpersonal redistribution matters. That is, a poor person is a poor person and should be aided irrespective of where he or she happens to live. Thus, in this view, regional disparity as such is not a real issue. It is true that transfers in favor of low-income areas are not guaranteed to benefit the poorer citizens of these areas, but a reduction of interpersonal disparities does not necessarily lead to a reduction in interspatial disparities either. As Prud'homme points out, "If the lower income region has a more equal income distribution than the higher income region, then transfers to the poorer citizens might well benefit primarily the richer region, increasing interregional disparities." See Remy Prud'homme, "On the Dangers of Decentralization," p. 19. It is therefore necessary to pay attention to both interpersonal and interregional disparities.

33. Douglas Hibbs, *Mass Political Violence;* Yannis Venieris and Dipak Gupta, "Income Distribution and Socio-Political Instability as Determinants of Savings," pp. 873–83; Dipak Gupta, *The Economics of Political Violence;* Abhijit Banerijee and Andrew Newman, "Risk Bearing and the Theory of Income Distribution," pp. 211–35; Alberto Alesina and Roberto Perotti, *Income Distribution, Political Instability, and Investment.*

34. Milica Zavkovic Bookman, *The Political Economy of Discontinuous Development;* Stuart Holland, *The Regional Problem.*

35. Dijana Plestina, *Regional Development in Communist Yugoslavia;* Dinko Dubravcic, "Economic Causes and Political Context of the Dissolution of a Multinational Federal State."

36. *Inter Press Service,* June 11, 1994.

37. UNDP, *Human Development Report, 1994,* p. 140.

38. Yehuda Gradus, "The Role of Politics in Regional Inequality," pp. 388–403.

39. Sen, *On Ethics and Economics,* pp. 4–9.

40. Bertil Ohlin, *Interregional and International Trade;* Simon Kuznets, "Economic Growth and Income Equality," pp. 1–25; Albert O. Hirschman, *The Strategy of Economic Development;* Walter Isard, *Methods of Regional Analysis;* Jeffrey G. Williamson, "Regional Inequality and the Process of National Development," pp. 3–45; Peter Haggett, *Locational Analysis in Human Geography;* B. J. L. Berry, "Hierarchical Diffusion"; K. Mera, *Income Distribution and Regional Development;* N. M. Hansen, "An Evaluation of Growth-Centre Theory and Practice"; M. Hechter, *Internal Colonialism;* Holland, *The Regional Problem;* D. M. Smith, *Geography, Inequality and Society;* Harry Richardson, *Regional and Urban Economics;* Edward J. Malecki, "Technology and Regional Development"; C. Gore, *Regions in Question;* Harvey Armstrong and Jim Taylor, *Regional Economics and Policy.*

41. Gunnar Myrdal, *Economic Theory and Under-Developed Regions;* Hirschman, *The Strategy of Economic Development.*

2

Theoretical Framework

Why do regions grow at different rates? Numerous noteworthy attempts have been made to construct models of regional growth over the past decades. So far, however, no consensus about the causes of regional growth disparities has emerged.

The first two sections of this chapter review two dominant hypotheses in the field, namely, the neoclassical convergence hypothesis and the inverted U-curve hypothesis. Identifying different factors as the sources of regional inequality, these theories yield opposite predictions about the tendencies of regional development. Neither of them is satisfactory, however, because they both pay too little attention to factors other than economic variables. The third section presents an alternative hypothesis, a political-economy hypothesis, focusing on the interaction of political and economic factors that influence regional growth.

The Convergence Hypothesis

Neoclassical theories predict convergence. According to these theories, some regions may become richer than others thanks to historical "accidents" and "pure luck," as is often the case with successful individuals in society. But there is nothing to worry about, because disparities in income and productivity level tend to converge: Regional economies that start out poor tend to grow faster. Eventually, everything balances out.

Various models have been proposed to explain why economic convergence happens.

The most simplistic neoclassical model is a closed one-sector economy in which there is neither technical progress nor interregional trade. Output is determined entirely by local capital and labor inputs. Differences in output per worker can be explained by differences in the capital-labor ratio. Differences in the capital-labor ratio cannot grow indefinitely, however, because capital is assumed to suffer from diminishing marginal returns. If output per worker increases at a diminishing rate, once the marginal product of labor falls to a sufficiently low level, producers will have no incentive to increase the capital-labor ratio any further. On the other hand, output per worker can continue to increase in poor regions before the capital-labor ratio reaches its long-term equilibrium level. Assuming a fixed relation between the labor force and population, the closed-economy model thus predicts that the per capita growth rate tends to be inversely related to the starting level of output or income per person. In other words, there is a tendency for poor regions to grow more rapidly than rich regions.[1]

A major drawback of the closed-economy model is that it ignores the potential contribution of trade to growth. The export-base model remedies this weakness by allowing regions to produce more than one commodity and to trade with each other. According to this model, regional growth differences are attributable, at least in part, to regional differences in the level of export growth. Thus, success of the export base is the determining factor of regional growth. And growth initiated by the export base determines the income level of a region.

The export-base model also predicts convergence. Its main assumption, however, is no longer "diminishing returns," but "comparative advantage" and "equal exchange." The central proposition of the model is that the pattern of trade among regions is determined by their differing endowments of factors of production—land, natural resources, capital, labor, and so forth. A region tends to maximize its economic potential by specializing in the production and export of commodities that use its relatively abundant factors intensively. If, for example, a region is abundant in capital and short on labor, it will be better off by promoting economic activities that require a great deal of capital but limited labor. Conversely, a region with an abundant labor supply will be better off specializing in labor-intensive commodities. With each region concentrating its efforts on its economic strengths, the model predicts that free trade will gradually equalize factor (capital and labor) prices (profit and wage) across regions, leading to a long-term tendency toward diminishing regional inequalities.[2]

It needs to be noted that this model holds only under certain relatively stringent assumptions, among which is zero factor mobility across regional boundaries. If factors are allowed to be mobile, then it is impossible to predict the commodities in which a region has a comparative advantage. This assumption is obviously unrealistic, for labor and, even more, capital could be, indeed often are, highly mobile between regions.[3]

This is where the factor price equalization model comes into the picture. This model predicts that allowance for factor mobility will accelerate the process of convergence. According to this model, in an economy that allows for free factor mobility, capitalists will maximize profits by locating their investments in areas of high labor availability and low labor cost, and workers will maximize wages by moving between regions in response to differences in employment prospects and income levels. Thus, labor tends to migrate from regions of high unemployment and low income to regions of low unemployment and high income, while capital tends to migrate in the opposite direction. The two contrasting movements will lower the capital-labor ratio in places with initially high ratios and increase the capital-labor ratio in places with initially low ratios. Eventually, an equilibrium will be reached at which returns to factors, or incomes, are equalized among regions. In short, this model suggests that inequalities between regions are only temporary; they will disappear over time.[4]

What are the policy implications to be drawn from these neoclassical models? Very simple: laissez-faire, or letting market forces deal with regional disparities. Since unhampered economies are supposed to move "naturally" toward equilibrium, it is believed that a free market will lead sooner or later to the elimination of regional differences. Furthermore, if convergence is the natural tendency, then there is no role in regional development for the government. Governments should not intervene to prop up poor regions, because, by blunting necessary economic adjustments, government programs may prolong rather than cure interregional differences.

Many scholars who study China's regional disparities seem to have embraced the self-balancing assumption of neoclassical economics. They believe that the persistence of regional disparities in China can be explained, at least in part, by the existence of serious impediments to the free flow of production factors. Therefore, liberalization in the movement of goods and factors is the solution to the regional problem.[5] According to their logic, the freer factor mobility is, the more balanced regional development becomes. Thus, the rate of convergence is expected to speed up in the 1990s, since many restrictions on factor mobility were not relaxed until 1990. As we will see in the next chapter, this prediction fails to correspond with the observable trends of regional development in China.

The main problem with these neoclassical explanations is that they rely heavily on some unrealistic assumptions. Take the last model, the most realistic one of the three, as an example. It assumes, among other things, (1) that factors (e.g., capital, labor, and technology) are perfectly mobile and react to market signals in an instantaneous manner; and (2) that the factors move in the direction that the model predicts, namely, labor flows from low- to high-wage regions and capital flows in the opposite direction.[6] As long as these two assumptions hold, convergence will occur. If either assumption is dropped, however, we may derive quite different results.

There are good reasons to believe that factor mobility cannot be perfect. Some factors of production, such as land or mines, are completely immobile. Others (capital, labor, and technology) are mobile, but their mobility is by no means perfect. Significant impediments prevent them from responding to differences in interregional earnings, even if all institutional rigidities were removed.[7]

Most existing capital goods are "locked in" equipment and structure. Locationally tied to a specific place, they are, for all intents and purposes, immobile. Capital goods in the form of machinery may potentially be mobile, but freight costs are far from zero. Thus, only capital in the form of savings surplus could respond to regional differences in rates of return. In modern economies, however, some projects are very large, so large that capital investment must flow either in large lumps or not at all. "In such cases, marginal adjustments in response to slight regional differences in rates of return will be impossible."[8] In any event, new capital very quickly assumes a physical form, and hence becomes immobile. Moreover, it is unlikely that investors will possess perfect information about current investment opportunities in all regions and future regional differentials in rates of return to capital. Due to such uncertainty, even capital in a liquid form may fail to be perfectly responsive to factor price differences between regions.

Labor may be even less responsive than capital. Hicks believes that "differences in net economic advantages, chiefly differences in wages, are the main cause of migration."[9] This assumption is deficient for two reasons. First, because of incomplete information, workers may not be fully aware of such regional differentials. Second, even if such differentials are known, impediments to labor mobility may still persist. This is because mobility is costly for the mover.

There are four types of costs. The first type is information costs. Potential migrants need both job information for themselves and information for their families—including information about housing, schools, social life, recreational and cultural facilities, and so on. Lack of information may cause uncertainty; uncertainty, in turn, may reduce the willingness to migrate. Information can, of course, be obtained, but it is not costless. The second type of relocation costs is the cost of retraining. By migrating to another place, one may have to change jobs. For this, skills necessary for the new occupation must be obtained. The costs of retraining could be substantial. Transportation costs comprise the third type of costs. Especially in countries like China, where transport systems are backward and inefficient, migration is expensive. Lack of financial liquidity may prevent many of those who are willing to migrate from doing so, even though migration may well pay off in the long run.

While the first three types of relocation costs are pecuniary ones, the psychic costs, the fourth type of relocation costs, may be of even greater significance. People are often reluctant to leave the location in which they have developed strong loyalties and attachments. Family, friends, culture, language, landscapes, climates, a familiar environment, and a general sense of belonging may not always be compatible with a narrow definition of economic rationality. But these subjective locational preferences may have enormous influence on location decisions.[10]

Because migration is costly and even painful, labor mobility will never be perfect in the sense that workers instantaneously respond to regional differentials by migrating to the region offering the most lucrative returns.[11] It should also be noted that the propensity to migrate varies considerably among different social groups (e.g., age, education, race, job status).[12]

How about the mobility of technology? Neoclassical economists believe that technical knowledge is highly mobile between regions.[13] If they are right—that is, if technological advances diffuse rapidly and uniformly across space—then interregional differentials in innovation rates would not matter very much; the regions that started off technologically backward might have a chance to catch up. As a matter of fact, we simply do not know much about the spatial diffusion of technical progress. The limited empirical work done in this area seems to suggest that although technical knowledge does diffuse outward from the source region to other regions in the economy, such diffusion is by no means instantaneous.[14] If that is the case, some regions will always be in the forefront of developing and adopting new technologies while others lag behind (and, in so doing, lose competitiveness). Consequently, regional differences in the propensity to create and use new technologies will result in major differences in regional economic growth rates.[15]

Moreover, perfect mobility of factors does not guarantee that convergence will occur. It is one thing whether factors can move freely; it is quite another where these factors then flow. Clearly, only if factor flows move in the direction predicted by the neoclassical model will convergence occur. But this need not be the case.

Capital may not flow from rich to poor regions for two reasons. First, due to high information costs, investment in poor regions may be deemed more risky, even if relative marginal rates of return may be greater. Thus, investors may prefer to use their capital at home because there are fewer uncertainties. Second, location decisions are often based on criteria other than profitability and costs. Such factors as access to metropolitan living, social amenities, and environment preferences may also be important determinants of investment location, more important than neoclassical economists think.

If the above two arguments hold, then the direction of capital movement is not invariable. While there are certainly instances in which capital flows from rich to poor regions, it is also likely for capital to stay just where it is or even to flow from poor to rich regions. In any event, there is no universal tendency for capital to move only in one direction. Since prosperous regions are able to generate more savings, capital mobility may not necessarily help alleviate the polarization of economic activity between regions.

Nor does the migration of workers from poor to rich regions necessarily speed up the convergence of per capita income. Workers are not identical. Whether migration can bring about convergence depends on what the migrants are like. As noted above, migration is not costless.

Therefore, not all persons in low-wage areas are motivated and able to leave at a given point in time. If we allow for heterogeneity among persons, then the willingness and ability to move will differ in accordance with age, gender, education, income, marriage status, occupation, and so on. Because of limited opportunities in backward regions and higher opportunity costs, it is young, educated, skilled, and enterprising persons who tend to have stronger incentive and ability to move.[16] When they leave poor regions, they take with them something very scarce in these regions—human capital. The loss of better-qualified, more enterprising people thus not only represents a capital outflow from poor to rich regions, but also deprives poor regions of precisely the part of the labor force most attractive to prospective investors.[17] Thus, convergence may not occur if migrants from poor to rich regions are substantially above average in terms of human capital.

Finally, technological diffusion in itself may not be able to make backward regions grow more rapidly than advanced regions. The reason is very simple. Advanced regions are normally the source of basic inventions, and take the lead in applying these inventions. Diffusion normally proceeds along a hierarchical route. Therefore, the introduction of any new technology tends at first to sharpen spatial differentiation. The diffusion of this technology may eventually narrow regional differences in its particular area of technical progress. But long before this happens, other new innovations are introduced in the advanced regions, which again produce differentiating effects. The repetitive diffusion of myriad innovations thus does not change the basic fact that, at any given moment in time, there are significant regional differences in levels of technology.[18] Diffusion of technology does not mean technological convergence. As long as interregional differentials in levels of technology persist, "human and physical capital may move from poor to rich economies and thereby create a force toward divergence."[19]

The preceding paragraphs suggest that factors of production are not as mobile as the neoclassical model assumes, and that factors may flow in all directions, not necessarily along the expected routes. If either of the two propositions is right, we may logically conclude that factor mobility does not invariably lead to convergence.[20]

Empirical studies seem to support this conclusion. The evidence of convergence is very mixed. In fact, for every example of convergence, there are two or more cases of divergence. In some countries (e.g., the United States), a trend of decreasing regional inequality has been found.[21]

In others (e.g., Brazil), divergence has been more the rule.[22] Even in countries where convergence predominates, "perverse" results have been produced in some periods (e.g., industrialized countries after 1973).[23]

Looking beyond individual countries, we may be able to identify convergence among a sample of the "advanced capitalist" countries.[24] However, there is a selectivity problem. As Pritchett points out:

> Defining the set of countries as those that are the richest now almost guarantees the finding of historical convergence, as either countries are rich now and were rich historically, in which case they all have had roughly the same growth rate (like nearly all of Europe) or countries are rich now and were poor historically (like Japan) and hence grew faster and show convergence.[25]

Within the group of low-income countries, no convergence has been observed.[26] If we mix the two groups together and look at the world as a whole, rather than convergence, we would find "divergence, big time."[27] What can these conflicting findings tell us? Clearly, there is no universal tendency toward convergence.

The Inverted U-Curve Hypothesis

In neoclassical theory, regional disparities are considered an abnormal phenomenon that will not last. But in most countries, large regional disparities do exist. How can we explain the persistence of spatial inequality? To reconcile neoclassical theory with fact, neoclassical economists tend to blame regional barriers to trade and factor mobility. However, others believe that even free movement of goods, capital, and labor may not always be equilibrating, as neoclassical theory claims. On the contrary, factor mobility may increase regional inequality at certain stages of development. The two names most frequently associated with this second school of thought—the unbalanced-growth school—are Gunnar Myrdal and Albert Hirschman.

Myrdal's theory of unbalanced growth is centered around the philosophical notion of "cumulative causation." In his understanding, any social system contains opposing forces. These forces, by themselves, do not automatically reach an equilibrium. This is so because social change tends to give rise to changes in the same direction, rather than to call forth countervailing changes. Thus, social processes are unlikely to move toward some sort of balance between forces. Instead, they tend to be cumulative, often gathering speed at an accelerating rate. Applying this insight to regional development, Myrdal argues that market forces tend to draw economic activity toward areas that possess initial advantages (e.g., natural resources, location, and transportation infrastructure), thus giving rise to regional disparities.

Hirschman's model of unbalanced growth is quite similar to Myrdal's, though it is not based on the cumulative-causation hypothesis. Hirschman simply does not believe that economic progress can appear everywhere at the same time. In order to reach higher levels of income, an economy must first develop one or several regional centers of economic strength. In other words, interregional inequality of growth is a condition of growth itself. Growth, therefore, is necessarily unbalanced.

If, at the initial stage of development, an economy contains two types of regions—expanding growth centers on the one hand, and lagging or depressed hinterlands on the other—are the latter going to converge with the former, as the neoclassical model predicts? Myrdal and Hirschman do not believe that linear convergence is likely. In their view, once growth takes hold in some parts of the national territory, it will set in motion certain forces that have direct economic repercussions on the remaining parts—some favorable, some adverse. Myrdal calls these forces spread effects and backwash effects, which are nearly analogous to what Hirschman calls trickling down and polarization effects.

Spread effects may help stimulate growth in lagging regions. For instance, expansionary momentum in economic centers may generate a growing demand for agricultural products and raw resources from depressed areas, which may in turn result in increased employment and even a capital inflow into these regions. If a sufficient number of workers become employed in these regions, consumer goods industries may benefit. It is also possible for regions around a nodal center of expansion to benefit from diffusion of innovation, if new investments bring new technologies. In addition, growth centers may absorb some of the disguised unemployment of the lagging regions, and thereby raise the marginal productivity of labor and per capita consumption in the latter. If spread effects are sufficiently strong, the expansionary momentum of growth centers may trickle down to lagging regions, making them, in turn, new centers of self-sustained economic expansion.

If the growth centers only produced favorable spread effects in other regions, convergence would, of course, occur. However, along with the spread effects, there is a second set of residual forces known as back-wash effects, which may further debilitate lagging regions. Myrdal and Hirschman doubt very much that the movement of labor, capital, goods, and services, by itself, necessarily leads to convergence. In their view, migration, capital mobility, and trade may act as the mechanisms through which a cumulative process evolves.

Given their higher levels of income and greater employment opportunities, growth centers may attract net immigration from other parts of the country. As migration is always selective, it may deprive lagging regions of their skilled workers, technicians, managers, and entrepreneurs, as well as their more enterprising young men and women. While growth centers may benefit from such inflows of high–human-capital labor, the migration may be undesirable not only from the point of view of lagging regions but also from that of the country as a whole. The loss to lagging regions represented by the departure of migrants may be greater than the gain to growth centers.

Capital movement tends to have a similar effect of increasing inequality. The expansion of growth centers will increase income and demand, and thereby spur investment, which in turn will further increase income and demand and cause a second round of investment. In growth centers, savings will increase as a result of higher incomes, but the supply of capital may fall short of a strong demand for new investment. In lagging regions, however, due to the lack of expansionary momentum, the demand for investment capital may be relatively weak, even compared to the low supply of local savings. Therefore, an unregulated banking system could become an instrument for siphoning off the savings from poorer regions to more prosperous ones where returns to capital are higher and more secure.

Similarly, trade of goods and services may operate in favor of more-developed regions. Usually working under conditions of increasing returns to scale, industries in already established centers of expansion tend to enjoy competitive advantages over producers in lagging regions. As a result, goods and services produced in growing regions may inundate lagging regions, and thus thwart the development of indigenous enterprises.[28]

Moreover, if left to themselves, the quality of infrastructure (e.g., transportation and communications facilities) and the level of public services (e.g., health and education) are likely to be inferior in lagging regions, thus further impairing their competitive advantages where investment is concerned. History shows that cheap labor alone does not usually attract investment to backward regions.

These backwash effects may reinforce the tendency for interregional divergence and polarization.

Given the coexistence of spread effects and backwash effects, three situations may emerge. First, if the two kinds of effects balance each other, the current spatial pattern of income distribution will persist. But, according to Myrdal, this balance is not a stable equilibrium, for any change in the forces will start a cumulative movement upwards or downwards. Second, if the spread effects are stronger than the backwash effects, the process of cumulative causation will lead to the development of new economic centers, and hence convergence. Third, in the case in which backwash effects outweigh spread effects, market forces will lead to polarization or divergence.

Myrdal and Hirschman hypothesize that in a poor economy, if things were left to market forces, the backwash effects would overshadow the spread effects. When national growth accelerates, economic activities tend to cluster in certain regions, leading to more rapid growth in already developed regions and stagnation in the rest of the country. Thus, the free play of market forces tends to increase, rather than to decrease, regional inequalities in a poor country.

Only at a substantially higher level of economic development, Myrdal and Hirschman predict, will the spread effects of growth become strong enough to neutralize the backwash effects. At higher levels of development, wages and prices of other factors may be driven up to such a high level that other regions finally get a real chance to compete successfully.[29] Meanwhile, industry will become congested in the growth centers, and expansion forces will be hampered by the insufficient size of the home market resulting from depressed income levels in lagging regions. Also, "a high average level of development is accompanied by improved transportation and communications, higher levels of education, and a more dynamic communication of ideas and values—all of which tends to strengthen the forces for the centrifugal spread of economic expansion or to remove the obstacles for its operation."[30]

Perhaps more importantly, in a highly developed economy, spread effects are likely to be strengthened by public policies intended to spur the development of lagging regions. At the early stages of development, the government may have incentives to favor maximum aggregate economic growth rather than balanced regional development. Its policies, therefore, might further compound growing regional dispari- ties caused by market forces. At higher levels of development, how- ever, policymakers may be compelled to consider the growth potential of lagging regions. By then, it is clear that if the country fails to utilize fully the resources of lagging regions, it will harm its own economic future. High levels of development may also allow the government "the luxury of equality in the geographic distribution of income and to pursue an active policy of income transfer to the poor regions."[31]

Both Myrdal and Hirschman envisioned a long-term trend toward interregional equilibrium, although they expected large and growing regional disparities at early stages of development. Myrdal supported this prediction in his study of regional development in Western Eu- rope. While regional disparities were large and increasing in poorer countries, he observed, they were small and diminishing in richer ones. A few years after Myrdal published his 1957 book, his findings seemed to have been confirmed by Jeffrey Williamson's study. Based on a much larger set of cross-sectional and time-series data, William- son identified "a systematic relationship between national development levels and regional inequality," or an inverted U in the national growth path—that is, regional gaps tended to increase in earlier stages of development and to diminish in later stages.[32] Since then, the inverted U-curve pattern of regional development has often been called the Williamson law.

To be sure, the Williamson law does not sound as reassuring as the neoclassical convergence hypothesis. If it were to prove true, however, we could still be confident that spread effects would eventually overtake backwash effects, and that regional inequalities would lessen over time.

In recent years, the Williamson law has found currency among some Chinese economists. Since China is still in an early stage of develop- ment, these economists maintain, it should focus its attention on how to accelerate the growth of the national economy as a whole rather than working on the reduction of regional disparities. If regional gaps are widening, in their view, there is no reason to panic; China has not yet reached the peak of the inverted U-shaped curve.[33] Of course, no one knows when that great historical moment will finally arrive, including Williamson himself.[34] This is not the only problem with the Williamson law. In fact, the so-called law can be challenged on several fronts.

First, the inverted U-shaped curve may not be an accurate description of patterns of regional development even in rich industrialized countries. A number of studies have shown that in those countries, per capita income levels have been diverging since 1973, after steady and strong convergence from the mid-1950s to the early 1970s.[35] In other words, a non-inverted U-shaped curve is probably a more accurate description of growth patterns over the last five decades. As far as most low-income countries are concerned, they are still climbing the upward slope of the supposedly inverted U-curve. Only the former centrally planned economies are exceptions.[36]

Second, even for those countries that experienced an inverted U-shaped curve during certain stages of their economic development, not all inverted U-shaped curves look the same. The timing of the convergence phase is very different. Some countries are able to achieve the reduction of interregional income variation at much earlier stages of economic development than others. Similarly, the peak levels of spatial income differentials from which convergence began are much lower in some cases than others. Moreover, the actual speed of change along the upward or downward slope of the curve varies considerably from country to country.[37] For these reasons, one may doubt that a predictable relationship between level of development and regional inequality really exists, as Williamson assumes.

Third, even if a correlation could be established between levels of development and regional inequality, such a finding might lead to either of the following two conclusions: (1) regional gaps tend to diminish when the national economy reaches higher levels of development; (2) a country will not be able to develop its economy unless it first manages to reduce regional gaps. It is difficult to demonstrate which of the two conclusions is more valid. Indeed, both may be true: Diminishing regional gaps and higher levels of growth may reinforce each other. There are reasons to believe that the more balanced regional development is in a country, the greater the opportunity for mutual reinforcement.[38] In any event, the Williamson law provides no grounds for the prescription offered by some Chinese economists, namely, that to eliminate regional disparities, China should first adopt policies designed to accelerate national economic growth even at the expense of poor regions.[39]

Finally, if convergence has ever taken place in any country, it was probably brought about not so much by "natural" market forces as by deliberate policy interferences. In the Western European countries where Williamson found strong convergence tendencies in the period from the end of World War II to the early 1970s, for instance, state policies played an important role in offsetting backwash effects and supporting spread effects. To counterbalance the outflow of capital and talent from poor regions, governments organized an even larger flow in the opposite direction. To offset the locational advantages of rich regions, governments offered special tax advantages to those willing to invest in poor regions.[40] Without such deliberate governmental intervention, the spread effects might never have been able to outweigh the backwash effects, and thereby postwar convergence might never have occurred.[41] This conclusion is borne out by developments since the early 1970s. Under growing pressure to reduce public expenditure, many countries have become much less enthusiastic about implementing regional policies. The new key words are *adjustment, austerity,* and *self-reliance,* which mean that regions have to try to develop their economies largely by their own means, whether they are poor or rich.[42] The result is the end—indeed, the reversal—of convergence.

What do the analyses in the above two sections tell us? To begin, there is no natural tendency toward equilibrium, whether in the short run or the long run. Left to themselves, market forces bring about neither convergence nor an inverted U-shaped curve. Convergence, divergence, the inverted U-shaped curve, and the non-inverted U-shaped curve are all possible, depending to a large extent on whether the government intervenes and how it intervenes. Therefore, to study the pattern of regional development in a country, one should never ignore the role played by the government in intensifying or lessening the degree of regional inequality. Ironically, while those who subscribe to the Williamson law blindly wait for market forces to perform a miracle, Williamson himself attached great importance to the effects of government policy in his 1965 analysis of regional inequality. For him, only when market forces are combined with deliberate governmental policy can they produce spread effects strong enough to reverse the differential rates of growth between backward and advanced regions and thereby ensure balanced regional growth.[43] Similarly, both Myrdal and Hirschman consider governmental intervention to be a special type of spread effect. Both, in turn, recognize its importance in effecting changes in interregional inequality. Although they firmly believe that spread effects will eventually triumph over backwash effects, the lag time before this actually takes place could be very long;[44] the society may not be able to withstand the political strain generated by growing interregional inequality. Thus, when market forces fail to restore an equilibrium among competing regions, both hold it necessary to channel public investment to depressed areas.[45]

Our Hypothesis

The two hypotheses discussed above share one feature in common: Both assume that regional development has an inherent natural tendency, and that the process is largely determined by economic forces. What they overlook are political forces that may directly or indirectly affect patterns of regional development. Economic determinism is the fatal weakness of both hypotheses. Their assumption of a politics-free world is unrealistic and unreasonable.

In what follows, we provide an alternative hypothesis to explain regional differences in economic performance. Unlike the above two hypotheses, ours is a political-economy one. We do not believe that any natural tendency in regional development exists, be it convergence, the inverted U-shaped curve, or otherwise. In our view, patterns of regional development are determined as much by economic forces as by political forces. Thus, our hypothesis allows all kinds of situations to exist. The hypothesis consists of two propositions.

First, we agree with the two above hypotheses that convergence or divergence is, to a large extent, attributable to differences in the growth of factor inputs. If production factors flow in the ways envisioned by neoclassical theories, convergence would occur. Otherwise, divergence would occur. However, we do not believe that, left to market forces, labor, capital, and technology would necessarily move in the direction predicted by neoclassical theories.

Second, the causes of labor migration, capital movement, and technology diffusion are many and complex. Among them, the role of government intervention is critical. As a matter of fact, in few countries is the movement of production factors left to the free play of market forces. All governments play some role in directing the movement of factors, even when economists say that they should not. Even if a government chooses not to intervene at all, that in itself represents a policy posture. Government intervention can either facilitate or impede factor mobility. It can also affect whether factors will move in one direction or in another. We are not suggesting that government intervention is always good for correcting regional imbalances. Far from it. Government intervention can intensify backwash effects just as it can strengthen the spread effects of economic forces. It all depends on what the government is willing and able to do. The important point here is that the role of the government should not be ignored in the search for explanations about various patterns of regional development. In other words, wherever regional disparities are present, they should not be viewed as the culmination of a natural economic process. Instead, the causes of uneven development should be sought in both the economic realm and the political realm.

Whether government intervention exacerbates or alleviates regional disparities depends on two variables: the government's desire and its capacity to countervail the inherent imbalance of market forces.

As Figure 2.1 shows, four scenarios are possible. Obviously, it is unlikely for regional gaps to narrow in Regime I, where the government's desire and capacity to intervene on behalf of poor regions are both weak. Regional disparities would continue to exist in Regime III as well, because, despite the government's strong desire to reduce regional gaps, its capacity to do so is limited. The situation in most developing countries probably resembles either Regime I or III. In Regime II, the desire to help poor regions is lacking. Thus, the government's strong capacity to intervene would offer little help to disadvantaged areas. What is worse, its strong capacity might even be used to intensify a cumulative process of regional divergence. In this regard, the reversal of the postwar convergence of income levels in rich industrialized economies in the mid-1970s is evidence of the pervasive influence of ideology. Only in Regime IV, where the government's desire and capacity to narrow regional gaps are both strong, is it likely for economic development to become more balanced. This at least partially explains why industrialized countries witnessed strong convergence from the mid-1950s to the mid-1970s, and why the former state-socialist countries were able to achieve convergence when their per capita income was still relatively low.[46]

To test this hypothesis, analyses need to be conducted at two levels. The first step is to identify the key economic determinants of regional performance differences. In particular, we need to investigate to what extent regional performance differences can be explained by differences in the growth of factor inputs. If a strong correlation can be established, then our next step is to explain the differences in the

Figure 2.1 **Theoretical Relationship between State Preference and State Capacity**

| | | Ability to affect capital movement | |
		Weak	Strong
Desire to narrow regional gaps	Weak	I	II
	Strong	III	IV

growth of factor inputs. Why do factor inputs grow at different rates across regions? Unless we can answer this question, we are still very much in the dark about the root cause of uneven regional development. This is why we should introduce political factors into the picture: namely, to examine the extent to which the direction and volume of factor movements are affected by the government's desire and capacity to narrow regional disparities.

Because our hypothesis emphasizes the interactive influence of both economic and political factors on regional development, it is obviously much harder to formalize than the other two hypotheses. As a result, our explanation will certainly be less rigorous and elegant. Some scholars have chosen to explain the world in terms of forces they know how to model, putting those forces that could not be modeled to the side. As Paul Krugman points out, they follow "the line of least mathematical resistance."[47] However, we think it is wrong to turn a blind eye to forces that we know play a crucial role in regional development, simply because they cannot be modeled with rigor. For us, realism is more important than rigor.

In this study, our hypothesis serves as an analytical framework for explaining changes in China's regional development. Of course, a single case study can neither verify nor refute any hypothesis. And we make no such claim. The whole purpose of this exercise is to show that the political economy hypothesis is a viable alternative to the two established hypotheses.

However, before trying to explain why some of China's regions have been more successful than others in developing their economies, we first have to examine how serious regional disparities are in today's China. So, too, must we consider how the patterns of regional development have changed in the period under discussion. These are the subjects of the next two chapters.

Notes

1. Robert M. Solow, "A Contribution to the Theory of Economic Growth," pp. 65–94.

2. Bertil Ohlin, *Interregional and International Trade;* G. H. Borts and J. L. Stein, *Economic Growth in a Free Market.*

3. Harvey Armstrong and Jim Taylor, *Regional Economics and Policy,* p. 76.

4. Walter Isard, *Methods of Regional Analysis.*

5. Tianlun Jian, Jeffrey D. Sachs, and Andrew M. Warner, "Trends in Regional Inequality in China," pp. 1–21; Song Xueming, "Zhongguo quyu jingji fazhan jiqi shoulianxing," pp. 38–44.

6. It also assumes that returns to scale are constant or declining. This assumption can be, and has been, challenged. See, for instance, Paul M. Romer, "Increasing Returns and Long-Run Growth," pp. 1002–37. Technological change has figured prominently in growth theory, and hence in explaining why different regional economies have developed at different rates. However, technology exhibiting increasing returns to scale would imply divergence instead of convergence whether the economy is open or closed. Robert J. Barro and Xavier Sala-i-Martin, *Economic Growth,* p. 383.

7. Harry W. Richardson, *Regional Economics,* p. 106.

8. Ibid., pp. 106–7.

9. J. R. Hicks, *The Theory of Wages,* p. 76.

10. Richardson, *Regional Economics,* p. 108; Armstrong and Taylor, *Regional Economics and Policy,* pp. 192–93.

11. In a study of the relationship between migration and regional growth in Japan and the United States, two market economies, Robert J. Barro and Xavier Sala-i-Martin found that the response of migration to regional income differentials was rather slow. See Barro and Sala-i-Martin, "Regional Growth and Migration," pp. 312–46.

12. Richardson, *Regional Economics,* p. 108.

13. Moses Abramovitz, "Catching Up, Forging Ahead, and Falling Behind," pp. 385–406; and William J. Baumol, "Productivity Growth, Convergence, and Welfare," pp. 1072–85.

14. Edward J. Malecki, "Technological Innovation and Paths to Regional Economic Growth"; idem, *Technology and Economic Development.*

15. Alex Bowen and Ken Mayhew, eds., *Reducing Regional Inequalities,* pp. 95–97.

16. For a discussion of the characteristics of migrants in the United States, see George J. Borjas, *Friends or Strangers.* For an excellent analysis of the characteristics of migrants in contemporary China, see Cai Fang, "An Economic Analysis of Labor Migration and Mobility in China," pp. 120–35.

17. Stuart Holland, *The Regional Problem,* p. 27.

18. G. William Skinner, "Differential Development in Lingnan," p. 20.

19. Barro and Sala-i-Martin, "Convergence Across States and Regions," p. 111.

20. In their comparative study of the United States and Japan, Barro and Sala-i-Martin find evidence of "conditional convergence" in both countries. But they also find that the effect of labor and capital mobility on convergence is either small or difficult to pin down, which means that greater labor and capital mobility may not lead to higher rates of convergence. Thus, if convergence does occur, it needs to be explained by variables other than factor mobility. See Barro and Sala-i-Martin, "Convergence Across States and Regions" and "Regional Growth and Migration."

21. Two massive descriptive-analytical volumes on the process of interregional growth in the United States, published in 1960, provided detailed empirical evidence of convergence tendencies in regional per capita incomes. See H. S. Perloff, E. S. Dunn, Jr., E. E. Lampard, and R. F. Muth, *Regions, Resources and Economic Growth;* and S. Kuznets, A. R. Miller, and R. A. Easterlin, *Population Redistribution and Economic Growth.* Also see R. A. Easterlin, "Long Term Regional Income Changes," pp. 313–25; G. H. Borts, "The Equalization of Returns and Regional Economic Growth"; G. H. Borts and J. L. Stein, *Economic Growth in a Free Market;* R. C. Estall, "Economic Geography and Regional Geography," pp. 297–310; Barro and Sala-i-Martin,. "Convergence Across States and Regions," "Regional Growth and Migration," and *Economic Growth,* chap. 11.

22. W. Baer, "Regional Inequality and Economic Growth in Brazil," pp. 268–85; W. T. Endres, "Regional Disparities in Industrial Growth in Brazil," pp. 300–310. In addition, regional inequality was also found to have increased for extensive periods of time in Indonesia, Mexico, Pakistan, Tanzania, Tunisia, Colombia, Peru, Italy, and Spain. See W. V. Ginneken, *Rural and Urban Income Inequalities in Indonesia, Mexico, Pakistan, Tanzania and Tunisia;* G. S. Fields and T. P. Schultz, "Regional Inequality and Other Sources of Income Variation in Colombia," pp. 447–68; E. M. Falaris, "The Determinants of Internal Migration in Peru," pp. 231–54; H. B. Chenery, "Development Policies for Southern Italy," pp. 515–47; J. R. Lasuen, "Regional Income Inequalities and the Problem of Growth in Spain," pp. 69–88.

23. Dowrick and Nguyen point out that "the postwar convergence of income levels in the rich industrialized economies appears to have slowed down or even reversed after 1973." Steve Dowrick and Duc-Tho Nguyen, "OECD Comparative Economic Growth 1950–85," p. 1011. Also see William J. Baumol and Edward N. Wolff, "Productivity, Growth, Convergence, and Welfare: Reply," pp. 1155–59; Mick Dunford, "Regional Disparities in the European Community," pp. 727–43; Abramovitz, "Catching Up, Forging Ahead," pp. 385–406.

24. Dowrick and Nguyen, "OECD Comparative Economic Growth 1950–85." Nevertheless, Baumol and Wolff find that, for the sixteen richest industrialized countries, per capita income began to diverge around 1975. See Baumol and Wolff, "Productivity, Growth, Convergence, and Welfare: Reply."

25. Lant Pritchett, "Divergence, Big Time," p. 6.

26. Baumol, "Productivity Growth."

27. Pritchett, "Divergence, Big Time."

28. Richardson, *Regional Growth Theory,* p. 16. "The hampering of industrial

growth in the poorer southern provinces of Italy, caused by the pulling down of internal tariff walls after Italy's political unification in the last century, is a case in point which has been thoroughly studied: industry in the northern provinces had such a lead, and was so much stronger that it dominated the new national market, which was the result of political unification, and suppressed industrial efforts in the southern provinces." See Gunnar Myrdal, *Economic Theory and Under-Developed Regions,* p. 28.

29. Albert O. Hirschman, *The Strategy of Economic Development,* pp. 183–201.

30. Myrdal, *Economic Theory and Under-Developed Regions,* p. 34.

31. Jeffrey G. Williamson, "Regional Inequality and the Process of National Development," p. 9.

32. Ibid.

33. Lu Dadao, *Quyu fazhan jiqi kongjian jiegou.* Fan Gang, a Chinese economist, has expressed a similar view on many occasions. Also see Li Zhou and Cai Fang, "Shouru chaju lada: nongcun fazhan bupingheng de shizheng fenxi yu zhanlue sikao," pp. 14–16.

34. Williamson, "Regional Inequality and the Process of National Development," p. 10.

35. Abramovitz, "Catching Up, Forging Ahead, and Falling Behind"; Baumol and Wolff, "Productivity, Growth, Convergence, and Welfare: Reply." Barro and Sala-i-Martin also find that in Japan and the United States the trend toward long-run convergence stopped in the mid-1970s. See their "Regional Growth and Migration," p. 329.

36. Baumol, "Productivity Growth."

37. For a comparison between China and a number of other cases, see Nicholas R. Lardy, "Regional Growth and Income Distribution in China," pp. 167–69; and Thomas P. Lyons, "Interprovincial Disparities in China," p. 499.

38. Benjamin Higgins and Donald J. Savoie, eds., *Regional Economic Development,* pp. 204–5.

39. See the discussion of gradient theory in Chapter 6.

40. Hirschman, *Strategy of Economic Development,* pp. 183–95.

41. In some countries where a certain degree of convergence has been achieved in recent decades (e.g., Brazil, Greece, Italy, Malaysia, Thailand), it has been the result of explicit regional policies rather than of free market forces alone.

42. Costis Hadjimichalis, *Uneven Development and Regionalism,* p. 28.

43. Williamson, "Regional Inequality," pp. 7, 9, 45.

44. Barro and Sala-i-Martin studied the behavior of states of the United States since 1880, the prefectures of Japan since 1930, and the regions of eight European countries since 1950. In all three contexts, the convergence of income across regions is robust. But they also found that the speed of convergence was rather slow, only around 2 percent per year. This implies that it would take thirty-five years to eliminate one half of an initial gap in per capita income. See Barro and Sala-i-Martin, *Economic Growth,* p. 413.

45. Hirschman, *Strategy of Economic Development,* p. 187.

46. Baumol, "Productivity."

47. Paul Krugman, *Geography and Trade,* p. 6.

3

Changes in Regional Disparity since 1978

Measurement

As a vast country, China has always displayed significant geographical variation in economic development. This chapter examines the extent of regional disparities in today's China as well as the issue of whether the market-oriented reforms implemented since 1978 have ameliorated or aggravated existing inequalities. These two seemingly simple empirical questions do not appear to have simple answers, however. Some researchers conclude that the post-1978 economic reforms have resulted in a divergence trend, while others insist that the Chinese economy has converged across provinces. As for the current state of regional disparities, fundamental differences of assessment also exist. While a growing number of scholars now believe that regional disparities have reached an alarming level, some suggest that recent trends are perfectly normal. How could scholars investigating the same phenomenon arrive at such conflicting conclusions? There are several possibilities:

First, they are in fact looking at different dimensions of regional disparity.

Second, although studying the same dimension, they have chosen different indicators.

Third, although using the same indicators, they have applied different methods of measurement.

Fourth, although applying the same method, they have employed different price indices.

Finally, although everything else is the same, their units of analysis are different.

Let us examine these key parameters of measurement one by one, for change in any one of them may lead to different conclusions.

Dimensions

Development has many dimensions. So, too, do regional disparities in the level of development. Care is needed when studying regional disparities because different dimensions may highlight different features. For instance, if fiscal equalization is a national policy, regional differences in the provision of public goods and services could be much smaller than regional differences in income. Thus, it is important to clarify which dimension of disparity is being investigated. Among all the dimensions, the economic one is probably the most consequential, because it has direct implications for regional disparities measured along other dimensions. For this reason, this chapter focuses on the economic dimension. Other dimensions, however, are by no means insignificant. Regional equality/inequality is a multidimensional phenomenon. It should be treated as such. To fully appreciate the complexity of the phenomenon, we will examine some other dimensions in the next chapter.

Indicators

Measuring the economic dimension alone is not as straightforward as it appears, for the result may be very sensitive to the particular indicator chosen. Many indicators can be used to characterize the economic welfare of regions. Examples include the unemployment rate, per capita income, and per capita consumption.[1] However, gross domestic product (GDP) per capita has been widely accepted as the best approximation of the overall level of development and well-being. GDP is a measure of the value of the goods and services produced in a region during a given period of time. Variations in GDP, accordingly, indicate differences in the productive capacities of different regions. Through the production of goods and services, incomes are created.[2] Therefore, the per capita GDP of a region can serve as an indicator of regional economic welfare in much the same way as the per capita GDP of a country can be used to measure national economic welfare.

In this chapter, provincial per capita GDP is adopted as the indicator of overall economic performance. In addition to the reason given above, its adoption is also based upon two other considerations. First, as the next chapter will show, many other key indicators of socioeconomic development are highly correlated with per capita GDP. Second, it is relatively easier to make international comparisons with this indicator than with others.

Of course, any attempt to use one indicator to describe overall performance must be treated with extreme caution, because no single indicator can fully reflect economic welfare. When a whole array of indicators are measured, measures of regional inequality can increase in certain aspects and simultaneously decrease in others. For this reason, the next chapter will utilize multiple indicators to study regional disparities, in the hope that each will reflect one aspect of China's uneven regional economic development.

Measurement Methods

If a country were composed of only two regions, A and B, the per capita GDP differences between them could be measured by two methods. One is to measure the absolute gap, or the difference in per capita income between A and B. The other is to measure the relative gap, or the ratio of the per capita income of A to the per capita income of B. When a country has more than two regions, as China does, then summary measures are needed to index the overall absolute and relative gaps.[3] In this chapter, we use the standard deviation (SD) to measure absolute disparities and the coefficient of variation (CV) to capture relative disparities. In either case, the higher the value, the larger the variation across regions. Conversely, the lower the value, the less regional variation. Because regions vary significantly in population size, the two measures are weighted by the region's share of the total population.[4]

While the standard deviation has been firmly established as the most common measure of absolute dispersion, the coefficient of variation, as a representation of relative dispersion, has a number of alternatives, such as the Gini coefficient. We have chosen the coefficient of variation over other measures for two reasons. First, studies that employ several measures, such as Tsui's 1991 study, found the aggregate results to be similar for different measures.[5] Second, since most studies of regional disparity employ the coefficient of variation as a summary measure of relative inequality, its adoption would make international comparisons relatively easier.

Some have argued that the relative measure is better than the absolute measure in depicting trends of regional convergence or divergence.[6] It is hard to see why this would be the case. If the direction of change in regional disparities measured by both methods always coincides, there may be grounds to believe that one measure is preferable to the other. However, it is possible for relative disparities to narrow while absolute disparities widen. When their directions of change diverge, both measures seem to be necessary. We take the view, moreover, that individuals are more concerned about the absolute difference in economic welfare than about the relative difference. If absolute gaps indeed have a greater impact on people's perceptions of regional disparity and thereby are more politically relevant, it becomes necessary to include an absolute measure in any study of regional disparities.

Both relative and absolute measures fall into the category of objective measures. It goes without saying that they are needed in any serious effort to investigate regional disparities. At the same time, however, we think it necessary and important to pay attention to subjective measures of spatial inequality, by which we mean perceived gaps rather than real gaps. As many researchers have noted, conclusions drawn from objective studies of regional disparities are often strikingly at odds with the popular perception.[7] Why does the correlation between objective and subjective assessments of regional gaps appear to be low in China? The reason is very simple. As the television set becomes a household item, millions of peasants are on the move, and the general educational level of the population increases, China has been experiencing an information revolution, which has in turn considerably broadened people's framework of comparison. No longer comparing their own level of welfare to the level in nearby communities, people are now exposed to a much wider world. Regional gaps that were previously indiscernible to them are now quite visible, thus magnifying the perception of regional disparities. Another reason why it is important to pay attention to subjective measures is that perceived disparities are probably more politically relevant than real disparities.

Price Index

If the prices of goods and services do not change at all, there is obviously no need to worry about the effect of price changes on the measurement of regional disparities. If prices change, but they fluctuate in much the same manner for all regions at each point in time, nominal figures remain just as good as real ones. Only if inflation rates vary across time and space would using current price figures result in faulty findings. However, deflation by national inflation rates would not make things any better. In countries where there are substantial regional price differentials, regional deflators would undoubtedly differ from one another and from the national one. Thus, to reflect changes in patterns of regional development accurately, it is necessary to deflate nominal figures by relevant regional price indices.

In this study, per capita GDP figures are expressed in 1978 yuan, and are generated by using the region-specific GDP deflator to deflate the nominal per capita GDP for each province. The significance of such an adjustment will become clear in Figure 3.6, which shows that using current price values tends to substantially exaggerate the magnitude of changes in regional disparities.

Units of Analysis

Measuring regional disparities may be further complicated by the problem of choosing the level of territorial subdivision at which observations are to be made.

Studies of China's regional inequality often divide China in one of the following ways:

- Two units: the coastal and interior regions.
- Three units: the eastern, central, and western regions.
- Seven units: Far West, North Hinterland, South Hinterland, Central Core, North Coast, East Coast, South Coast.[8]
- Nine units: Manchuria, Yungui, the Upper Yangzi, Middle Yangzi, Gan Yangzi, Lower Yangzi, Lingnan, Southeast Coast, and Northeast Coast.[9]
- Thirty units: all the province-level administrative units.[10]
- 2,143 units: all the county-level administrative units.

Which regional classification is the most appropriate one? To answer this question, one must be aware that the degree of regional inequality detected is highly sensitive to the size of the observational units adopted. The magnitude of real regional disparities is likely to be underestimated when the size of the unit increases. The fact that measured inequality decreases with the level of territorial disaggregation is, of course, not unexpected, because "at high levels of aggregation, differences within are often averaged out."[11] This is one of the reasons that we have chosen the province as our unit of analysis in this study. China's thirty provinces are already very large by international standards, with each having a population of around 40 million on average. Grouping them into even larger units of analysis would result in huge agglomerates whose sizes exceed those of most countries. As a result, conclusions drawn from observations at any level higher than the province would overlook substantial intraregional inequalities.

There are several additional reasons why the province is preferable to other units of analysis. First, the province is a functional economic, administrative, and political unit. Provinces are deeply involved in the process of regional planning. They can also, in varying degrees, exercise political leverage over central policy-making on spatial resource allocation. An analysis at this level, therefore, provides data to assess the effects of specific regional development policies that may otherwise be unavailable at any other level. Second, measured regional disparities depend not only on the level of spatial disaggregation, but also on the choice of regional boundaries. Just as the delimitation of electoral districts may shape the outcome of elections, the choice of boundaries may affect the measurement of regional disparities. Except for the province and county, however, the other units mentioned above are the products of arbitrary geographical aggregation and do not conform to institutional boundaries. Third, the county is also a political unit. Analysis at this level could well reveal the extent of regional disparities. We are forced, however, to operate at the provincial level because county-level data are often incomplete and inconsistent.

One problem with using the province as the unit of analysis is how to classify the three metropolitan areas that also enjoy provincial status (Beijing, Shanghai, and Tianjin). It would be problematic to treat them in the same way as we treat the rest of the provinces, because they are far more urbanized and hence have substantially higher incomes than the others. Many have noted that changes in regional disparities display different patterns when the three cities are excluded.[12] In order to present an unbiased picture, we present two sets of statistics wherever appropriate in this chapter—one including the three cities, and the other excluding them.

Regional Disparity in 1978 and 1994

This section examines the magnitude of regional disparities in 1978 and 1994, the first and last years of the period under study. These, in turn, provide reference points for us to discern the trend in disparity between 1978 and 1994 in the next section.

Table 3.1 presents data on per capita GDP in China's thirty provinces for these two years. By measuring the deviations of provincial per capita GDP from the national average, we may divide the thirty provinces into the following three groups:

- The low-income group includes provinces where per capita GDP equals less than 80 percent of the national average.
- The middle-income group includes provinces where per capita GDP equals 80 to 120 percent of the national average.
- The high-income group includes provinces where per capita GDP is greater than 120 percent of the national average.

Table 3.2 ranks the provinces in ascending order of per capita GDP for 1978 and 1994. In 1978, ten provinces fell into the low-income category and five into the high-income category. Most provinces were somewhere in between. It is clear that regional gaps were fairly large on the eve of reforms. At that time, in Guizhou, China's poorest province, per capita GDP amounted to only 175 yuan, less than one-half of the national average. At the other end of the spectrum, per capita GDP in Shanghai, China's leading industrial center, was almost seven times the national average and more than fourteen times that of Guizhou. Even if we exclude the three metropolitan centers (Beijing, Tianjin, and Shanghai) and compare Guizhou with Liaoning, the fourth-richest province, the latter's per capita GDP was still 3.87 times that of the former.

In 1978, variations in per capita GDP already demonstrated some geographical patterns. For instance, except for Fujian, a province on the frontier facing Taiwan, all the low-income provinces were located in the interior, while four of the five high-income provinces were located along the east coast. However, such patterns were not entirely

Table 3.1

Provincial Per Capita GDP, 1978 and 1994

Provinces	Per capita GDP (in 1978 yuan)			As % of national average		
	1978	1994	Change	Index 1978	Index 1994	Change
Beijing (M)	1,267.8	4,148.3	2,880.5	334.5	306.6	−27.9
Tianjin (M)	1,160.0	3,435.3	2,275.3	306.1	253.9	−52.2
Hebei (E)	364.1	1,325.9	961.8	96.1	98.0	1.9
Shanxi (C)	365.0	1,097.3	732.3	96.3	81.1	−15.2
Inner Mongolia (C)	317.0	1,047.0	730.0	83.6	77.4	−6.2
Liaoning (E)	677.0	2,125.6	1,448.6	178.6	157.1	−21.5
Jilin (C)	381.0	1,369.2	988.2	100.5	101.2	0.7
Heilongjiang (C)	564.0	1,405.8	841.8	148.8	103.9	−44.9
Shanghai (M)	2,498.0	8,044.9	5,546.9	659.1	594.6	−64.5
Jiangsu (E)	430.0	2,381.3	1,951.3	113.5	176.0	62.5
Zhejiang (E)	331.0	2,214.9	1,883.9	87.3	163.7	76.4
Anhui (C)	244.0	871.3	627.3	64.4	64.4	0.0
Fujian (E)	273.0	1,677.7	1,404.7	72.0	124.0	52.0
Jiangxi (C)	276.0	1,051.3	775.3	72.8	77.7	4.9
Shandong (E)	316.0	1,543.8	1,227.8	83.4	114.1	30.7
Henan (C)	232.0	913.3	681.3	61.2	67.5	6.3
Hubei (C)	332.0	1,271.8	939.8	87.6	94.0	6.4
Hunan (C)	286.0	870.0	584.0	75.5	64.3	−11.2
Guangdong (E)	370.0	2,321.8	1,951.8	97.6	171.6	74.0
Guangxi (W)	227.0	732.0	505.0	59.9	54.1	−5.8
Sichuan (W)	253.0	953.9	700.9	66.8	70.5	3.7
Guizhou (W)	175.0	576.4	401.4	46.2	42.6	−3.6
Yunnan (W)	225.0	786.1	561.1	59.4	58.1	−1.3
Tibet (W)	375.0	918.7	543.7	98.9	67.9	−31.0
Shaanxi (W)	294.0	1,001.2	707.2	77.6	74.0	−3.6
Gansu (W)	348.0	1,029.6	681.6	91.8	76.1	−15.7
Qinghai (W)	428.0	930.9	502.9	112.9	68.8	−44.1
Ningxia (W)	370.0	1,017.5	647.5	97.6	75.2	−22.4
Xinjiang (W)	313.0	1,244.8	931.8	82.6	92.0	9.4
Hainan (E)[a]		1,589.0			117.4	
NATIONAL AVERAGE	379.0	1,353	974.0	100.0	100.0	0.0

Note: (W): western provinces; (C): central provinces; (E): eastern provinces; (M): metropolitan cities.

[a]Hainan used to be part of Guangdong province. It became a separate province in 1988.

clear-cut, for the middle-income group contained provinces situated in all three geographical regions (eastern, central, and western).[13]

In 1994, sixteen years after the introduction of market-oriented reforms, Shanghai and Guizhou were still China's richest and poorest

Table 3.2

Provincial Per Capita GDP as % of National Average, 1978 and 1994

1978		1994	
Low-Income		Low Income	
Guizhou (W)	46.2	Guizhou (W)	42.6
Yunnan (W)	59.4	Guangxi (W)	54.1
Guangxi (W)	59.9	Yunnan (W)	58.1
Henan (C)	61.2	Hunan (C)	64.3
Anhui (C)	64.4	Anhui (C)	64.4
Sichuan (W)	66.8	Henan (C)	67.5
Fujian (E)	72.0	Tibet (W)	67.9
Jiangxi (C)	72.8	Qinghai (W)	68.8
Hunan (C)	75.5	Sichuan (W)	70.5
Shaanxi (W)	77.6	Shaanxi (W)	74.0
		Ningxia (W)	75.2
Middle-Income		Gansu (W)	76.1
Xinjiang (W)	82.6	Inner Mongolia (C)	77.4
Shandong (E)	83.4	Jiangxi (C)	77.7
Inner Mongolia (C)	83.6		
Zhejiang (E)	87.3	Middle-Income	
Hubei (C)	87.6	Shanxi (C)	81.1
Gansu (W)	91.8	Xinjiang (W)	92.0
Hebei (E)	96.1	Hubei (C)	94.0
Shanxi (C)	96.3	Hebei (E)	98.0
Guangdong (E)	97.6	Jilin (C)	101.2
Ningxia (W)	97.6	Heilongjiang (C)	103.9
Tibet (W)	98.9	Shandong (E)	114.1
Jilin (C)	100.5	Hainan (E)	117.4
Qinghai (W)	112.9		
Jiangsu (E)	113.5	High-Income	
		Fujian (E)	124.0
High-Income		Liaoning (E)	157.1
Heilongjiang (C)	148.8	Zhejiang (E)	163.7
Liaoning (E)	178.6	Guangdong (E)	171.6
Tianjin (M)	306.1	Jiangsu (E)	176.0
Beijing (M)	334.5	Tianjin (M)	253.9
Shanghai (M)	659.1	Beijing (M)	306.6
		Shanghai (M)	594.6

provinces, respectively. Moreover, two-thirds of the provinces remained in the same income group they had been in sixteen years earlier. In particular, the same six provinces remained at the very top and very bottom of the development scale in both years. Does this mean that no changes occurred in the intervening sixteen years?

A close look at Figure 3.1 suggests otherwise. Four conspicuous changes seem to have occurred in the years between 1978 and 1994. First, the relative position of China's poorest provinces as well as the three metropolitan centers declined. While in 1978 Guizhou registered a per capita GDP of 46.2 percent of the national average, the corresponding percentage in 1994 was even lower, only 42.6 percent. At the opposite end of the scale, Shanghai suffered the biggest blow. Its relative position declined by 64.5 percentage points. However, the magnitude of the relative gap between Shanghai and Guizhou, the richest and the poorest, shrank only marginally—from 14.27 times higher in 1978 to 13.96 times higher in 1994. Second, the relative position of all but two western provinces declined. The two exceptions were Sichuan and Xinjiang. Third, it was the southeastern coastal provinces, Guangdong, Fujian, Zhejiang, and Jiangsu, that were able to make considerable headway during the reform era. In Guangdong, for instance, per capita GDP had been 2.4 percent lower than the national average in 1978, but by 1994, per capita GDP in that province had jumped to 71.6 percent above the national average. Fourth, China appeared to be more polarized in 1994 than it had been sixteen years earlier. Among China's thirty provinces, more than two-thirds now fell into either the low-income group or the high-income group, while in 1978 half of the provinces fell into the middle category. And, excluding the three metropolitan centers, the gap between the most-developed province (Liaoning/Jiangsu) and the least-developed province (Guizhou) increased from 3.87 times higher to 4.13 times higher.

As a consequence of these four changes, geographical patterns of regional disparity now became unmistakable: the coastal provinces were better off than the central provinces, which, in turn, surpassed the western provinces. Only one western province (Xinjiang) was able to make the middle-income group, and none the high-income group. On the other hand, the ten provinces with the highest per capita GDP were all eastern ones. Hebei was the only eastern province where per capita GDP was below the national average—yet it was only 2 percentage points lower.

Trends in Regional Disparity between 1978 and 1994

It is, of course, impossible to discern any long-term trends by looking at only two years. This section therefore turns from the starting and ending points of the study to the whole period.

Figure 3.1 **Per Capita GDP as % of National Average, 1978 and 1994**

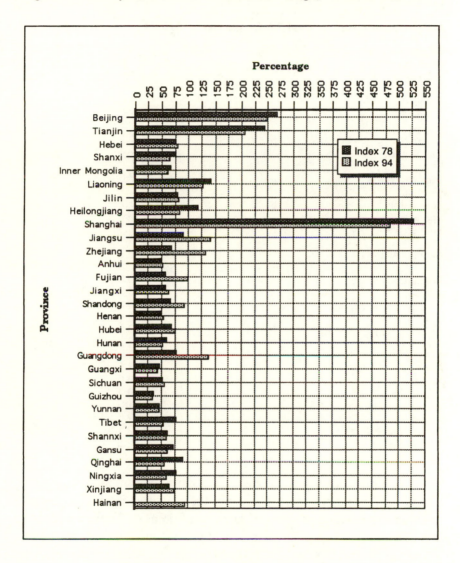

Table 3.3

Annual Growth Rate of Real Per Capita GDP, 1978-94

Qinghai (W)	5.0
Tibet (W)	5.8
Heilongjiang (E)	5.9
Ningxia (W)	6.5
Tianjin (M)	7.0
Gansu (W)	7.0
Shanxi (C)	7.1
Hunan (C)	7.2
Liaoning (E)	7.4
Shanghai (M)	7.6
Guangxi (W)	7.6
Guizhou (W)	7.7
Beijing (M)	7.7
Shaanxi (W)	8.0
Yunnan (W)	8.1
National Average	8.3
Anhui (C)	8.3
Jilin (C)	8.3
Inner Mongolia (C)	8.3
Hebei (E)	8.4
Sichuan (W)	8.6
Jiangxi (C)	8.7
Hubei (C)	8.8
Henan (C)	8.9
Xinjiang (W)	9.0
Shandong (E)	10.4
Jiangsu (E)	11.3
Fujian (E)	12.0
Guangdong (E)	12.1
Zhejiang (E)	12.6

Since a province's growth rate is the most important factor affecting changes in its relative position within the nation as a whole, we start with an examination of regional growth differences. Table 3.3 reports the average annual growth rates of real per capita GDP in twenty-nine provinces from 1978 to 1994. All the provinces seem to have grown rapidly. Even the slowest-growing province, Qinghai, was able to grow at 5 percent annually, a respectable growth rate for any economy. However, provincial growth rates fluctuated widely around the national average (8.3 percent), varying from 5 percent to 12.6 percent. Growth was slower than the national average in fifteen provinces, and equal to, or faster than, the national average in the other fourteen.

Some patterns seem to be identifiable here. Two types of provinces appear to have grown slowly. The first were western provinces, such as Qinghai, Tibet, Ningxia, and Gansu. The second were old industrial bases, namely, those that had ranked among the top five in per capita GDP in 1978. On the other hand, the fastest growth was observed in those southeastern coastal provinces where growth potential had been repressed due to the government's concern about possible foreign invasion before 1978. Examples were Guangdong, Fujian, Zhejiang, Jiangsu, and Shandong. The central provinces tended to grow at a speed of no more than 1.2 percentage points above or below the national average.

Neoclassical economists have long argued that there is a general tendency for poor countries or regions to grow more rapidly than rich countries or regions. Such a model of convergence (the so-called β-convergence)[14] has recently been applied to the study of regional growth in China.[15] These studies generally find supporting evidence for β-convergence in the reform period. Figure 3.2 presents our finding. Although, by showing a descending slope, the figure seems to support the conclusion reached in previous studies, Figures 3.3 and 3.4 suggest that if β-convergence occurred at all, it was during the early years of the reform era, in the infancy of China's market-oriented reform. In the mid-1980s, China accelerated its reform. Convergence, however, subsequently disappeared. More significantly, as Figure 3.5 shows, after 1990 provinces with above-average levels of per capita GDP tended to grow faster, resulting in divergence rather than convergence. This was exactly the period in which marketization and liberalization were in full swing. Those who argue that convergence in China was "strongly associated with the extent of marketization and openness"[16] need to answer two questions. First, what evidence supports a long-term tendency toward β-convergence in post-Mao China? Second, why did the deepening of market-oriented reform coincide with the disappearance of convergence in the economy as a whole?

Even with β-convergence, regional inequality need not decline. β-convergence is a necessary, but not sufficient, condition for regional per capita GDP inequality to diminish over time. Convergence of the first kind (poor economies tending to grow faster than their rich counterparts), of course, could generate convergence of the second kind (the so-called α-convergence, namely, reduced inequality of per capita GDP).[17] If there is no β-convergence, α-convergence simply would

Figure 3.2 **Growth Rate vs. Initial Per Capita GDP, 1978–94**

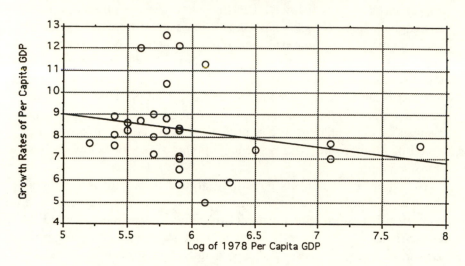

Figure 3.3 **Growth Rate vs. Initial Per Capita GDP, 1978–85**

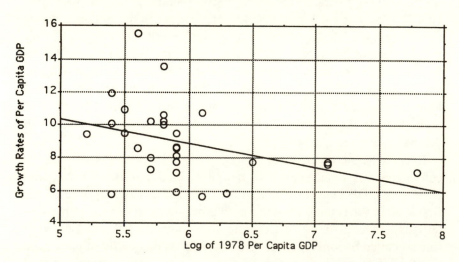

Figure 3.4 **Growth Rate vs. Initial Per Capita GDP, 1985–94**

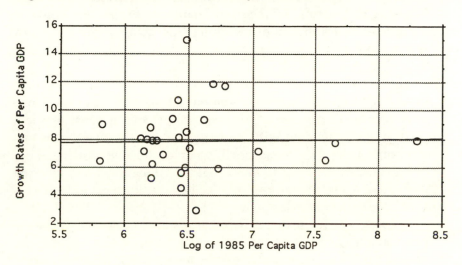

Figure 3.5 **Growth Rate vs. Initial Per Capita GDP, 1990–94**

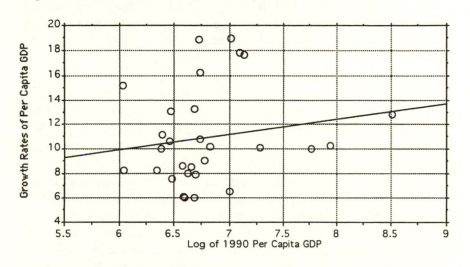

not happen. However, regional disparities may increase even when β-convergence occurs.[18] Since our main interest in this study is changes in the distribution of per capita GDP across regions, we now turn our attention to α-convergence, which is measured here by the coefficient of variation.

Figure 3.6 plots two measures of relative dispersion. Although both are unweighted coefficients of variation (CV) of per capita GDP, one set is calculated using current prices and the other using constant prices (1978 yuan). Contrary to Williamson's inverted U-hypothesis, the two time paths yield similar uninverted U-curves. Relative dispersion declined between 1978 and 1990–91, but the falling trend was reversed afterwards. All in all, however, regional disparities seem to have narrowed during the reform era.

Of course, one has reason to question whether changing CVs convey an accurate picture of real changes in relative dispersion, because the unweighted CV is determined in part by the somewhat arbitrary administrative division of regional units.[19] Even so, Figure 3.6 is still important, for it clearly demonstrates the significance of adjusting data by using provincial deflators. Measured in current prices, the coefficient of variation fell from 0.983 in 1978 to 0.669 in 1994, a steep drop of 0.314. After being adjusted by individual provincial deflators, however, the coefficient of variation only showed a marginal decline of 0.115 in the same period. Obviously, using current price values tends to substantially exaggerate the degree of change. Due to the huge size and phenomenal diversity of China, there is always great regional variation in inflation rates.[20] Therefore, anyone who studies regional disparities has to exercise caution in drawing conclusions from unadjusted data.

Figure 3.7 displays two other sets of coefficients of variation (CV_w) of per capita GDP that are different from those shown in Figure 3.6 in that they are both weighted (based on share of total population) and measured in constant prices. The top and bottom curves differ only in sample size; the former includes Beijing, Tianjin, and Shanghai, while the latter excludes the three cities.

Let us first take a look at the top curve, which is supposed to be a better measure of relative dispersion than that given by the unweighted coefficient of variation. Interestingly, CV_w essentially shows a very similar time path to that of CV, with inequality declining from 1978 to 1991 and then reversing course. In terms of the degree of dispersion, however, CV and CV_w lead to different conclusions. The values of

Figure 3.6 **CV Measured in Current Price and Constant Price**

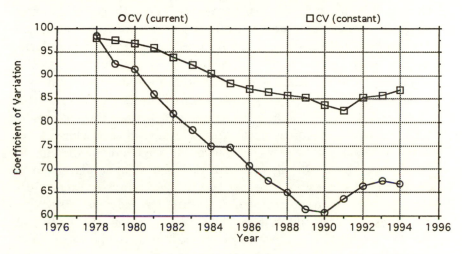

Figure 3.7 **Changes in CV_W, with and without BTS, 1978–94**

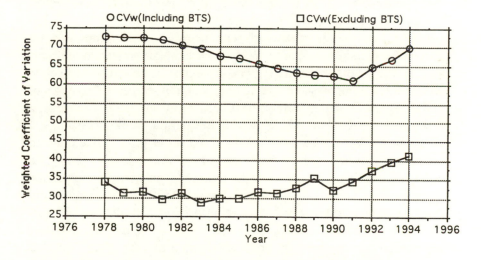

CV_w are approximately 0.25 below the corresponding figures of CV, suggesting that, in general, relative dispersion in per capita GDP is probably not as large as CV indicates. Moreover, while both CV_w and CV show a decline of relative dispersion between 1978 and 1994, the former suggests a much smaller magnitude of change (0.030) than the latter (0.115).

The bottom curve in Figure 3.7 differs from the top one in that Beijing, Tianjin, and Shanghai are not included. Compared to most provinces, the three centrally administered metropolises are much more urbanized and industrialized. As a result, they enjoy extraordinarily high levels of per capita GDP relative to the national average. For this reason, treating these metropolitan areas like other provinces may greatly bias our analysis of regional disparities. As the bottom curve shows, excluding the three cities yields two noteworthy changes in CV_w. First, CV_w becomes much smaller. Rather than fluctuating between 0.60 and 0.75, it now oscillates in the neighborhood of 0.35. In other words, once extreme cases are excluded, relative dispersion in per capita GDP does not appear to be alarmingly large in China. Second, the direction of change in CV_w is different. Regional dispersion did decrease marginally in the initial years of reform, but the twelve years following 1983 saw a steady increase in relative dispersion. Consequently, CV_w at the end of the period was 0.073 higher than its value in 1978 (increasing from 0.342 to 0.415). Thus, the relative dispersion across provinces seems to have widened during the reform era if the three cities are excluded.

Intuitively, when relative dispersion grows, it is impossible for absolute dispersion to decline. What would happen to absolute dispersion if relative dispersion falls? The answer is, it depends.[21] Absolute inequality may increase, and relative inequality decrease. The cases of Guizhou and Shanghai demonstrate this point. Guizhou's per capita GDP grew faster than Shanghai's in the period from 1978 to 1994 (7.73 percent vs. 7.58 percent). Although a faster growth rate allowed Guizhou to narrow the relative gap in income between itself and Shanghai from 14.27 to 13.96 times higher, the absolute gap expanded from 2,323 to 7,469 yuan. Figures 3.8 and 3.9 also make it abundantly clear that downward movements in relative dispersion do not necessarily lead to absolute convergence. Here, the absolute dispersion of per capita GDP is measured by both unweighted and weighted standard deviations (SD and SD_w). Figures 3.8 and 3.9 plot SD and SD_w from 1978 to 1994, with the former covering all the provinces and the latter excluding Beijing, Tianjin, and Shanghai. All four measures point to the same conclusion: Absolute dispersion increased continuously throughout the whole period, and accelerated after 1990. It is particularly interesting that, when the three metropolises are excluded, the time paths of SD and SD_w show an almost identical contour (Figure

Figure 3.8 **Standard Deviation of Per Capita GDP (BTS included), 1978–94**

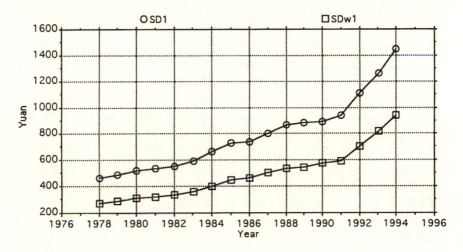

Figure 3.9 **Standard Deviation of Per Capita GDP (BTS excluded), 1978–94**

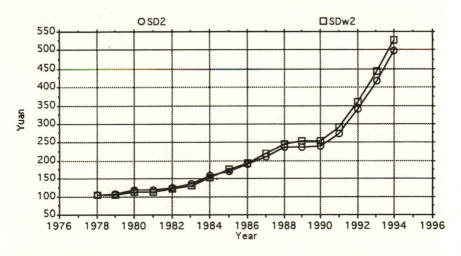

3.9). This figure presents a striking contrast with the situation when these cities are included (Figure 3.8). The comparison once again illustrates how drastically the three extreme cases affect the overall picture of regional disparity in China.

To sum up the findings in this section, it seems fair to divide the years after 1978 into three subperiods. Before 1985, poor provinces tended to grow faster than rich provinces. As a result, the general trend was for relative dispersion to diminish. Absolute dispersion was still on the rise, but it increased at a slow pace. This early trend came to a halt during the second half of the 1980s. The negative correlation between a province's initial level of per capita GDP and its growth rate, observed in the first subperiod, disappeared altogether (compare Figures 3.3 and 3.4). However, no positive correlation was found either. The overall relative dispersion appeared to continue falling if the three centrally administered metropolises were included. But once we controlled for the effects of the three extreme cases, a different picture emerged: The relative dispersion among the rest of the provinces began to grow. In the meantime, the absolute dispersion was increasing at a faster rate than before. After 1990, there was strong evidence of a secular increase in regional disparity, no matter which measure was used and whether or not the cases of the three big cities were counted. Between 1990 and 1994, provinces with above-average levels of per capita GDP grew faster. Consequently, both relative and absolute dispersions showed an upsurge. Having experienced convergence from the late 1970s to the early 1980s and stabilization in regional inequality in the second half of the 1980s, China now entered a period of divergence.

Intraprovincial Inequality: Guizhou and Guangdong

In addition to interprovincial differences, intraprovincial variations have also been characteristic of China. In a country where provinces often are as large and as populous as middle- or even large-sized countries, substantial intraprovincial inequality is to be expected. However, because the recent debate on China's regional-development strategy has focused on interprovincial inequalities, intraprovincial inequalities have attracted little attention. Many seem to have forgotten that regardless of the general level of economic development of any given province as a whole, internal variation in development levels can be great. Not all of the counties in the rich provinces are rich. A high

Table 3.4

Guizhou and Guangdong, 1994

Province	Population (millions)	As % of China	Area (sq. km.)	As % of China	GDP (1994 yuan, billions)	As % of China
Guizhou	34	2.89	176,100	1.85	52.1	1.12
Guangdong	67	5.73	178,500	1.87	424.0	9.09

average per capita GDP makes a province rich, but the broad picture delineated by aggregate data may mask sharp internal variations.[22] Studying intraprovincial disparities may help us to identify conditions and trends disguised by the aggregate data.

This section analyzes regional variations in two provinces, Guizhou and Guangdong. Due to data limitations, we focus on only one year— 1994. Table 3.4 provides information about the two provinces. Although Guangdong is about the same size as Guizhou, its population at the time was about twice as large as Guizhou's. In terms of the level of economic development, Guizhou fell far behind Guangdong, with its total GDP reaching only 12.3 percent of Guangdong's. As Table 3.2 shows, in 1994 Guizhou's per capita GDP was the lowest in China, whereas Guangdong's was among the highest.

As Table 3.5 shows, Guizhou was indeed very poor. Among its eighty-one counties/cities, sixty-four (79 percent) had a per capita GDP of less than 50 percent of the national average, and another twelve counties/cities (14.8 percent) less than 80 percent. Altogether, only five of its counties/cities had a per capita GDP higher than 80 percent of the national average. In other words, the overwhelming majority of the counties/cities in Guizhou, or more precisely 93.8 percent of them, belonged to the low-income group in our classification. Table 3.5, in fact, does not give a full picture of the level of poverty in Guizhou. For instance, it fails to tell us that there were seventeen counties/cities where per capita GDP did not even reach 20 percent of the national average. In the poorest county, Guanling, the corresponding percentage was merely 13.6 percent!

The situation in Guangdong was very different. Thirty-eight of its ninety-eight counties/cities belonged to the high-income group. Another twenty-eight fell into the middle-income group (80–120 percent

Table 3.5

Classification of Counties by Per Capita GDP, in Guizhou and Guangdong, 1994

Province	No. of counties	50%	50–80%	80–120%	120–400%	400%
Guizhou	81.0	64.0	12.0	3.0	2.0	0,0
%	100.0	79.0	14.8	3.7	2.5	0.0
Guangdong	98.0	8.0	24.0	28.0	32.0	6.0
%	100.0	8.2	24.5	28.6	32.7	6.1

National average per capita GDP = 100%.

of the national average) in our classification. This does not mean that there were no poor counties/cities in Guangdong, however. Indeed, there were thirty-two low-income counties/cities, including eight counties/cities where per capita GDP was lower than 50 percent of the national average. In Guangdong's poorest county, Heping, per capita GDP amounted to less than one-third of the national average.

Despite the differences between the two provinces, Table 3.6 shows that they shared two common features.

First, relative dispersion was very large. The coefficient of variation of per capita GDP was 0.67 in Guizhou and 0.81 in Guangdong. The ratio of the richest county/city to the poorest county/city was approximately 12 : 1 in Guizhou and 19 : 1 in Guangdong. Remember that when the province was used as the unit of analysis in the preceding section, the overall coefficient of variation was 0.67 (see Figure 3.6), and the ratio of per capita GDP between Shanghai and Guizhou was 13.96 : 1 in 1994.

Second, absolute dispersion was even more striking. The standard deviation of per capita GDP was 315 yuan in Guizhou and 1,665 yuan in Guangdong. Meanwhile, the difference in per capita GDP between the richest county/city and the poorest county/city was 2,058 yuan in Guizhou and 7,805 yuan in Guangdong. Again remember that the national standard deviation was slightly over 1,400 yuan, and the difference in per capita GDP between Shanghai and Guizhou was 7,469 yuan in 1994.

Without comparing these two cases to the other provinces, we cannot determine the extent to which the two cases were representa-

Table 3.6

Regional Disparities in Guizhou and Guangdong, 1994 (1978 yuan)

Province	Maxi-mum (yuan)	Mini mum (yuan)	Mean (yuan)	SD (yuan)	CV	Maximum/ Minimum	Maximum-Minimum (yuan)
Guizhou	2,242	184	473	315	0.666	12.18	2,058
Guangdong	8,246	441	2,060	1,665	0.808	18.70	7,805

tive. The point we intend to make here is that significant regional inequalities may be found within poor as well as rich provinces. Guangdong was one of China's most rapidly growing provinces during the 1978–94 period and, by 1994, was one of China's most affluent provinces. Yet, considerable variations were found even within such an economically advanced province. Moreover, the comparison between Guangdong and Guizhou seems to suggest that the unevenness of development tends to be more pronounced in rich provinces than in poor provinces.

The sharp geographic differences in per capita GDP within China's least-developed province and one of its most developed provinces suggest that regional inequality would be a far more serious problem were the county rather than the province taken as the unit of analysis. It is also likely that changes in regional disparities observed at the county level may not correspond to those at the provincial level. Therefore, anyone who studies China's regional disparities should not lose sight of the importance of intraprovincial inequalities.

Minority Nationality Areas

China is a multinational country. Apart from the Han people, there are fifty-five other nationalities. Unlike in the former Soviet Union, where just over one-half of the population was Russian, minority nationalities in China are a true minority. The fourth national census in 1990 found that the minority nationalities altogether accounted for only slightly more than 8 percent of China's total population. But in absolute terms, the total population of minority nationalities amounted to nearly 100 million, comparable to the size of a large country. More importantly, the fifty-five minority nationalities occupy two-thirds of China's total land territory. Their economic well-being, therefore, has a great bearing on the stability of the country. In this section, we examine the economic gaps between minority nationality areas and the rest of the country.

In China, five provinces are designated as autonomous regions (Tibet, Xinjiang, Inner Mongolia, Guangxi, and Ningxia). In addition, there are three provinces (Yunnan, Guizhou, and Qinghai) in which minority nationalities comprise over one-third of the population.

In 1978, among these eight provinces, only Qinghai enjoyed a level of per capita GDP higher than the national average. Tibet and Ningxia were below the average, but came close to it. The other five were well below the national average (see Table 3.2). During the reform era, however, Qinghai, Tibet, and Ningxia were among the slowest-growing provinces. The other minority-concentrated provinces did not do well either. As a matter of fact, except for Xinjiang, their annual growth rates of real per capita GDP were lower than the national average (see Table 3.3). As a result, all minority-concentrated provinces except Xinjiang found their relative positions in the nation worsened. And by 1994, none of the eight provinces had a per capita GDP higher than the national average, and seven of them fell into the low-income group by our definition (see Table 3.2).

Below the provincial level, thirty minority-nationality autonomous prefectures are scattered across nine provinces (Guizhou, Sichuan, Yunnan, Qinghai, Gansu, Jilin, Hubei, Hunan, and Xinjiang). Figure 3.10 compares the levels of per capita GDP in these autonomous prefectures with the national average. There were great variations in the level of per capita GDP among the thirty prefectures. Leading the list was Haixi Mongolian and Tibetan Autonomous Prefecture of Qinghai, where per capita GNP was 61.5 percent above the national average. At the bottom of the list was Wenshan Zhuang and Miao Autonomous Prefecture of Yunnan, where per capita GDP was merely 20 percent of the national average. Taken as a whole, the levels of per capita GDP of the thirty autonomous prefectures were far lower than the national average. In 1994, the average per capita GDP of the thirty autonomous prefectures was 805 yuan, which was less than 60 percent of the national average (1,353 yuan). Twenty-five of them belonged to the low-income. In twelve out of the thirty prefectures, per capita GDP did not even reach 50 percent of the national average.

At the county level, the contrast between minority-concentrated areas and the rest of the Han areas appears to be even more striking.

Figure 3.10 **Per Capita GDP as % of National Average in 30 Autonomous Prefectures, 1994**

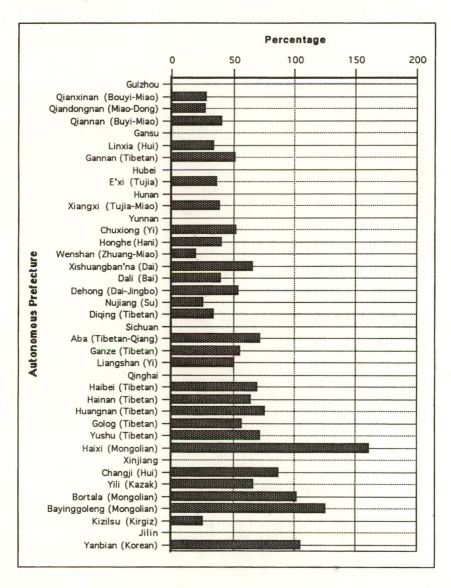

Table 3.7

Minority-Concentrated Counties in Poverty, 1992

Province	Counties in province	Counties in poverty	Minority-concentrated counties in poverty
Inner Mongolia	84	31	31
Xinjiang	85	25	25
Ningxia	18	8	8
Guangxi	80	28	28
Tibet	77	5	5
Yunnan	123	73	51
Guizhou	80	48	34
Qinghai	39	14	12
Sichuan	172	43	21
Gansu	75	41	12
Hubei	68	25	9
Hunan	90	10	4
Liaoning	44	9	4
Jilin	41	5	1
Heilongjiang	68	11	1
Hebei	139	39	5
Hainan	17	5	4
Guangdong	78	3	1
Zhejiang	64	3	1
Shanxi	100	35	0
Anhui	68	17	0
Fujian	63	8	0
Jiangxi	84	18	0
Shandong	95	10	0
Henan	116	28	0
Shaanxi	92	50	0
Beijing	8	0	0
Tianjin	5	0	0
Shanghai	6	0	0
Jiangsu	64	0	0
Total	2,143	592	257

Source: Difang caizheng (January 1996), pp. 62-64.

During the Eighth Five-Year Plan Period (1991–95), altogether 592 counties were designated as impoverished counties. Nearly half of them (257 or 43.4 percent) were minority-concentrated counties. Table 3.7 gives the distribution of impoverished counties in China's thirty provinces. By definition, in the five officially designated autonomous regions, all impoverished counties were minority-concentrated counties. In Yunnan, Guizhou, and Qinghai, while minority nationalities accounted for one-third to three-sevenths of the total population, over 70 percent of the impoverished counties were minority-concentrated. In several provinces, such as Sichuan, Gansu, and Hubei, where minority nationalities comprised only a small fraction of the total population, minority-concentrated counties often represented a large proportion of the impoverished counties.

It is clear that there are huge gaps between minority-concentrated areas and Han areas, whichever administrative level is chosen as the unit of analysis. Based on such an observation, a professor at the South-Central Institute of Ethnology came to the following conclusion: "In the final analysis, regional disparities in today's China are disparities between Han areas along the east coast and minority-concentrated areas in the west."[23]

China in Comparative Perspective

How bad is China's regional inequality? Only in a comparative context can one make a meaningful judgment about the degree of regional inequality in China. Table 3.8 compares the distribution of per capita GDP in China in 1994 with available recent estimates of the distribution of income in selected countries. Due to data limitations, the following two measurements of regional inequality in per capita GDP (or income) are used: the ratio of the maximum to the minimum (Max./Min.) and the coefficient of variation (CV). We calculate two sets of estimates for China. China(a) covers all provincial units, and China(b) excludes Beijing, Tianjin, and Shanghai. We also present two sets of estimates for Indonesia, with Indonesia(a) including the capital city, Jakarta, and Indonesia(b) excluding Jakarta.

In comparison with the other countries included in the table, regional disparities in China appear to be the largest if China(a) is adopted. Even if China(b) is chosen, the degree of interregional inequality in China is still substantially higher than in all countries except the former Yugoslavia. Among industrialized countries, Italy and France are often regarded as classic cases of north-south dualism. In the Third World, meanwhile, India and Indonesia are treated as examples of uneven development. However, China fares worse than all of these cases.

It needs to be noted that such international comparisons must be interpreted with care, because the unit of analysis varies greatly in size

Table 3.8

International Comparison of Regional Disparities in Per Capita GDP or Per Capita Income

Country	Year	Max/Min	CV
China(a)	1978	14.27	0.73
China(b)	1978	3.87	0.34
China(a)	1994	13.96	0.87
China(b)	1994	4.13	0.39
Yugoslavia	1988	7.80	0.54
Greece	1988	1.69	0.10
Spain	1988	2.23	0.17
Germany	1988	1.93	0.13
France	1988	2.15	0.26
Canada	1988	2.30	0.28
Japan	1981	1.47	0.12
Italy	1988	2.34	0.26
Portugal	1988	1.66	0.23
Belgium	1988	1.61	0.15
Britain	1988	1.63	0.15
Netherlands	1988	2.69	0.19
United States	1983	1.43	0.11
Australia	1978	1.13	0.05
South Korea	1985	1.53	0.15
India	1980	3.26	0.36
Indonesia(a)	1983	5.30	0.46
Indonesia(b)	1983	4.00	0.34

Source: For data on China, see *China Statistical Yearbook, 1995* (Beijing: China Statistical Press, 1995), p. 38; 1995 statistical yearbooks of thirty provinces and autonomous regions (Beijing: China Statistical Press, 1995). For data on Yugoslavia, Italy, Greece, Portugal, Spain, Belgium, Germany, UK, France, and Netherlands, see Daniel Ottolenghi and Alfred Steinherr (1993), p. 229. For data on Canada, see Donald J. Savoie (1992), p. 191. For data on the United States, see David M. Smith (1987), p. 41. For data on Japan, see Institute of Japan Studies and Chinese Academy of Social Sciences (1994), p. 235. For data on Australia, see Benjamin Higgins (1981), pp. 69–70. For data on India, see K. R. G. Nair (1985), p. 9. For data on Indonesia. see Hal Hill and Anna Weidemann, in Hill (1989), pp. 6–7. For data on South Korea, see Kyung-hwan Kim and Edwin S. Mills (1990), p. 415.

from one country to another. China is an extraordinarily large country in terms of population. On average, a province in China has a population of about 40 million, which is bigger than many of the world's medium-sized countries. The population of Sichuan, China's largest province before the city of Chongqing was chopped out in 1997, was close to that of Japan; Henan and Shandong, the second- and third-largest provinces, have populations as large as Germany and much larger than Britain, France, and Italy. Ranging in population size from 30 to 60 million, even China's medium-sized provinces exceed the size of Greece, Spain, Canada, Portugal, Belgium, the Netherlands, Australia, South Korea, and the former Yugoslavia. Of course, no province even comes close to the size of India, the United States, or Indonesia. However, India's population of 800 million is divided into thirty-one states, the United States' population of 250 million into fifty states, and Indonesia's population of 200 million into twenty-seven provincial units. Thus, it is safe to say that the units of analysis used for studying all the other cases included in Table 3.8 must be much smaller than the unit we use to study China.

As pointed out above, measures of regional inequality are very sensitive to the level of aggregation of the data. The higher the aggregate level, the lower the estimate of the degree of inequality. For this reason, the picture presented by Table 3.8 has to be regarded as somewhat misleading, for it must have grossly underestimated the degree of interregional inequality for China. If units of the same size were to be used to study both China and the former Yugoslavia, the China of 1994 would undoubtedly have higher levels of regional inequality than did Yugoslavia in 1988, just a few years before its disintegration.

Subjective Regional Disparities

In the preceding sections, we used various measures to examine changes in China's regional disparities since 1978. All of these measures fall into the broad category of what we call objective measures. As pointed out above, in social and political life, perceived regional gaps are as important as, and probably even more important than, objectively existing regional gaps. Therefore, this section turns its attention to the subjective dimension of regional disparities.

Before 1978, China was a closed society. Not only did the country close its doors to the outside world, but localities within the country were also largely cut off from one another. No wonder China was described as a "honeycomb society."[24] At that time, peasants had little chance of leaving their villages. To them, regional disparities were nothing but differences between production brigades or among different communes. Nor did urban dwellers have much chance of traveling. They knew that there were regional gaps, but without travel and access

Figure 3.11 **Measures of Subjective Regional Disparities**

(A)

Do you think China's regional disparities have (1) widened, (2) narrowed, or
(3) not changed much since the beginning of the 1980s?

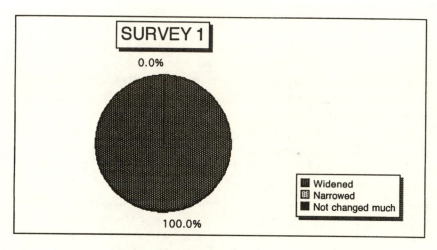

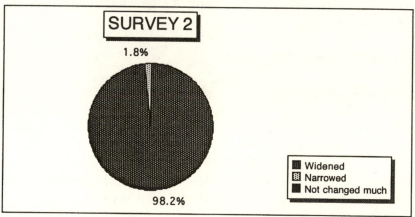

Figure 3.11*(continued)*

(B)

Are regional gaps in per capita income between developed and less-developed
areas (1) too large, (2) too small, or (3) normal?

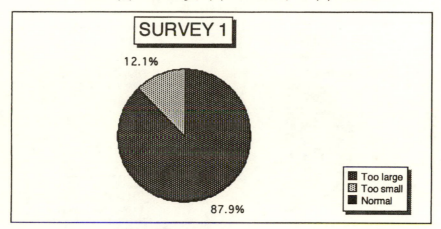

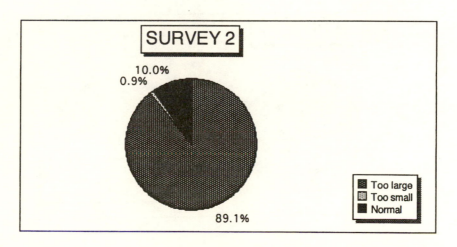

Figure 3.12 **What Is the Worst Possible Consequence That May Be Brought about by Excessively Large Regional Disparities?**

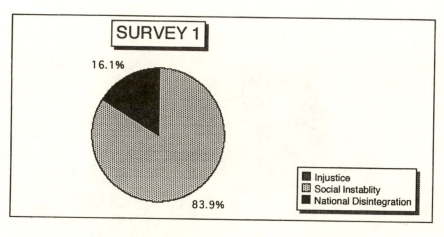

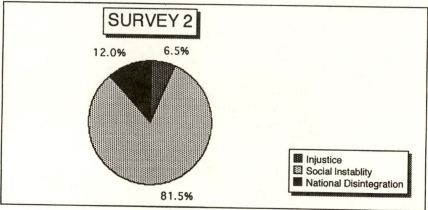

to television, it was hard for them to imagine how serious regional inequality really was. Quite possibly, perceived regional gaps were smaller than objective ones during the pre-reform years.

Thanks to economic reform, China has quickly moved into the information age. TV sets, radios, tape-recorders, and VCRs are now household items. The computer, publication, and tourism industries are booming. And what is more, millions of peasants are leaving their villages and flowing into county seats, provincial capitals, and coastal areas. As the mass media become all-pervasive and people's radii of action expand, it is inevitable that their reference points for drawing interregional comparisons will change.

No longer comparing their localities to neighboring communities, people may now use what they know of the most advanced regions in the country as the benchmark for comparison. Consequently, perceived gaps may now be much bigger than real ones. It is also possible that perceived gaps will increase even as objective regional disparities are declining. Although the perceived gaps may misrepresent the economic reality, such perceptions could have significant political repercussions if widely shared by the populace. The reason is simple: People's responses to regional inequality are influenced most deeply, not by objective indices, however accurate, but by their perceptions of regional disparities. Thus, failure to appreciate the importance of the subjective dimension of regional disparities could have fatal political consequences.

In order to gauge perceived regional gaps, we conducted two small-scale surveys. One (Survey 1), conducted in June 1994, involved seventeen provincial leaders and sixteen prefectural leaders attending a training program at the Central Party School. The other (Survey 2), carried out in June 1995, had 109 participants, all of whom were prefectural or county leaders from minority-concentrated areas. Figure 3.11 reports how the participants in the two surveys responded to the following two questions:

- Do you think China's regional disparities have (1) widened, (2) narrowed, or (3) not changed much since the beginning of the 1980s?
- In your view, are regional gaps in per capita income between developed and less-developed areas (1) too large, (2) too small, or (3) normal?

To the first question, all the respondents in Survey 1 chose the first answer. None opted for the second or the third. Although two partici- pants (1.8 percent) in Survey 2 believed that regional gaps had nar- rowed, the overwhelming majority (98.2 percent) agreed with the intervicwccs of Survey 1 that regional disparities had worsened.

The answers to the second question were more interesting. Four out of the thirty-three respondents (or 12.1 percent) in Survey 1 reported that regional gaps were too small to provide sufficient incentive for economic growth. One person (or 0.9 percent) in Survey 2 shared this view, and another eleven respondents (or 10 percent) claimed that the gaps were neither too large nor too small, but just about right. To protect the anonymity of the participants, since both samples were very small, we intentionally did not ask them to identify the province or prefecture from which they came. Hence, there was no way for us to tell whether or not those who chose the second or third answers were from relatively affluent areas. In any event, most of the participants in both surveys believed that regional disparities were already excessive.

What is the worst possible consequence of excessively large re- gional disparities? Figure 3.12 reports the participants' answers to this question across the two surveys. Over 80 percent of them responded that China's political stability might be undermined if the growing disparities were not halted. Some feared that excessively large regional disparities might result in such dire consequences as national disinte- gration. One-eighth in Survey 1 and one-sixth in Survey 2 shared this view. Among the 142 officials interviewed in the two surveys, only seven were so optimistic that they excluded the possibility of political instability or national disintegration altogether. Widening regional gaps particularly worried officials working in minority-concentrated areas in our Survey 2. Over 95 percent of them claimed that the gaps had already negatively affected the relations between Han Chinese and minority nationalities, and two-thirds believed that such effects were dreadful. This finding was confirmed by another survey of minority officials conducted in late 1995.[25]

Notes

1. Which indicator is more adequate depends on which aspect of economic life is of greater concern to the people in a country. In industrialized countries, the unemployment rate is often used to gauge regional disparities, because per capita

income does not vary as much as the unemployment rate among different regions. See, for example, Harvey Armstrong and Jim Taylor, *Regional Economics and Policy.*

2. But the income that results does not necessarily accrue to a region's inhabitants. Where the inhabitants of other regions are employed within a region, there may be an outflow of income. The distribution of original income can also be modified by the redistributive transfers that result from government taxation, benefits, and social security expenditures. Moreover, GDP estimates do not include the value of those goods and services that people produce for their own use, and the value that results from informal and hidden economic activities. Both values are large in developing countries like China, and in all probability vary significantly from one place to another. See Mick Dunford, "Regional Disparities in the European Community," p. 727.

3. Douglas Rae, *Equalities,* chap. 6.

4. If n denotes the number of regions, p_i the population of the ith region ($i=1,2,3 \ldots n$), and x_i the per capita GDP of the ith region, there are two ways to define the mean per capita GDP in the nation, namely:

$$x = \Sigma x_i/n \text{ and}$$

$$x = \Sigma x_i p_i/\Sigma p_i$$

Then the unweighted standard deviation is:

$$SD = [\Sigma (x_i - x)^2 /n]^{1/2}$$

The weighted standard deviation is:

$$SD_W = [\Sigma (x_i - x)^2 \, p_i/\Sigma p_i]^{1/2}$$

The unweighted coefficient of variation is given by the equation:

$$CV = SD/x$$

and the weighted coefficient of variation is given by the equation:

$$CV_W = SD_W/x$$

5. Kai-yuen Tsui, "China's Regional Inequality," pp. 1–21.

6. C.P. Lo, "The Geography of Rural Regional Inequality in Mainland China," pp. 466–86; C. Cindy Fan, "Regional Impacts of Foreign Trade in China," p. 137.

7. E. Walter-Busch, "Subjective and Objective Indicators of Regional Quality of Life in Switzerland," pp. 337–91; Gabriel Lipshitz, "Divergence or Convergence in Regional Inequality, pp. 13–20.

8. Albert Keidel, "China: Regional Disparities."

9. G. William Skinner divides China into nine macroregional systems. See his "Differential Development in Lingnan." But he does not give a full list of all nine regions in the article.

10. Today, China has thirty-one provincial units, including twenty-two provinces (Anhui, Fujian, Gansu, Guangdong, Guizhou, Hainan, Hebei, Heilongjiang,

Henan, Hubei, Hunan, Jiangsu, Jiangxi, Jilin, Liaoning, Qinghai, Shaanxi, Shandong, Shanxi, Sichuan, Yunnan, Zhejiang), five autonomous regions (Guangxi, Inner Mongolia, Ningxia, Tibet, Xinjiang), and four centrally administered municipalities (Beijing, Chongqing, Shanghai, Tianjin). Among them, Hainan was separated from Guangdong and became a province in 1987, and Chongqing was separated from Sichuan and became a municipality directly under the central government in 1997. In addition, China considers Taiwan to be its thirty-second province. For the sake of convenience, we refer to the centrally administered municipalities and autonomous regions as provinces in this study. Twenty-nine provinces are covered for the 1978–86 period, and thirty provinces for the 1987–95 period.

11. Mick Dunford, "Regional Disparities," p. 732.

12. For example, see Hiroyuki Kato, "Regional Development in the Reform Period," p. 119.

13. Guangxi is usually classified as an eastern coastal province. But actually "much of its population is cut off from the sea by hills and mountains." See Keidel, "China," p. 4. Also see Sasunne Yabuki's classification in his, *A Great Country, Where Is China Going?* p. 219. Therefore, Guangxi is treated as a western province in this study.

14. The β-convergence measures whether poor economies tend to grow faster than rich ones. We may say that there is β-convergence if regression of growth against the initial level of per capita GDP is negative and statistically significant.

15. Tianlun Jian, Jeffrey D. Sachs, and Andrew M. Warner, "Trends in Regional Inequality in China," pp. 1–21; Summer J. La Croix and Richard F. Garbaccio, "Convergence in Income and Consumption in China During the Maoist and Reform Regimes."

16. Jian, Sachs, and Warner, "Trends in Regional Inequality," p. 18.

17. We say that there is α-convergence if there is a decline over time in the spatial dispersion of per capita GDP.

18. See Robert J. Barro and Xavier Sala-i-Martin, "Convergence Across States and Regions," p. 112; idem, *Economic Growth,* pp. 383–86.

19. Jeffrey G. Williamson, "Regional Inequality and the Process of National Development," p. 11.

20. Zhao Xiaobin Simon and Tong S. P. Christopher, "Inequality, Inflation, and Their Impact on China's Investment Environment in the 1990s and Beyond," pp. 66–100.

21. Suppose there are only two regions, A and B. The per capita GDP values of the two regions (measured in each year over a period of n years) are $Y_{a,i}$ and $Y_{b,i}$ ($i = 0,1,2, \ldots ,n$), respectively. Let $Y_{a,0}$ $Y_{b,0}$, and the average growth rates of the two regions be g_a and g_b. It can be proved that:

if $g_b > g_a$ and $g_b > (Y_{a,0}/Y_{b,0}) \cdot g_a$, both absolute dispersion ($Y_{a,i} - Y_{b,i}$) , and relative dispersion ($Y_{a,i}/Y_{b,i}$) will decline from the first year on;

if $g_b > g_a$ but $g_b = (Y_{a,0}/Y_{b,0}) \cdot g_a$, both absolute dispersion and relative dispersion will decline after the first year; and

if $g_b > g_a$ but $g_b < (Y_{a,0}/Y_{b,0}) \cdot g_a$, relative dispersion will decline all along, but absolute dispersion will increase for x years before it begins to decline, and in t years it will decline to zero, where

$$x = \{\ln[Y_{b,0} \cdot \ln(1+ g_b)] - \ln[Y_{a,0} \cdot \ln(1+ g_a)]\}/\{\ln(1+ g_a) - \ln(1+ g_b)\},$$

and

$$t = [\ln Y_{a,0} - \ln Y_{b,0}]/[\ln(1+ g_b) - \ln(1+ g_a)]$$

See Wei Wei, *Zhongguo jingji fazhen zhong de quyu chayi yu quyu xietiao* [Regional Disparities and Coordination in China's Economic Development], pp. 27–29. With thirty provinces, it is impossible to predict precisely how changes in relative dispersion would affect changes in absolute dispersion.

22. Chor Pang Lo and Kok Chiang Tan studied two of the most affluent subprovincial regions in coastal China, the Zhujiang Delta and the city of Wenzhou, where they found considerable variations within these "open areas." See Chor Pang Lo, "The Pattern of Urban Settlements in the Zhujiang Delta, South China," pp. 171–205; and Kok Chiang Tan, "Small Towns and Regional Development in Wenzhou," pp. 207–34.

23. Yang Qingzhen, "Narrowing the East-West Gaps and Developing the Western Minority-Concentrated Regions," p. 2.

24. Audrey Donnithorne, "China's Cellular Economy," pp. 605–19.

25. Yang Jingchu, "1995–1996 nian minzu diqu jingji shehui xingshi," pp. 212–20.

4

Multidimensional Facets
of Regional Disparity

In Chapter 3, per capita GDP was adopted as a summary measure of the overall level of development across China's thirty provinces. In studying regional inequality, no other indicator has been more widely used as a proxy of human well-being than per capita GDP. But it was never designed to serve as such a measure. In the final analysis, GDP is merely a measure of the value of the output (goods and services) produced in a region in a given period of time. Owing to several conceptual limitations, per capita GDP alone cannot capture the full picture of regional differences in human welfare.

First, GDP estimates may misrepresent the productive capacities of different regions. GDP estimates do not include the value of those goods and services that people produce for their own use, which in all probability varies significantly from one place to another. Generally speaking, the more developed a region is, the more commercialized such activities are likely to be. Thus, higher GDP may reflect a transfer of production from the nonmarket to the market sector rather than a truly greater volume of production. Also excluded from GDP estimates are the economic activities of informal and hidden economies, which are particularly significant in contemporary China and which also vary in importance from place to place. For this reason, too, variations in GDP may fail to accurately indicate regional differences in economic prosperity, even when calculated on a per capita basis.

Second, incomes created through the production of goods and services within a region do not necessarily accrue to the region's inhabitants. By definition, gross provincial product is the total of the income accruing to persons supplying different productive factors (wages and salaries, profits, including undistributed corporate profits, etc.), but factor owners may reside in other provinces. Where the inhabitants of other regions have property rights in a region, there is an outflow of income, as there is if the human capital of other regions is used locally. Given the massive migration across provinces in China in recent years, average personal income may substantially diverge from per capita GDP. Moreover, the original distribution of income can be modified in varying degrees by the redistributive transfers that result from central taxation and the government's provision of public goods and services.[1]

Third, GDP is one-dimensional, whereas economic development is multidimensional. Spatial differentiation extends across a wide range of variables—from per capita GDP to physical environment, to levels of industrialization, and to life expectancy—some of which may not be directly related to income. Thus per capita GDP alone cannot be expected to capture many important aspects of regional development, particularly the circumstances in which growth occurs and the consequences brought about by growth. For instance, China is an extremely diversified country. However, per capita GDP is silent about how its provinces differ in resource endowment, geographic conditions, ethnic makeup, demography, infrastructure, and the like, although these factors are crucial for understanding the past growth records of various provinces, and the future directions in which those provinces are heading. Similarly, economic development has been transforming China, but per capita GDP tells us nothing about the shifting regional structures of industry, employment, and ownership. Other indicators, therefore, are needed to supplement GDP per capita if we are to understand and analyze regional disparities.

Finally, and most important, per capita GDP only reveals how much goods and services people living in a region possess on average, while what we are really interested in knowing is their actual state of well-being. It might well be argued that higher levels of per capita GDP would translate into a better human condition, but that does not necessarily happen. As numerous empirical studies have shown, the quality of human life in a country or region may or may not be highly correlated with its per capita GDP;[2] convergence in per capita GDP may or may not be accompanied by convergence across other relevant dimensions of human welfare.[3] The question of whether there is a direct link between economic growth and human progress needs to be proved, not simply assumed. If we accept that human welfare is the ultimate purpose of development, then regional development should be judged not only by how much a region is producing, but also by how its people are faring. Accordingly, in studying regional disparities, we must look beyond variations in per capita GDP. In terms of human well-being, income may be no more important than better nutrition, a more secure livelihood, greater access to knowledge and health services, a clean physical environment, and the ability to enjoy life's simple pleasures. Therefore, it is necessary to employ a whole class of multidimensional indices to assess China's interprovincial inequalities with respect to attributes of human well-being other than per capita GDP.

By using a broad array of indicators to further our investigation of regional inequality, this chapter attempts to remedy the above-mentioned deficiencies of relying solely on per capita GDP. We will systematically examine, apart from income gaps, how China's thirty provinces differ from one another along three other dimensions: resource endowment, economic structure, and human development. The primary purpose of this exercise is to provide a more comprehensive picture of China's regional disparities. As the following sections will show, regional inequality is indeed a multidimensional phenomenon. No matter which dimension we look at, notable regional variations are always observed. Once this fact is established, we will be in a much better position to discuss three key issues in the study of regional disparity.

The first issue is the extent to which the indicators of the other three dimensions are positively or negatively correlated with per capita GDP. If they all are highly correlated, then it will be easy to make out distinct regional patterns of development differentiating poor and rich provinces. Development economists have long been trying to identify the special features that typify less- or more-developed economies. Examples are structural transformation from agriculture to industry to services, rising savings rates, and urbanization.[4] We will see whether their generalizations accord with our cross-province data.

Even if all other variables either reflect or are influenced by regional differences in per capita GDP, it does not mean that the use of other variables is unnecessary. It is still possible for certain aspects of regional inequality to be more serious than others. For instance, consumption may be more evenly distributed than output in both relative and absolute terms.[5] Furthermore, residents' access to nonmarket public goods and services may show much smaller regional differences than does the consumption of private goods and services. Of course, neither scenario needs to be true in contemporary China.

The second issue we would like to explore in this chapter is the extent to which public policy modifies the original distribution of incomes and how such redistribution affects the well-being and growth potential of different regions.

Finally, the most interesting issue in the study of regional disparity is why some regions can reach a high income level whereas others lag behind. Of course, the factors that affect a region's development include those that affect the overall performance of the national economy. However, factors specific to each region must have an even greater bearing on the region's own performance. Otherwise, it would be impossible to account for the gaps between regions. Among the possible determinants of regional growth patterns are natural resource endowments, infrastructure, capital, labor force, technology, and foreign trade, the spatial variations of which will be closely examined in this chapter. Thus, the exercise conducted in this chapter will give us a chance to gauge which variables may be crucial in explaining regional disparities and also to assess their relative importance. The next chapter will build upon this examination of the variables, providing a fuller, more rigorous treatment of the issue.

Resource Endowment

Geographical Conditions

Geography has always been one of the important factors shaping the economy of a region, particularly before the dawn of industrialization. Resource endowment, geographic location, and historical accident may give certain regions within a country an initial advantage in developing a modern economy and restrict others. Although such effects may gradually weaken, natural conditions are nevertheless something that is hard to surmount by human efforts. In this sense, the observed regional disparities may be attributable in part to underlying differences in location and endowments.

Geographically, China is an extremely heterogeneous country.

Mountainous topography is a major factor that defines China's geo-graphical heterogeneity. More than two-thirds of the country consists of high plateaus, mountains, and hills. Land less than 500m above sea level comprises only 25.2 percent of the total land area, while that above 3,000m occupies 25.9 percent.[6] However, not all of China's provinces are hilly and mountainous. In fact, over the millennia, most Chinese have settled in low-elevation alluvial areas.[7] More than 80 percent of the land in eleven of China's thirty provincial units is less than 500m above sea level.[8] Most of the eleven are coastal provinces. At the other end of the spectrum are the eleven northwestern and south-western provinces where highlands, mountains, and hills dominate the landscape. Over 80 to 100 percent of their land is more than 500m above sea level, and many parts are extremely mountainous. Because of their high elevation and steep hills, mountainous areas are prone to water loss and soil erosion. In between the two extremes are eight relatively hilly provinces where at least 50 percent, and as much as 80 percent, of the land is less than 500m above sea level (see Table 4.1).

China's mountainous topography exerts a great influence on the climate in its various provinces. As everywhere else, the distribution of temperature in China is chiefly determined by latitude. There is a great difference in temperature between the south and the north; the annual mean temperature in the southernmost province, Hainan, is 22–27°C, whereas in the northernmost province, Heilongjiang, it is below 4°C.[9] However, topography also affects temperature. The vertical zonation of temperature is conspicuous in high-elevation and mountainous areas. Generally speaking, temperature decreases by 0.5–0.6°C with each 100m increase in elevation, roughly corresponding to the average temperature change for each 100km northward movement in latitude.[10] It is clear from Table 4.1 that the eastern provinces tend to have warmer climates than their western counterparts in the same latitude. For instance, Qinghai is located in about the same latitude as Shandong but has a much lower annual mean temperature.

Topography also redistributes moisture. Because moisture in the atmosphere over China comes mainly from the warm, moist summer maritime monsoon, precipitation is closely related to distance from the sea. The greater the distance from the sea, the less plentiful the precipi-tation, and the drier the climate.[11] With generous monsoons, the south-ern and southeastern provinces (e.g., Guangdong and Zhejiang) enjoy abundant precipitation. In contrast, the weather patterns in the northern

Table 4.1

Geographical Profiles of Provinces, 1994

Province	Land area below 500m as % of total land area	Annual mean temper- ature (C)	Annual mean precipitation (mm)	Arable land as % of total land	Irrigated land as % of arable land	Han as % of total popu- lation
Beijing	64.5	10 to 12	600	23.9	76.8	96.5
Tianjin	99.9	12	550–650	37.8	81.6	97.9
Hebei	54.0	4 to 13	400–800	34.8	60.7	98.4
Shanxi	5.3	3 to 14	350–700	23.4	32.5	99.7
Inner Mongolia	12.5	−1 to 10	50–450	4.5	33.0	84.5
Liaoning	82.8	4 to 10	400–1,200	23.4	34.7	91.9
Jilin	66.4	−3 to 7	350–1,000	21.1	23.0	91.9
Heilongjiang	82.3	−6 to 4	250–700	19.6	11.4	95.1
Shanghai	100.0	15 to 16	1,000	46.3	99.2	99.6
Jiangsu	100.0	13 to 16	800–1,200	43.5	85.1	99.8
Zhejiang	73.4	15 to 19	850–1,700	16.1	87.3	99.6
Anhui	92.5	14 to 17	700–1,700	31.0	66.9	99.5
Fujian	53.6	15 to 22	800–1,900	9.8	77.5	99.0
Jiangxi	86.8	16 to 20	1,200–1,900	13.9	78.5	99.9
Shandong	98.5	11 to 14.5	560–1,170	42.9	69.1	99.5
Henan	84.7	12 to 16	500–900	40.9	57.6	98.9
Hubei	66.4	13 to 18	750–1,500	18.1	66.3	96.3
Hunan	72.9	16 to 18.5	1,250–1,750	15.4	82.2	95.9
Guangdong	84.5	>19	>1,500	13.1	63.0	98.2
Guangxi	70.6	17 to 23	1,000–2,800	11.0	57.2	61.7
Sichuan	19.6	−1 to 19	500–1,200	10.9	46.3	96.3
Guizhou	6.3	10 to 20	900–1,500	10.4	33.0	74.0
Yunnan	1.2	4 to 24	600–2,300	7.2	41.3	68.3
Tibet	2.4	−3 to 12	60–1,000	0.2	73.0	4.9
Shaanxi	8.1	7 to 16	400–1,000	16.6	38.8	99.5
Gansu	0.0	−1 to 15	30–860	7.7	26.3	92.1
Qinghai	1.7	−5 to 8	50–700	0.8	30.3	60.6
Ningxia	0.9	5 to 10	190–700	15.6	34.4	68.1
Xinjiang	7.8	−4 to 14	150	1.9	89.6	40.4
Hainan	NA	22 to 27	>1,600	40.4	40.4	NA

and northwestern provinces (e.g., Inner Mongolia and Gansu), sur-rounded by high mountains, are little influenced by the summer mari-time monsoons. Consequently, the climate in these areas is semi-arid or arid.[12]

Overall, the southern provinces, especially the southeastern ones, have the most favorable temperature and moisture conditions for agri-cultural production. With good temperature and rainfall, the central and northern provinces are also fairly productive in agriculture. Given the hilly and mountainous terrain and cold dry weather in Northwest China, however, natural conditions there are fairly adverse to agricultural development. In consequence, this region is one of the areas where China's officially designated poor counties are concentrated. Examples include southern Gansu province, the Xihaigu area of Ningxia, the three southern prefectures and Haidong prefecture of Qinghai, the Taibajin high mountain area of southern Shaanxi, the Baiyu mountainous area of northern Shaanxi, and four prefectures in southern Xinjiang.[13]

In addition to its effect on temperature and precipitation, this mountainous topography makes China quite poor in arable land. With nearly a quarter of the world's population to be fed, China has only 7 percent of the world's total arable land. And scarce as they are, arable land resources are unevenly distributed among China's thirty provinces. In Tibet, arable land accounts for only 0.2 percent of total land area, while in Shanghai nearly one-half of the total land is arable. A careful reading of Table 4.1 reveals that the more mountainous a province is, the smaller the ratio of arable to total land tends to be (r = 0.72), a correlation that is by no means surprising. Centered in Guizhou province, Southwest China (including Yunnan, Guangxi, and parts of Hunan and Sichuan) is the largest karst area in the world. The limited arable land there is not only extremely scattered but also suffers virulent water loss and soil erosion. This is another region where China's poor counties are concentrated—and all five provinces in the region are among the poorest in the country.

A final factor contributing to varying levels of agricultural production is irrigation. Irrigated land tends to be more productive. However, how large a proportion of arable land is irrigated in a province depends on two factors: the availability of irrigation water and the province's financial ability to build dams, water reservoirs, and irrigation canals. There are three main sources of irrigation water: precipitation, surface water, and groundwater. As pointed out above, precipitation is unevenly distributed. So are surface water and groundwater.[14] Financial capacity, which will be discussed in Chapter 6, varies even more widely. As a result, the provincial ratios of irrigated land to total arable land fluctuate greatly from slightly higher than 10 percent (Heilongjiang) to nearly 100 percent (Shanghai). Table 4.1 confirms that provinces with poor precipitation tend to have a lower proportion of their arable land irrigated. The inadequate supply of arable land and irrigation water is another critical factor that limits food production and agricultural development in the northwestern provinces.[15]

Furthermore, China's mountainous topography allows some provinces to enjoy certain locational advantages that the others cannot share. In China, just as is the case elsewhere, modern commerce and industry first took shape in coastal and river mouth areas. Even today, these are still the core areas where such key resources as capital, technology, and markets are concentrated. Moreover, these areas have much easier access to foreign capital, technology, and markets than others. It is no wonder that in 1994, all the high-income provinces were coastal ones and no coastal province fell into the low-income category (see Table 3.1).[16] On the other hand, due to long distances and rough terrain, interior provinces have to pay high prices in order to gain access to major domestic economic centers and international markets. The access advantages of the coastal provinces and the substantial distance-related costs for the interior provinces may be another reason why the latter lag far behind the former.

Ethnic Makeup

China features great diversity not only in natural conditions but also in ethnic makeup across its thirty provinces. There are fifty-six ethnic groups in China, among which the Han is the largest, accounting for over 90 percent of the total population. Proportionally, the other fifty-five groups may appear to be small, representing only about 9 percent of the population. In terms of absolute size, however, they together amount to over 100 million, larger than the population of all but nine countries.[17] More importantly, they are widely dispersed and can be found in over two-thirds of China's territory. Nevertheless, with their overwhelming majority, the Han dominate twenty-eight of the thirty provinces. As Table 4.1 shows, the Han account for more than 90 percent of the population in twenty-two provinces, and in nine of them even exceed 99 percent. The Han even dominate three of the five autonomous regions (Inner Mongolia, Guangxi, and Ningxia). For instance, 84.5 percent of the population of Inner Mongolia is of the Han nationality. In Xinjiang, the Han fail to form a majority but they account for over 40 percent of the total population, about the same size as the Uygur.[18] Only in Tibet do the Han comprise a real minority (less than 5 percent).[19] Geographically, the ethnic minorities are concentrated in the border areas and in mountainous areas.[20] For this reason, none of the provinces in which more than 10 percent of the population are ethnic minorities make it into either the high-income or the middle-income category (see Table 3.1).

All of the factors discussed in this section and the preceding one are rather stable. They do not change much over a long period of time. However, their impact on regional patterns of development should not be underestimated. In a sense, they constitute a deep structure that conditions each region's growth potential.

Capital

Capital accumulation is a necessary ingredient for economic growth. The rapid expansion of China's economy over the last two decades would not have been possible without the enormous investments the country undertook during this period. By the same token, investment may be viewed as one of the driving forces of regional economic growth. More specifically, the growth rates of regional economies may be directly related to their capital investment; the more a region is able to invest, the greater will be the growth of its GDP.

However, in order to invest, a region has to save first. Although, in an open regional economy, investment can be financed by borrowing from other provinces or other countries, local savings nevertheless is still the single most important source of investment in all of China's provinces. In this sense, the rate of investment that is physically possible in a region is limited by the local population's self-imposed cut in current consumption. Of course, a high level of voluntary savings is unlikely when the average income is very low. Because savings involves a trade-off between present and future consumption, it is hard for the poor to give up much of their current consumption. Thus, savings rates are expected to be somehow correlated with the level of per capita GDP (see Chapter 6).

As the left-hand column of Table 4.2 shows, rich provinces tended to save more. All of the nine provinces with savings rates (savings/GDP) higher than 50 percent, for instance, were coastal ones. In Beijing, the savings rate was as high as 63.4 percent. Conversely, all of the four provinces whose savings rates were below 30 percent were poor western provinces. In Guizhou, China's poorest province, the savings rate was barely 25.4 percent, less than half of Beijing's.

Table 4.2

Capital and Labor Force in Provinces, 1994

Province	Savings rates (%)	Investment rates (%)	Per capita investment (yuan)	Labor force as % of population
Beijing	63.4	83.3	8,551.6	72.3
Tianjin	55.4	59.4	4,849.4	69.6
Hebei	52.5	41.2	1,390.9	66.6
Shanxi	42.0	45.2	1,274.2	66.1
Inner Mongolia	40.3	48.6	1,464.3	69.4
Liaoning	50.1	42.7	2,735.4	71.2
Jilin	40.4	40.2	1,539.3	71.8
Heilongjiang	37.0	35.0	1,549.8	72.2
Shanghai	55.7	58.4	8,879.1	70.9
Jiangsu	57.6	49.8	2,880.9	69.2
Zhejiang	56.0	44.5	2,736.3	70.7
Anhui	40.7	40.2	1,013.4	67.0
Fujian	44.8	45.3	2,439.9	63.3
Jiangxi	39.6	41.0	1,060.3	65.8
Shandong	53.8	48.7	2,178.4	67.8
Henan	47.0	40.2	983.3	64.3
Hubei	43.7	39.8	1,329.7	65.5
Hunan	34.3	34.3	926.4	66.4
Guangdong	48.5	46.7	2,979.5	61.3
Guangxi	34.2	38.5	1,067.2	63.1
Sichuan	38.8	38.3	963.6	69.2
Guizhou	25.4	29.7	460.9	63.6
Yunnan	41.4	44.5	1,108.1	64.4
Tibet	28.6	50.3	998.0	61.7
Shaanxi	30.4	48.1	1,169.3	66.4
Gansu	29.3	39.3	756.5	67.2
Qinghai	33.3	43.5	1,265.8	65.6
Ningxia	29.0	51.6	1,385.5	64.4
Xinjiang	44.3	72.4	2,862.7	60.5
Hainan	52.7	67.7	3,263.1	61.2

As expected, provinces with higher savings rates tended to invest more. With the highest savings rate, Beijing also ranked number one in terms of investment ratio (investment/GDP), which was as high as 83.3 percent. In the meantime, Guizhou's investment ratio was also the lowest in the country (29.7 percent). Overall, there appears to be a strong correlation between savings rates and investment rates ($r = 0.71$) if we exclude China's five autonomous regions (Inner Mongolia, Guangxi, Tibet, Ningxia, and Xinjiang). The autonomous regions are excluded because they enjoy special preferential policies, which explains why their investment rates are universally higher than their savings rates.

Since the savings rate tends to be higher in rich provinces and is highly correlated with investment rates, the logical conclusion would be that the more developed a region is, the more it is able to invest. That was exactly the case in 1994. On the one hand, among the twelve provinces where per capita GDP was higher than the national average, eleven invested more than 40 percent of their GDPs in new capital stock. On the other hand, all of the seven provinces whose investment ratios were lower than 40 percent happened to be relatively poor ones. The only exception to this observed pattern was Heilongjiang, where per capita GDP was slightly higher than the national average but the investment ratio was less then 35 percent.

Given the big regional disparities in per capita GDP discussed in the last chapter, the differences in investment ratios mean even greater gaps in per capita investment. Per capita investment ranged from 2,000 to over 8,000 yuan in almost all of the coastal provinces. But it was below 1,000 yuan in six provinces, all of which were poor interior ones. In Shanghai, per capita investment was as high as 8,879 yuan, 19.3 times Guizhou's 461 yuan!

The growth-savings relationship is a tricky one. While growth often precedes a significant increase in savings rates, rising savings rates may in turn boost growth through new investments. It seems fair to conclude that growth and savings mutually reinforce each other, manifesting what Myrdal calls "circular and cumulative causation."[21] We will further explore the relationship between investment and growth in the next chapter. What is important here is to take note of the great regional disparities in savings rates and investment ratios.

Labor Force

Labor has long been viewed as one of the primary sources of economic growth. If we do not consider variations in worker quality or effort, then labor here means the sum of productive manpower. Other things being equal, it is commonly believed that output will increase if more productive manpower is available. However, many parts of China have surplus labor. Therefore, it is not clear whether greater manpower supply in a region exerts a positive or negative influence on the region's economy. It may depend on the extent to which the region is able to productively employ all able-bodied workers. This is an ability that may be closely related to the availability of complementary factor inputs, such as physical capital or experienced management. Nevertheless, it is important to know how the labor force is distributed across China's various regions.

The relative size of the labor force varies from province to province, but within a rather narrow range. The highest ratio was observed in Beijing, where citizens between the ages of 15 and 64 made up over 72 percent of the total population, while the lowest ratio was seen in Xinjiang, where the corresponding figure was about 61 percent. Only a difference of eleven percentage points existed between the two extremes. Not only is the range of variations small, but also no clear regional patterns of workforce distribution can be identified. There were as many poor provinces as rich with more than 65 percent of their population active in the labor market. For instance, the labor force accounted for only 61.17 percent of the population in Hainan and 61.25 percent in Guangdong, both of which were lower than Tibet's 61.72 percent and Guizhou's 63.65 percent. The lack of discernible regional patterns in this respect suggests that neither the labor supply's impact on the level of income nor the income level's impact on the labor supply is significant.

Infrastructure

Infrastructure refers to the amount of physical capital embodied in transportation, communications, electricity, and the like. These physical investments are of real importance to any economy, because they play an indispensable role in facilitating and integrating economic activities within the region and in linking the region with the outside world. Without them, it is hard to imagine how an economy could ever grow. The level of infrastructural development in a region, therefore, is a crucial factor determining its economic performance.

Due to limited space, we focus only on transportation here. Let us look at how the density of inland waterways, roads, and railroads—three pillars of China's transport network—varies across regions.

China is a country with more than fifty thousand rivers, containing over 54,000 km of navigable waterways. In addition, there are more than nine hundred navigable lakes. Before the advent of railroads and automobiles, transport in China was principally dependent on waterways. Nearly all of the navigable waterways are located in southern

China, however. As shown by Figure 4.1, navigable waterways were completely absent in four provinces and almost nonexistent in another twelve. The density of waterways was higher than 0.01 km/sq. km only in fourteen provinces, among which Heilongjiang was the only northern province. And what is more, over 80 percent of China's navigable waterways were concentrated in two drainage systems, the Yangzi and the Zhujiang.[22] Little wonder that the provinces in these two regions (Shanghai, Jiangsu, Zhejiang, Hubei, Hunan, and Guangdong) have long been famed in China as "the land of plenty" (*yumi zhixiang*) in China.

As of 1994, China had 77,000 km of railroads (including local railroads). Most of them were concentrated in eastern China.[23] If we use the Beijing-Wuhan-Guangzhou railroad as a dividing line, then more than three-fourths of the total railroad length lay east of the line. West of it, especially on the Tibetan Plateau and in Northwest China, railroads were very sparsely distributed. Of the thirty provinces, nine had relatively high railroad density (higher than 0.02 km/sq. km). They were Beijing, Tianjin, Hebei, Shanxi, Jilin, Liaoning, Shanghai, Shandong, and Henan. In contrast, Tibet did not yet have any railroad.[24]

Compared to waterways and railroads, roads seem to be a more important form of transportation in China. In 1994, there was a total of 1,117,821 km of highway, which was nearly fifteen times longer than the total length of railroads and ten times longer than the length of inland waterways. In areas inaccessible by waterways and railroads, such as much of Northwest and Southwest China, roads were often the only form of transportation. This was the case in nine provinces (Inner Mongolia, Guizhou, Yunnan, Tibet, Gansu, Qinghai, Ningxia, Xinjiang, and Hainan). All of the provincial capitals and all but one county seat (Medog in Tibet) are now connected by road transportation, but most roads are still concentrated in coastal and central provinces.[25] Road density was generally higher than 0.3 km/sq. km along the coast, and between 0.2 and 0.3 km/sq. km in the central provinces. However, in the western provinces, road density was normally below 0.1 km/sq. km. It was less than 0.05 km/sq. km in Xinjiang, Tibet, Qinghai, and Inner Mongolia, which happen to be the country's four largest provinces.[26]

In addition, those provinces with long coastlines and good seaports have exclusive access to coastal waterways and oceanic navigation

Figure 4.1 **Density of Transport Networks in Provinces, 1994**

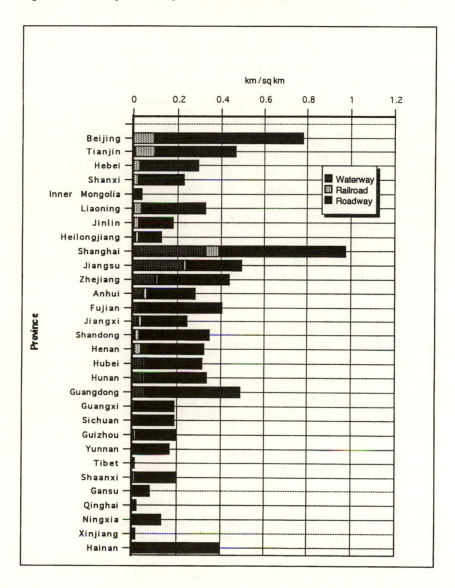

lines. They are Liaoning, Tianjin, Shandong, Jiangsu, Shanghai, Zhejiang, Fujian, Guangdong, Hainan, and to a lesser extent, Hebei and Guangxi.[27]

Overall, the coastal provinces possess great advantages in terms of a dense transport network. Even if we exclude coastal navigation, the aggregate density of waterways, railroads, and roads, as shown by Figure 4.1, was generally higher in these provinces than in others in 1994. Especially in the three metropolises (Shanghai, Beijing, and Tianjin) and the southern coastal provinces (Jiangsu, Zhejiang, Fujian, Guangdong, and Hainan), the density was above 0.4 km/sq. km. The density in the northern coastal provinces (Liaoning, Hebei, and Shandong) was lower, around 0.3 km/sq. km, about the same as in some of the central provinces (Henan, Hubei, Hunan, Shanxi, and Jiangxi). In the other provinces, transportation facilities were rather primitive, with aggregate density less than 0.2 km/sq. km.

The well-developed transport networks in the coastal provinces substantially reduce travel time in these areas, thus enhancing the movement of raw materials, commodities, and human and capital resources in all directions. Much of the development in these provinces can be attributed to their transport advantages. By contrast, remoteness from lucrative markets and deficient transportation facilities may be an important factor contributing to the low levels of development in the central and western provinces. In fact, the aggregate density of the transport network can serve as a very good predictor of a region's development level. The coefficient of correlation between the two variables was as high as 0.71 in 1994.

Economic Structure

Regional disparities may manifest themselves not only in per capita GDP and resource endowment, but also in economic structure. It has been noted in development economics that as the economy moves forward, its structure tends to change in certain ways. Thus, we may expect great structural diversity among regions that have achieved different levels of development. In this section, we attempt to identify some of the most important structural differences among China's thirty provinces. Any portrayal of regional structural differences in China requires an examination of four critical components: production, employment, ownership, and the degree of openness.

The Structure of Production

Let us first examine the structure of production. Table 4.3 provides a breakdown of each provincial economy by sectors. The primary sector consists of agriculture, including forestry and fishing; the secondary, mostly of industry; and the tertiary, of commerce, finance, transport, and services. Note in particular the relative importance of agriculture in different provincial economies. Developed regions relied much less on agricultural production. The contribution of agriculture to GDP was lower than 7 percent in Beijing and Tianjin, and as low as 2.5 percent in Shanghai. In the other provinces, it ranged from 12.34 percent in Liaoning to 46.03 percent in Tibet. Agriculture's contribution to GDP was generally below 20 percent in coastal areas. However, it exceeded 25 percent in most of the interior provinces. In any case, there was a clear pattern—the more developed a region, the less important its agricultural sector.

Since 1978, all of China's provinces have greatly accelerated the growth of their industrial output and are rapidly becoming industrialized. In the meantime, the service sector has been expanding everywhere. As expected, there were wide variations in the relative importance of the industrial and service sectors across provinces (see Table 4.3). Some developed provinces had both a large industrial sector and a large service sector (e.g., Beijing, Tianjin, Liaoning, Shanghai, and Guangdong), while others had either a large industrial sector (e.g., Jiangsu, Zhejiang, Shandong) or a large service sector (e.g., Hainan). But both sectors tended to be small in less-developed provinces (e.g., Xinjiang, Gansu, Yunnan, Guizhou, Sichuan, Guangxi, Hunan, Hubei, Jiangxi, Inner Mongolia).

In the international context, it has been noted that the weight of a country's production structure tends to shift from the secondary sector to the tertiary sector as the economy develops.[28] However, this does not seem to be the case in China. As a matter of fact, the service sector was proportionally smaller in such rich coastal provinces as Jiangsu, Shandong, Zhejiang, Guangdong, Fujian, and Liaoning than in such poor western provinces as Tibet, Shaanxi, Qinghai, and Ningxia. What is also worth noting is that, compared to other countries, the service sector in China is universally small no matter which part of the country we look at. Even in China's three metropolises (Shanghai, Beijing, and Tianjin), for instance, this sector's contribution to GDP was less than

Table 4.3

Structure of Production and Structure of Employment, 1994

	Percentage of GDP			Percentage of the Labor Force		
Province	Agriculture (1)	Industry (2)	Service (3)	Agriculture (4)	Industry (5)	Service (6)
Beijing	6.90	46.11	46.99	11.02	40.99	47.99
Tianjin	6.42	55.72	37.86	16.69	48.05	35.26
Hebei	21.04	49.04	29.92	55.46	25.93	18.61
Shanxi	14.51	51.63	33.86	45.41	31.32	23.27
Inner Mongolia	30.58	38.39	31.03	51.92	21.78	26.30
Liaoning	12.34	53.46	34.20	31.24	38.49	30.27
Jilin	26.78	44.47	28.75	45.65	27.46	26.89
Heilongjiang	19.54	52.70	27.76	36.80	35.37	27.83
Shanghai	2.46	57.98	39.56	9.58	56.08	34.34
Jiangsu	16.56	53.90	29.54	44.54	34.36	21.10
Zhejiang	16.64	52.05	31.31	45.19	34.75	20.06
Anhui	22.62	49.99	27.38	51.98	17.53	30.49
Fujian	22.11	43.88	34.01	51.17	23.93	24.90
Jiangxi	30.46	40.90	28.64	56.14	24.57	19.29
Shandong	20.02	49.08	30.90	58.01	25.07	16.92
Henan	23.69	48.75	27.56	64.41	19.42	16.17
Hubei	26.69	43.25	30.06	55.07	22.43	22.50
Hunan	31.45	36.48	32.07	61.06	21.50	17.44
Guangdong	16.38	50.46	33.16	42.32	33.58	24.10
Guangxi	28.81	39.10	32.09	68.02	11.47	20.51
Sichuan	28.38	41.98	29.64	61.39	19.59	19.02
Guizhou	35.21	37.56	27.23	74.66	9.95	15.39
Yunnan	24.39	44.11	31.50	77.87	10.23	11.90
Tibet	46.03	17.28	36.69	77.38	3.69	18.93
Shaanxi	21.47	43.30	35.23	61.34	19.37	19.29
Gansu	22.98	44.13	32.89	65.07	17.85	17.08
Qinghai	22.94	42.21	34.85	56.33	16.78	26.89
Ningxia	22.34	41.64	36.02	60.63	19.44	19.93
Xinjiang	27.86	39.39	32.75	58.37	18.36	23.27
Hainan	32.50	25.28	42.22	60.95	11.95	27.10

50 percent. Industry is still the most important sector in all but three provinces (Beijing, Tibet, and Hainan).

"Industry" is an all-embracing concept that covers a broad range of economic activities. However, some regions may possess a more favorable industry mix than others. Regions that possess a high proportion of nationally fast-growing industries can expect to have faster growth rates than regions with a high proportion of nationally slow-growing industries.

Before reform, Chinese policymakers placed emphasis on the development of heavy industry. Even then, the coastal provinces tended to have relatively larger light industry sectors than did the others. Since 1978, there has been a general trend for the share of heavy industry to drop and the share of light industry to increase. However, the fastest growth of light industry has occurred in such southern coastal provinces as Zhejiang, Jiangsu, Fujian, and Guangdong.[29] Consequently, by 1994, the share of light industry in total industrial output tended to be higher in the coastal provinces than in the rest of the country.

As shown by Figure 4.2, Hainan had the highest proportion of light industry, closely followed by Zhejiang, Guangdong, Yunnan, Fujian, Jiangsu, and Shandong. Yunnan was able to top the list solely because it was a large tobacco producer. Except for Yunnan, these coastal provinces also happened to be the fastest-growing regions in China between 1978 and 1994 (see Table 3.3). On the other hand, provinces with extraordinarily large shares of heavy industry (e.g., Shanxi, Ningxia, Qinghai, Gansu, Liaoning, and Heilongjiang) were precisely the ones that had experienced the slowest growth during the same period.

The striking contrast in growth rates between the two groups of provinces was by no means accidental. It has to do with price distortions, which are reflected in differences in rates of return on fixed assets.[30] In 1995, for instance, the average rate of return was 11.23 percent in industry as a whole. However, the rate varied from 6.5 percent in coal mining to nearly 23 percent in beverages and 142.8 percent in tobacco. Overall, the rate of return in light industry was about five percentage points higher than in heavy industry.[31] Since the proportion of light industry was relatively large in the southern coastal provinces, these provinces stood to gain from such price distortions. Relying too much on mining and raw material industries, the western provinces were the ones that bore the costs of price distortions.

One of the most prominent features of China's recent economic history is the rapid pace of rural industrialization. Since the reforms, rural industry has been the fastest-growing sector of the Chinese economy. This development, however, is not evenly dispersed across the Chinese countryside. Table 4.4 provides information about the regional distribution of rural industrial output. Column 3 reveals that rural industrialization is largely a coastal phenomenon. Among the ten provinces where rural industry produced more than one-half of total rural output (including outputs of agriculture, industry, transportation, construction, and commerce), nine were coastal. Shanxi was the only ex-

Figure 4.2 **Industrial Structure in Provinces, 1994**

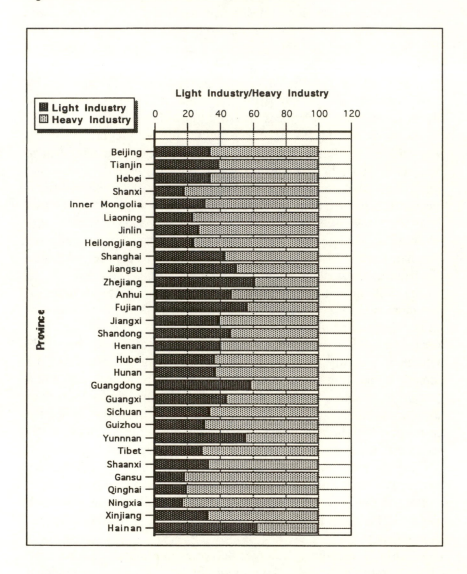

Table 4.4

Rural Industrialization, 1994

Province	(1) Total rural output (billion yuan)	(2) Rural industrial output (billion yuan)	(3) Rural industrial output as % of rural total	(4) Provincial rural industrial output as % of national total
Beijing	106.159	72.18	67.99	2.23
Tianjin	86.107	72.94	84.71	2.26
Hebei	335.013	182.31	54.42	5.64
Shanxi	124.992	66.66	53.33	2.06
Inner Mongolia	55.532	11.81	21.27	0.37
Liaoning	297.552	156.00	52.43	4.82
Jilin	88.928	25.66	28.85	0.79
Heilongjiang	113.787	30.47	26.78	0.94
Shanghai	118.494	104.47	88.16	3.23
Jiangsu	788.723	607.88	77.07	18.80
Zhejiang	551.761	447.67	81.13	13.84
Anhui	226.963	103.67	45.68	3.21
Fujian	155.485	69.58	44.75	2.15
Jiangxi	179.296	82.74	46.15	2.56
Shandong	819.093	505.14	61.67	15.62
Henan	267.942	116.65	43.54	3.61
Hubei	244.294	101.90	41.71	3.15
Hunan	211.286	77.55	36.70	2.40
Guangdong	335.338	167.93	50.08	5.19
Guangxi	102.671	28.15	27.42	0.87
Sichuan	320.233	127.67	39.87	3.95
Guizhou	36.153	6.30	17.43	0.19
Yunnan	64.468	14.04	21.78	0.43
Tibet	2.306	0.00	0.00	0.00
Shaanxi	88.378	33.17	37.53	1.03
Gansu	45.001	11.85	26.33	0.37
Qinghai	5.497	0.72	13.10	0.02
Ningxia	6.910	1.47	21.27	0.05
Xinjiang	37.537	3.94	10.50	0.12
Hainan	23.509	3.09	13.14	0.10

ception. Meanwhile, there were twelve provinces where rural industry accounted for less than 30 percent of the rural economy. All but one (Hainan) were interior provinces. Column 4 further demonstrates that rural industry is concentrated in coastal areas. About three-fourths of China's total rural industrial output in 1994 emanated from eleven coastal provinces. In fact, four coastal provinces—Jiangsu, Shandong, Zhejiang, and Guangdong—alone produced over one-half of the nation's total rural industrial output. Conversely, the combined rural industrial outputs in twelve western provinces (Shanxi, Inner Mongolia,

Guangxi, Sichuan, Guizhou, Yunnan, Tibet, Shaanxi, Gansu, Qinghai, Ningxia, and Xinjiang) did not reach even a half of Jiangsu's. As of 1994, rural industrialization did not seem to have started in West China.

It is widely accepted that rising regional inequality is attributable, to a large extent, to the differential rates of rural industrialization.[32] However, the uneven development of rural industry is a symptom of widening regional disparities, not a cause. The latter cannot be explained by the former, because the former itself needs to be explained. Many recent studies have shown that the following factors are conducive to rapid development of rural industry: locational advantages, favorable endowment of physical and human capital, abundant inflows of foreign capital and technology, preferential tax and credit policies, relatively dense transport network, and the like.[33] These are also the factors that favor economic growth in general.

Moreover, it is around urban centers that the bulk of China's rural enterprises cluster. To a large extent, rural industrialization is in fact suburban industrialization.[34] This explains why, despite their coastal location, Fujian and Hainan are lagging in developing rural industry. Unlike the other coastal provinces, they do not have any major urban centers within their boundaries or in nearby areas. If rural industrialization is indeed a by-product of urban spillover, as some hypothesize,[35] then what really needs to be explained is why some urban centers have been able to grow faster than others in the first place.

The Structure of Employment

Table 4.3 provides information on the distribution of the labor force among the primary, secondary, and tertiary sectors in China's thirty provinces, in 1994. Given the spatial variations in production structure, regional disparities in employment structure are expected. However, the latter seem to be much greater than the former. The proportion of the labor force involved in agricultural activities varied from less than 10 percent in Shanghai to nearly 80 percent in Yunnan and Tibet. In twenty provinces, including four coastal ones (Hebei, Shandong, Fujian, and Hainan), agriculture was still the principal economic activity in terms of the occupational distribution of the labor force, if not in terms of proportionate contribution to the gross domestic product. The proportion of farmers in the working population was higher than 60 percent in most of the western provinces. Only in two groups of provinces was more than one-half of the labor force engaged in nonagricultural activities. One group consisted of the northeastern provinces (Liaoning, Heilongjiang, and Jilin), which were China's old industrial bases. The other included several coastal provinces (Beijing, Tianjin, Shanghai, Jiangsu, Zhejiang, and Guangdong). Shanxi, China's chief coal producer, was the only exception.

The proportion of the labor force employed in industry also varies widely across provinces, from a minuscule 3.69 percent in Tibet to over 56 percent in Shanghai. While over one-third of the labor force was hired by industrial enterprises in most of the coastal provinces, no western province had more than 20 percent of its labor force employed in this sector. The regional pattern of the labor force in the service sector largely resembled that for the industrial population. However, compared to the other two sectors, variations in this sector were relatively small, ranging from about 12 percent in Yunnan to 48 percent in Beijing. Beijing had the largest service sector, because, as the national capital, it was the home of a huge central bureaucracy.

In China, "the labor force in the countryside" (*nongcun laodongli*) and "the labor force in agriculture" (*nongye laodongli*) are different concepts. Many workers who are engaged mostly in nonfarming activities are categorized as rural laborers because they hold rural household registrations (*nongcun hukou*). Comparing the first column of Table 4.5 and the fourth column of Table 4.3, it is clear that the proportion of the labor force in the countryside was generally ten to twenty percentage points higher than that of the labor force in agriculture. There were three exceptions, Gansu, Hainan, and Xinjiang, where the situation was exactly the opposite, although the differences between the two ratios were rather small in the cases of both Gansu and Hainan. Xinjiang was the only real exception, probably because many large state farms, whose employees were not classified as rural residents, were located there. In any event, in most parts of China, including such prosperous provinces as Jiangsu, Zhejiang, and Guangdong, the overwhelming majority of the labor force (70 percent or more) still lived and worked in the countryside.

However, the official rural-urban classification is outdated and extremely misleading. In the suburbs of Shanghai, Beijing, and Tianjin, for instance, two-thirds to three-quarters of the so-called rural labor force was actually involved in nonfarming activities (see Table 4.5). Although the rural share of the total labor force was high in Jiangsu,

Table 4.5

Distribution of Rural Labor Force, 1994

Province	Rural labor force as % of total labor force (1)	Labor force in nonfarming as % of rural labor force (2)	Labor force in rural industry as % of rural labor force (3)
Beijing	25.83	59.97	29.37
Tianjin	33.53	51.56	31.16
Hebei	79.21	30.54	11.57
Shanxi	66.83	32.59	12.68
Inner Mongolia	56.09	13.79	2.73
Liaoning	42.66	31.55	10.13
Jilin	51.47	13.96	3.77
Heilongjiang	37.98	18.28	5.89
Shanghai	29.63	73.09	48.84
Jiangsu	76.45	42.81	19.15
Zhejiang	79.56	43.49	20.78
Anhui	81.50	25.03	6.68
Fujian	73.00	30.94	8.72
Jiangxi	75.86	28.02	6.39
Shandong	81.28	28.98	9.75
Henan	83.57	23.10	6.43
Hubei	71.29	24.46	6.66
Hunan	80.12	22.16	5.79
Guangdong	71.37	42.50	13.84
Guangxi	82.84	18.93	2.98
Sichuan	82.48	22.01	4.68
Guizhou	85.04	12.60	2.87
Yunnan	85.43	10.23	2.43
Tibet	80.97	6.08	1.10
Shaanxi	76.17	19.94	4.95
Gansu	60.32	22.75	4.00
Qinghai	63.20	13.22	3.41
Ningxia	67.36	14.08	2.72
Xinjiang	46.32	8.99	2.62
Hainan	60.02	19.09	2.77

Zhejiang, and Guangdong, over 40 percent of the rural working population in these provinces had jobs in industry, construction, transport, trade, and other services in 1994. But such employment opportunities were open only to less than one-fifth of the rural labor force in Inner Mongolia, Jilin, Heilongjiang, Guangxi, Guizhou, Yunnan, Tibet, Shaanxi, Qinghai, Ningxia, and Xinjiang.

One thing revealed by the third column of Table 4.5 is interesting to note. Important as it is, rural industry is not a major source of employment in rural China. In nineteen provinces, fewer than one in fifteen rural laborers was employed in industrial enterprises, and in another two provinces, the ratio was less than one in ten. Only in nine provinces was the ratio above 10 percent—and all but one of these provinces (Shanxi) were coastal.

The Structure of Ownership

Before reforms, the state sector dominated the national economy. At that time, the structure of ownership was rather simple everywhere. An important change brought about by China's market-oriented reforms was the rapid rise of the non-state sectors. Take the industrial sector as an example.[36] In 1978, nearly four-fifths of total industrial output was produced by state-owned enterprises. By 1994, however, the overall share of the state sector had dropped to one-third. The other two-thirds was accounted for by the non-state sector.[37] While the non-state sector has expanded throughout China, its development is by no means even. It has grown much faster in some provinces than in others. As a result, great variations have emerged in terms of the structure of ownership across provinces.

The non-state sector should not be confused with the private sector. In Chinese statistics, this sector is composed of "collectives" (collectively owned enterprises) and "others" (enterprises in other forms of ownership). The latter is a hotchpotch, including private enterprises, foreign-invested firms, joint ventures, and companies whose ownership is mixed. In what follows, we will use two indicators to measure the relative size of the state and non-state sectors. One is the share of the total value of fixed assets in industry, and the other the share of total industrial output.

By the first measure (see Figure 4.3), the state sector still seems to dominate in most provinces. In particular, in all the western provinces, the share of fixed assets owned by state enterprises was more than 80 percent. In Qinghai, it was nearly 95 percent. On the other hand, the share was barely 31 percent in Guangdong, followed by other southern coastal provinces such as Zhejiang (41.91 percent), Jiangsu (44.71 percent), Fujian (47.23 percent), Shanghai (57.84 percent), and Hainan (59.19 percent). It needs to be noted, however, that non-state sector had a different meaning in different provinces. In Zhejiang and Jiangsu, the non-state sector was composed chiefly of collective enter-

Figure 4.3 **Value of Fixed Assets in All Industrial Enterprises at Township Level and Above, 1995**

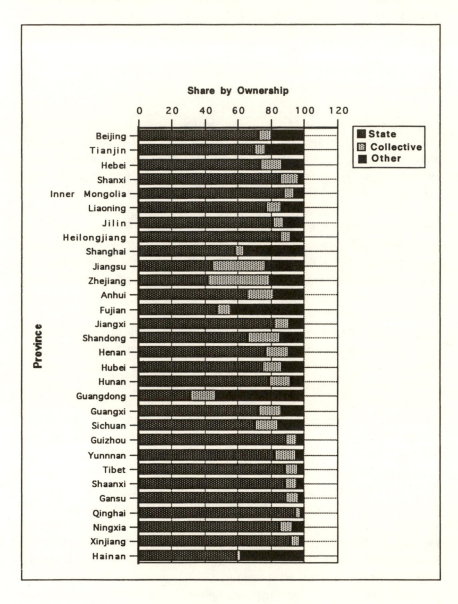

prises, whereas in Guangdong, Fujian, Hainan, and Shanghai, its components were mainly "others." As will be shown in a moment, foreign-invested firms constituted a large part of the "others."

The observations made in the last paragraph should be treated with caution, though, because they were drawn from a data set that includes only enterprises at the township level and above. There were millions of additional industrial enterprises at the village level and below. Individually, they might be small, but together they were responsible for a quarter of total industrial output. Since none of them were state-owned, excluding them would definitely lead to a gross overestimation of the relative size of the state sector, especially in provinces where enterprises at the village level and below were flourishing. Figure 4.4 confirms this conjecture.

Figure 4.4 provides two separate estimates of the state's share of total industrial output in the provinces, one based on data excluding enterprises below the township level, and the other including them. Obviously, once the enterprises below the township level are taken into consideration, the share of the state sector shrinks, in some cases dramatically. In Tianjin, Hebei, Shanxi, Jiangxi, Henan, Guangxi, and Shaanxi, for instance, the reduction was more than 20 percent. Viewed in this context, the state sector no longer appeared to be a dominating player in many provincial economies. In four coastal provinces, Zhejiang, Jiangsu, Guangdong, and Shandong, the state sector actually produced less than one-quarter of total industrial output. In no coastal province was the state share higher than 50 percent. However, two regions still appeared to be dominated by the state sector, whether or not the enterprises below the township level were included. These were the northern interior provinces (e.g., Inner Mongolia, Jilin, and Heilongjiang) and the western interior provinces (e.g., Gansu, Qinghai, Ningxia, Xinjiang, Tibet, Guizhou, and Yunnan).

Thus, no matter which indicator is applied, the spatial patterns of ownership structure are very clear: The more developed a province is, the more diversified its ownership structure tends to be. This observation has led some to argue that enlarging the non-state sector was a recipe for high growth.[38] There is no doubt that the non-state sector has grown much faster than the state sector (otherwise, it is impossible for its share in the economy to rise). Logically, therefore, provinces with relatively larger non-state sectors are expected to grow at rates higher than those provinces with a high share of state-owned industries. The

Figure 4.4 Industrial Output by State Sector, 1994

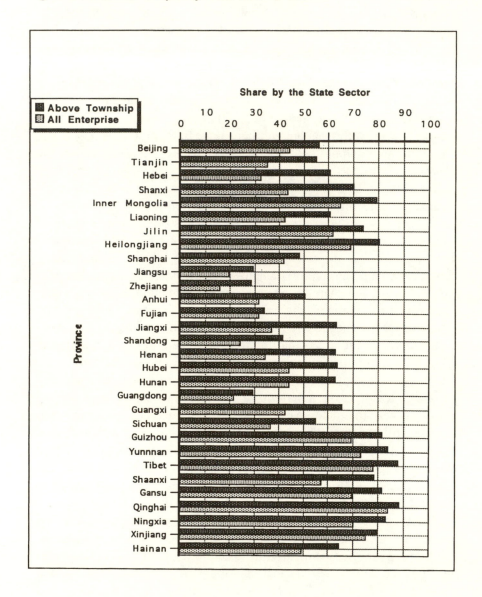

problem with this argument is that it ignores a fundamental fact of the Chinese reform: The relative weight of the non-state sector has increased not because many state-owned enterprises have been privatized, but because a great number of non-state-owned enterprises have emerged and gradually overshadowed the state sector. In other words, the rise of the non-state sector is a function of the formation rate of new non-state-owned firms. The higher the formation rate in a province, the larger its non-state sector. What really needs to be explained, then, is the spatial disparities in the new-firm formation rate. The same conditions that favor high new-firm formation rates may also favor high-output growth rates in general. If that is the case, the relationship between the two phenomena cannot be a causal one.

The Degree of Openness

The open-door policy is a cornerstone of China's reform program. It is widely accepted in China that trade allows each economy to explore its comparative advantages and to bring in scarce foreign exchange earnings. The inflow of foreign funds can supplement domestic savings and increase overall investment. In addition, new technology and managerial skills embodied in foreign investments are essential for raising productivity. Therefore, foreign trade and foreign investment have been actively pursued by government at all levels. However, despite a more or less equally strong desire to open their economies, the performance records of the provinces are worlds apart.

First of all, the expansion of exports has been very uneven. Export income is now vital to coastal China. In this regard, Guangdong is far ahead of all the others. In 1994, it exported $53.3 billion worth of goods, accounting for 44 percent of total Chinese exports (Table 4.6). Guangdong was followed by Shanghai (8.21 percent of the national total), Jiangsu (5.75 percent), Shandong (5.38 percent), Zhejiang (5.36 percent), Fujian (5.02 percent), Liaoning (4.26 percent), Beijing (3.18 percent), and Tianjin (2.5 percent). The exports of these nine coastal provinces represented 83.7 percent of China's total, leaving the remaining twenty-one provinces far behind. In particular, the western provinces simply did not have much to export. Even adding exports by all of them together, they amount to less than 2.5 percent of the national total.

The importance of exports to the coastal economies can also be seen from the angle of export dependency, which is measured by the ratio of a province's exports to its GDP. In this regard, Guangdong again stands head and shoulders above the others. In 1994, its exports equaled 108 percent of its GDP. No other province came even close to this. Nevertheless, a regional pattern of export dependency is very clear. In the coastal provinces, export dependency rates ranged from 15 to 40 percent, while in the western provinces, the rate was nowhere higher than 10 percent.

A province's ability to attract foreign investment is another important indicator of its openness. Table 4.6 makes it abundantly clear that the distribution of foreign capital was extremely uneven. Guangdong alone took 43.48 percent of the national total, which was about the same amount as the combined shares of the other ten coastal provinces (44.25 percent). The rest of the country together received only 12 percent of total foreign investment. Foreign investors simply bypass many poor provinces. As little as 1.8 percent of foreign investment was found in a vast area covering ten provinces (Inner Mongolia, Shanxi, Xinjiang, Tibet, Qinghai, Gansu, Ningxia, Shaanxi, Yunnan, and Guizhou), although this area covers about two-thirds of China's territory. Of course, these provinces were not as densely populated as the coastal provinces. To take the density of population into consideration, let us turn to the level of per capita foreign investment.

Differences in per capita foreign investment were equally striking. Based on this indicator, Shanghai led the nation with $182.38 per head, followed by such coastal provinces as Guangdong, Hainan, Beijing, Fujian, and Tianjin. In these provinces, per capita foreign investment was in three digits. For the other coastal provinces, except Hebei, the comparable figures were in two digits. Only in one interior province (Hubei), however, was a figure in two digits found.

A glance at Table 4.6 reveals that there is an almost perfect correspondence between major exporting provinces and provinces attracting most of the foreign capital. By no means accidentally, both categories include the same group of coastal provinces. This is because the degree of a province's engagement in the world economy is clearly related to its geographical location. With close ties to overseas Chinese communities, easy access to international shipping, sound internal transport networks, and skilled labor, the coastal provinces have inherent advantages in exploring foreign markets and in attracting foreign investment. These advantages are further enhanced by preferential tax, trade, and investment policies specifically granted to them by the central govern-

Table 4.6

Openness of Provinces, 1994

Province	Exports as % of provincial GDP	Provincial exports as % of national total	Provincial foreign investment as % of national total	Per capita foreign investment (US$)
Beijing	30.60	3.18	3.15	121.92
Tianjin	35.92	2.50	2.65	108.56
Hebei	7.61	1.57	1.21	8.19
Shanxi	11.03	0.90	0.12	1.04
Inner Mongolia	6.07	0.40	0.11	1.77
Liaoning	17.20	4.26	3.46	35.41
Jilin	14.73	1.37	0.56	9.40
Heilongjiang	15.40	2.39	0.80	9.47
Shanghai	43.40	8.21	5.90	182.38
Jiangsu	14.77	5.75	8.65	53.60
Zhejiang	20.93	5.36	2.64	26.79
Anhui	5.59	0.80	0.94	6.21
Fujian	31.07	5.02	8.51	116.66
Jiangxi	5.45	0.54	0.68	6.52
Shandong	14.47	5.38	5.94	29.44
Henan	4.26	0.90	1.06	4.28
Hubei	6.90	1.24	1.53	10.52
Hunan	6.38	1.04	0.78	5.21
Guangdong	108.19	44.01	43.48	141.48
Guangxi	9.27	1.10	1.94	18.61
Sichuan	4.72	1.26	2.19	8.22
Guizhou	4.46	0.22	0.15	1.84
Yunnan	7.80	0.73	0.16	1.65
Tibet	3.57	0.02	0.00	0.00
Shaanxi	8.36	0.68	0.56	6.86
Gansu	5.97	0.26	0.22	3.69
Qinghai	7.16	0.10	0.01	0.51
Ningxia	6.49	0.08	0.02	1.44
Xinjiang	5.84	0.38	0.45	2.96
Hainan	11.35	0.36	2.14	129.13

ment. Given the circumstances, it would be surprising if the landlocked interior provinces could achieve the same degree of openness as the coastal ones do.

Human Well-Being

As pointed out at the beginning of this chapter, the ultimate purpose of development is to enrich people's lives and enlarge their choices. If

improving the quality of people's lives is indeed the goal of development, then no study of regional disparities can be regarded as satisfactory unless it examines spatial discrepancies in human well-being.

Two aspects of human well-being are examined in this section. One
is people's standard of living and the other what Mahbub ul Haq calls
human development. The concept of the standard of living is straightforward, and needs no further explanation. One's standard of living
depends, to a large extent, on how much disposable income one pos-
sesses and how high one's consumption level is. Human development
refers to a process of enlarging people's choices. Obtaining income is
certainly one means of expanding choices, for higher income allows
one at least more choices of consumer goods and services. However,
higher income does not automatically translate into a wider range of
choices in many other aspects of human life. Access to information,
education, and health care may be just as important for enlarging the
choices in people's social, cultural, and political lives as income is in
their economic lives. For this reason, we will examine both monetary
and nonmonetary dimensions of welfare in the following paragraphs.

Urbanization

Any study of income and consumption inequalities in China must
begin with a discussion of the rural-urban divide. The rural-urban
divide exists everywhere. Due to strict control over rural-urban migration in China, however, the dichotomy between the rural and
urban sectors has become one of the most distinctive features of
Chinese society.[39] Urban residents enjoy higher incomes as well as
many social welfare benefits that are not available to rural residents.
Numerous studies have established that in virtually every aspect of
economic life, the rural-urban difference is much greater than that
within either rural or urban China.[40] Thus, we may expect that the
more urbanized a province is, the higher its income and consumption levels will tend to be.

Which provinces are more urbanized? Due to the lack of data on the
share of urban population, we use the ratio of nonagricultural population to total population as an approximation of the degree of urbanization. Figure 4.5 reports the findings. In the nation as a whole, less than
one quarter of the population was classified as nonagricultural, which is
probably lower than the average for low-income countries.[41] However,

Figure 4.5 **Level of Urbanization, 1994**

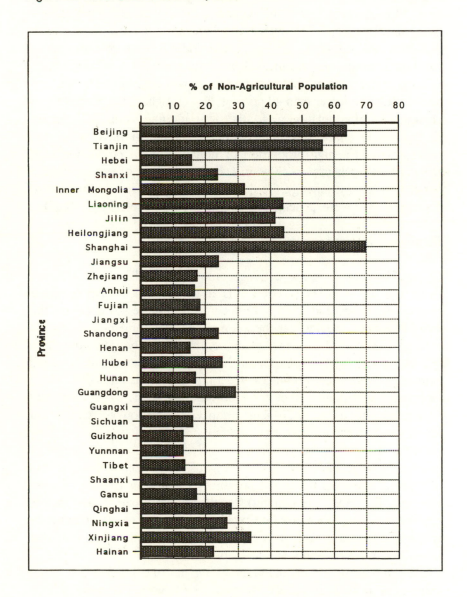

Shanghai, Beijing, and Tianjin were highly urbanized, with 70.1 percent, 64.13 percent, and 56.61 percent of their respective populations living in urban areas. The degree of urbanization in these three provincial units was similar to that in upper-middle-income countries. After the three metropolises, Northeast China was the most urbanized region. In none of the three northeastern provinces was the ratio of nonagricultural population lower than 40 percent. But elsewhere the percentage of nonagricultural population was rather low, ranging from 13.22 percent in Yunnan to 34.20 percent in Xinjiang. Although there were poor provinces with a high proportion of nonagricultural population (e.g., Qinghai) and rich provinces with a low proportion of nonagricultural population (e.g., Zhejiang), the degree of urbanization and the level of per capita GDP were, generally speaking, highly correlated ($r = 0.81$).

Disposable Income

Disposable income refers to the income which individuals or households may use at their discretion. It is an essential means for anyone to be well nourished and to enjoy a decent life. Figure 4.6 confirms that there is a huge income gap between urban and rural populations no matter which part of China we examine. In 1994, only in two provinces (Heilongjiang and Shanghai) was the ratio of urban to rural income below 2 : 1. In most provinces, the ratio fluctuated around 3 : 1. In Guizhou, Yunnan, and Tibet, the ratio was over 4 : 1.[42] It is interesting to note that the urban-rural income gap was somehow correlated with the degree of urbanization. For instance, Guizhou, Yunnan, and Tibet were the least urbanized provinces in the country. They also happened to have the largest urban-rural income gaps. On the other hand, in none of China's six most urbanized provinces (Shanghai, Beijing, Tianjin, Liaoning, Jilin, and Heilongjiang) was the ratio of urban to rural income higher than 2.2 :1. One possible explanation for this phenomenon is the spillover effect of urban centers. It is expected that the spillover effect would be stronger in more urbanized provinces.

Within the urban sector, Guangdong had the highest per capita disposable income, and Inner Mongolia the lowest. The ratio of highest to lowest urban income was 2.55, which was substantially lower than that of per capita GDP. If the four provinces where urban per capita incomes were exceptionally high (Guangdong, Shanghai, Beijing, and Zhejiang) were to be excluded, the regional variations in

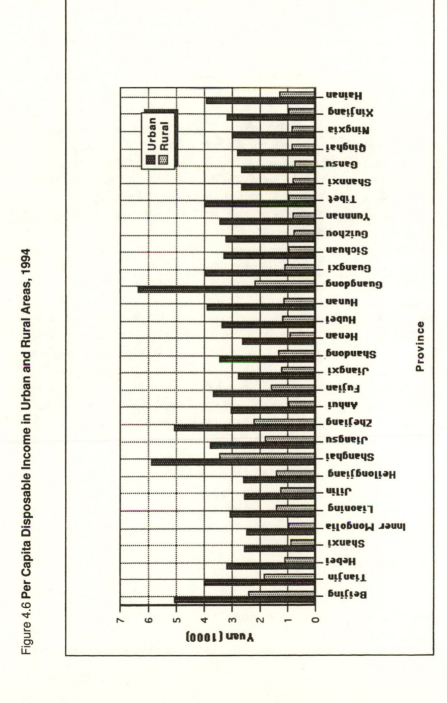

Figure 4.6 Per Capita Disposable Income in Urban and Rural Areas, 1994

urban income would be rather small. Urban residents in such poor provinces as Guizhou, Yunnan, and Guangxi, in fact, earned as much as their counterparts in Tianjin, Jiangsu, Fujian, and Shandong.

Turning to the rural sector, we find similar patterns. Rural per capita disposable income was highest in Shanghai and lowest in Gansu. The highest/lowest income ratio, 4.75, was higher than the corresponding figure for urban China, but nevertheless much lower than that for per capita GDP. If we exclude the four provinces with exceptionally high rural per capita income (Guangdong, Shanghai, Beijing, and Zhejiang, the same four that had the highest urban incomes), the regional variations in rural income were again found to be not very large. Unlike in urban China, however, the level of rural per capita income was almost perfectly correlated with the level of the provincial per capita GDP. In other words, peasants living in the least-developed parts of China also had the lowest per capita income in the country.

Despite the relatively small regional variations in per capita disposable income in both urban and rural China, the overall regional income inequality was probably still substantial, although we do not have any data to back up this conjecture. This hypothesis is based on the evidence that the urban-rural income gap existed in every province and that some provinces were more urbanized than others. Given Shanghai's highest degree of urbanization and very high levels of both urban and rural per capita income, the city almost certainly had the highest average per capita income in the nation. Since urban Shanghainese had a per capita income that was 7.5 times the per capita income of Guizhou peasants, the average per capita income gap between the two provinces would definitely be greater than either the rural per capita income gap (4.37 times) or the urban per capita income gap (1.83 times) between them. Urban-rural differences appear to be a major source of spatial income inequality. Had the urban-rural gap been narrower or had all provinces been equally urbanized, regional income inequality would have been much smaller.

Consumption

Strictly speaking, consumption is composed of two parts: social consumption and private consumption. Consumption here refers exclusively to private consumption. Issues related to social consumption will be discussed later. Some claim that per capita income does not by itself reflect the welfare of an individual. Rather, it is the level of private consumption that is more directly relevant to a person's well-being. As far as the year 1994 is concerned, however, using one or the other indicator makes virtually no difference. Comparing Figure 4.7 with Figure 4.6, we find that the former is just the mirror image of the latter, although one provides information about the regional distribution of per capita consumption, and the other about the regional distribution of per capita income. The only difference between the two figures is that the level of consumption is generally lower than the level of income. The identical contour of the two figures suggests that provinces with high levels of per capita income also have high levels of per capita consumption. In other words, consumption was no more evenly distributed than income in either the urban or rural sector. The overall consumption gap thus was likely to be as large as the overall income gap.

Access to Information

Among all consumer goods, information-access devices or media, such as television, newspapers, and telephones, deserve special attention, because people may use them not only as sources of entertainment but also to enrich themselves. Moreover, in an age in which information resources are just as important as material resources, people must possess these devices in order to gain access to information indispensable for their lives and well-being.

By 1994, the ownership of televisions in urban China had reached over 100 percent in all provinces but Hainan (95.2 percent) and Tibet (67 percent). Since urban China is saturated with TV, we focus our attention on rural China. As Table 4.7 shows, the ownership rate of televisions in rural China varied from 7.29 percent in Tibet to 117.34 percent in Shanghai. In coastal regions, television had become a household item found in over 80 percent of rural families. Only in Hainan was the TV ownership rate unexpectedly low (less than 30 percent). Television ownership had also penetrated most rural families in Central China. There over two-thirds of households had TV sets, mostly black-and-white ones. The TV ownership rate was lower in West China, particularly in Tibet (7.29 percent), Guizhou (33.80 percent), and Yunnan (49.91 percent). Nevertheless, the regional difference in terms of TV ownership was relatively small. A television seems to be

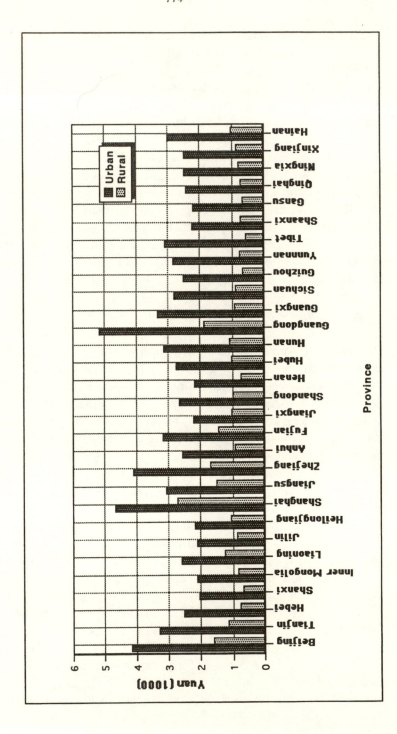

Figure 4.7 Per Capita Consumption in Urban and Rural Areas, 1994

Table 4.7

Access to Information, 1994

Province	Television sets per 100 rural households	Newspapers sold in 1994 (copies per person)	Telephones per 100 persons
Beijing	117.20	110.32	9.40
Tianjin	115.34	31.94	6.30
Hebei	95.19	17.73	1.73
Shanxi	76.95	16.79	1.48
Inner Mongolia	79.29	17.53	1.99
Liaoning	99.16	16.78	3.88
Jilin	91.44	15.84	3.46
Heilongjiang	88.10	14.57	2.99
Shanghai	117.34	79.68	12.18
Jiangsu	89.67	25.23	3.20
Zhejiang	93.81	18.78	4.09
Anhui	78.04	12.31	1.40
Fujian	85.99	16.89	3.77
Jiangxi	73.80	13.84	1.14
Shandong	85.47	13.10	1.51
Henan	65.19	11.35	0.99
Hubei	77.67	19.52	1.76
Hunan	61.51	19.23	1.69
Guangdong	81.13	21.56	6.63
Guangxi	59.82	12.14	1.10
Sichuan	68.04	10.70	0.92
Guizhou	33.80	10.60	0.56
Yunnan	49.91	15.75	1.19
Tibet	7.29	13.55	0.87
Shaanxi	67.57	16.16	1.27
Gansu	60.26	15.03	1.26
Qinghai	50.67	14.63	1.24
Ningxia	78.50	14.83	2.00
Xinjiang	63.87	21.05	1.68
Hainan	28.75	20.00	3.43

the first electronic device most rural families tend to buy, which is an indication of the burning desire of China's rural residents to embrace the outside world. Indeed, TV is probably the only window to the outside world for the majority of Chinese peasants, because they rarely read newspapers and do not have telephones installed in their houses.

As shown by Table 4.7, most Chinese, especially those living in rural areas, did not spend much on purchasing newspapers. In this regard, Beijing stood out as a category by itself. On average, the residents of the national capital bought (or their work units bought on their behalf) 110 editions of newspapers per person in 1994. With 80 newspapers per person, Shanghai ranked second. Left far behind was Tianjin, where, if counted on a per capita basis, only 32 newspapers per person were sold in that year. Nevertheless, the readership of newspapers in Tianjin was still much higher than in the other provinces. Elsewhere, the regional difference in newspaper readership was small, varying from 10.6 percent in Guizhou to 25.2 percent in Jiangsu. In any event, the regional pattern was unmistakable: the higher the per capita GDP, the higher the readership.

In 1994, ownership of telephones was correlated almost perfectly with per capita GDP ($r = 0.97$). Just as in the ranking of per capita GDP, Shanghai had the highest telephone ownership rate and Guizhou the lowest. In all of the coastal provinces except Shandong and Hebei, on average, every 100 persons owned three or more phone sets. However, the telephone ownership rate was generally below two sets per 100 persons in the rest of the country.

Poverty

Poverty is a negative indicator of quality of life. For those whose living standards are below any common concept of human dignity, quality of life is something beyond their reach, because they can hardly earn a bare living. In discussing quality of life, therefore, we should pay attention not only to the average levels of income and consumption in various provinces but also to the extent and magnitude of absolute poverty.

China's achievement in poverty reduction since 1978 has been universally acknowledged as historically unprecedented. However, by 1993, there were still about 80 million rural people languishing in absolute poverty.[43] Table 4.8 presents some information about the distribution of the rural poor for 1993. We see that in 1993, the highest poverty rate was found in Ningxia (28.5 percent), closely followed by Gansu (26.0 percent), Yunnan (23.7 percent), and Guizhou (21.9 percent). In fact, all the provinces with rural poverty rates higher than 15 percent were located in West China. Rural poverty was also a serious problem for many of the central provinces, especially Henan, Shanxi, and Inner Mongolia. By contrast, rural poverty rates were normally lower than 5 percent in the coastal provinces. The rate did not even reach 1 percent in Shanghai, Tianjin, Beijing, and Guangdong. Figure 4.8 suggests that terrain is probably the single most important factor

Table 4.8

Rural Poverty, 1993

Province	People living in poverty (1,000)	Provincial rate of poverty (%)	Provincial share of total poverty (%)
Beijing	21	0.54	0.0260
Tianjin	6	0.15	0.0074
Hebei	7,314	13.75	9.0683
Shanxi	2,673	11.75	3.3141
Inner Mongolia	1,536	10.23	1.9044
Liaoning	863	3.84	1.0700
Jilin	913	6.19	1.1320
Heilongjiang	964	4.83	1.1952
Shanghai	6	0.15	0.0074
Jiangsu	1,298	2.49	1.6093
Zhejiang	1,265	3.55	1.5684
Anhui	4,182	8.52	5.1850
Fujian	295	1.16	0.3658
Jiangxi	1,023	3.30	1.2684
Shandong	4,179	6.22	5.1813
Henan	9,616	12.61	11.9224
Hubei	2,514	5.90	3.1170
Hunan	1,664	3.20	2.0631
Guangdong	276	0.58	0.3422
Guangxi	2,999	8.03	3.7183
Sichuan	9,490	10.24	11.7662
Guizhou	6,371	21.89	7.8991
Yunnan	7,831	23.67	9.7093
Tibet	117	5.93	0.1451
Shaanxi	5,243	19.35	6.5005
Gansu	4,999	25.95	6.1980
Qinghai	531	16.53	0.6584
Ningxia	1,057	28.47	1.3105
Xinjiang	1,192	11.42	1.4779
Hainan	217	4.09	0.2690

that explains regional variations in rural poverty: The more mountainous a province is, the higher the incidence of poverty tends to be. Mountainous areas are normally characterized by "difficult hilly farming conditions, poor and degraded soils, scarce rainfall, underdeveloped transportation and other infrastructural facilities, and remoteness from lucrative urban markets."[44] All these conditions may contribute to the high poverty rates in such regions.

An alternative way of ranking provinces is to calculate the numeric magnitude of poverty. In terms of total numbers, as shown in Table

Figure 4.8 Geographical Location and Rural Poverty

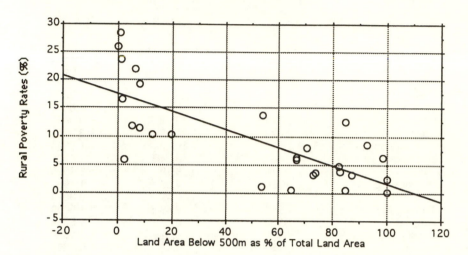

4.8, Henan, the second-most-populous province, ranked the highest, with nearly 10 million peasants living in poverty. Sichuan, China's most populous province, followed closely after Henan. Other populous provinces, such as Shandong, Hebei, and Anhui, also had millions of peasants who were barely achieving minimum subsistence incomes. In this sense, the numeric magnitude of poverty was a function of population size. However, the poverty rate in a province was still a very important determinant of the province's share of total poverty. Thus, no matter which method of ranking is chosen, the problem of poverty in Henan, Sichuan, and Hebei is unlikely to escape the attention of the central government. After all, the incidence of poverty was greater than 10 percent in each of these provinces, and together about one-third of China's rural poor resided in these three provinces.

Education

Are income and consumption inequalities in China accompanied by differential access of the residents of different regions to such non-market public goods and services as education and health care? For three reasons, this is an important question to ask in investigating regional inequality. First, the levels at which these key social services are provided directly affect people's current quality of life. Second, regions with healthier and better-educated labor forces are likely to grow faster in the future. Third, the answer to this question will reveal the extent to which the central government has used fiscal transfers to redress the issue of regional inequality. This subsection examines regional differences in the educational composition of the populations of various provinces, leaving the issue of health to the next subsection.

We use two variables to measure educational level, one negative and one positive. The negative indicator is the illiteracy rate, and the positive one the number of years of education attained by the average person. The findings are reported in Table 4.9. According to the State Statistical Bureau's 1995 survey of 1 percent of the population, regional gaps in illiteracy were quite visible in that year.[45] On the one hand, illiteracy rates were lower than 8 percent in six provinces, five of which were coastal ones. Beijing had the lowest illiteracy rate, just 6.38 percent. On the other hand, there were five provinces where over one-fifth of the population was illiterate. All of these were western provinces. The highest illiteracy rate was found in Tibet, where 40 percent of the population could not read. Between the two extremes, in Central China, provincial illiteracy rates varied within a rather narrow range, from 7.11 percent in Jilin to 14.09 percent in Anhui.

Turning to the positive indicator, we find that the same five provinces that had the highest illiteracy rates (Tibet, Qinghai, Gansu, Yunnan, and Guizhou) happened to be the provinces with the lowest average years of schooling. Similarly, the provinces with the lowest illiteracy rates tended to have the highest average years of educational attainment. Guangdong was a notable exception. Although the province had a far lower illiteracy rate than Jiangsu, Zhejiang, and Inner Mongolia, for instance, the average of schooling years was no higher than the corresponding figures in these three provinces. The mean number of schooling years was also relatively low in the other two southern coastal provinces, Hainan and Fujian. Hainan had a lower figure than Jilin, Heilongjiang, Shanxi, and Hebei, and was on a par with Hunan. The average years of schooling achieved in Fujian was not only lower than in all the central provinces but also was lower than in a number of western provinces. It is interesting to explore why the fastest-growing provinces were still lagging behind many other provinces in this regard.

The regional differences in length of schooling probably have little to do with regional variations in primary education, because education

Table 4.9

Education, 1995

Province	Illiteracy rates (%)	Mean school years
Beijing	6.38	8.71
Tianjin	7.17	7.67
Hebei	9.41	6.18
Shanxi	8.26	6.71
Inner Mongolia	12.26	6.40
Liaoning	7.31	7.09
Jilin	7.11	7.20
Heilongjiang	8.25	6.95
Shanghai	7.00	8.38
Jiangsu	11.31	6.62
Zhejiang	13.32	6.25
Anhui	14.09	5.50
Fujian	14.23	5.49
Jiangxi	12.75	5.66
Shandong	13.30	6.19
Henan	11.36	6.11
Hubei	12.00	6.00
Hunan	11.02	6.17
Guangdong	7.81	6.25
Guangxi	9.14	5.97
Sichuan	12.81	5.78
Guizhou	20.36	4.96
Yunnan	21.03	4.79
Tibet	40.00	2.21
Shaanxi	13.00	6.13
Gansu	24.28	4.86
Qinghai	26.95	4.63
Ningxia	17.94	5.45
Xinjiang	9.28	6.19
Hainan	10.00	6.17

at this level has largely been made universal in China by now. Rather, it is in the area of secondary education (both junior high and senior high school) that provinces differ. Figure 4.9 confirms that there was indeed a huge regional gap in secondary education in 1995. In Shanghai, over one-half of the population has received secondary education. However, the ratio drops off sharply as we turn our attention from the coastal to the central and western provinces. In Tibet, less than 7 percent of the population has ever had the opportunity to attend middle school. By showing a nearly perfect correlation between the average years of schooling and the share of the population receiving secondary education ($r = 0.97$), Figure 4.9 also confirms that the problem of

Figure 4.9 **Determinant of Mean Years of Schooling, 1995**

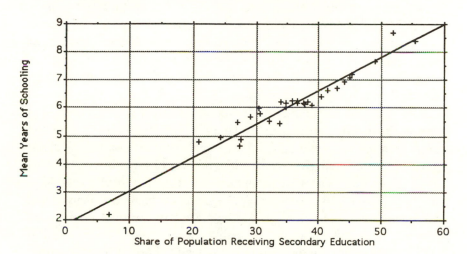

regional disparity in education lies in secondary education rather than in primary education. As Albert Keidel points out: "This interregional disparity in high-school education is perhaps the most significant for future economic development in the various regions, because a more mature educational background will almost certainly facilitate higher-productivity employment and easier migration to future concentrations of such jobs in coastal cities."[46]

Technological Capabilities

The characteristics of the local workforce may have a great effect on a region's growth prospects, because the higher the educational level of the workforce, the more capable it will be in applying new technological innovations. However, new innovations have to come from scientific and technological research. Without making efforts in R&D (research and development), it is impossible for a region to adapt and improve technologies obtained from elsewhere, not to mention inventing new products and processes on its own. It is now universally recognized that technology plays a crucial role in modern economic growth. Just as technological change may contribute to increasing productivity and economic growth at the national level, regional differences in the propensity to create and adapt new technologies can result in major differences in regional economic growth rates. Product innovations may help regions to improve their product range and hence their product mix, while process innovations may help regions to improve their efficiency and produce products of higher quality. Both types of innovations are necessary for maintaining competitiveness.[47] It is therefore important to examine how technological capabilities vary among regions.

R&D activities are conducted by scientists and engineers. Thus, it is reasonable to use the number of talented personnel who are in the forefront of creating and adopting new technologies as an approximation for the technological capabilities of various regions. The geographical distribution of technological talent by province for 1994 is shown in Table 4.10. Predictably, Beijing, Shanghai, and Tianjin had the highest ratios of scientists and engineers to the total population. This was especially noticeable in Beijing, where among every 100,000 people, there were 3,699 scientists and technicians. What is perhaps unexpected is that the proportion of scientists and engineers was relatively high in four northwestern provinces, Xinjiang, Qinghai, Shaanxi, and Ningxia, where the ratios were actually higher than the corresponding figures in such high-income coastal provinces as Jiangsu, Zhejiang, Fujian, Shandong, and Guangdong. At the same time, however, the ratios in four southwestern provinces, Tibet, Guangxi, Guizhou, and Yunnan, were among the lowest in the nation. Still, this observation should not lead to the conclusion that the distribution of technological talent showed no regional pattern. On the contrary, such a pattern did exist. A close look at Table 4.10 reveals that a province's proportion of scientists and engineers was highly correlated with its per capita GDP (r = 0.77). In other words, despite some exceptions, in general, it was the rich provinces that tended to have a higher proportion of scientists and engineers among their populations.

By using the relative numbers of scientists and engineers to measure the technological capability of various regions, we assume that provinces with relatively large numbers of scientists and engineers tend to be innovation-leaders. Is this a sound assumption? The right-hand column of Table 4.10 uses the number of patents per 100,000 population in a province to measure the province's innovation rate. Regressing the innovation rates against the relative numbers of scientists and engineers, we find that the two are highly correlated (r = 0.95), which confirms the importance of the number of R&D personnel. Neverthe-

Table 4.10

Selected Indicators of Technological Capability, 1994

Province	Engineers per 100,000 persons	Scientists per 100,000 persons	Engineers and scientists per 100,000 persons	Patents per 100,000 persons
Beijing	3,023	676	3,699	36.64
Tianjin	1,750	92	1,842	11.89
Hebei	336	14	350	2.50
Shanxi	569	19	588	1.85
Inner Mongolia	510	13	523	1.52
Liaoning	1,030	43	1,073	6.78
Jilin	747	42	788	3.65
Heilongjiang	792	22	813	4.15
Shanghai	2,011	166	2,177	11.19
Jiangsu	544	28	572	3.57
Zhejiang	354	17	371	4.67
Anhui	255	14	269	1.01
Fujian	355	11	366	2.34
Jiangxi	310	9	319	1.30
Shandong	380	12	392	3.06
Henan	241	14	256	1.41
Hubei	490	27	517	1.86
Hunan	313	17	330	2.57
Guangdong	381	14	395	4.71
Guangxi	301	9	310	1.42
Sichuan	350	19	369	1.77
Guizhou	301	10	311	0.73
Yunnan	308	15	324	1.14
Tibet	178	17	195	0.13
Shaanxi	595	44	639	3.86
Gansu	441	33	474	1.46
Qinghai	626	31	657	1.29
Ningxia	572	18	590	2.54
Xinjiang	649	31	681	2.23
Hainan	261	14	275	0.95

less, the relative numbers of R&D personnel could not fully explain the regional variations in innovation rates. A province's ability to finance R&D also seems to be very important. For instance, Xinjiang, Ningxia, and Qinghai were not able to compete with Jiangsu, Zhejiang, Shandong, and Guangdong in terms of innovation rates, despite the fact that the latter provinces had much lower ratios of scientists and engineers to their total populations. In fact, the number of patents per 100,000 population was higher than two in all but one coastal province (Hainan). In the rest of the country, however, most provinces failed to obtain more than two patents for every 100,000 population in 1994. The spatial differences in the ability to develop and apply new technologies will determine, at least in part, the country's future regional growth patterns.

Health

People's ability to lead healthy and well-nourished lives depends crucially on access to health services in the region where they live. As will be shown below, the residents of some of China's provinces have better access to health care than do those living elsewhere. For illustrative purposes, inequality in the access to public health is measured here by two indicators, namely, medical personnel (including physicians, pharmacists, laboratory specialists, and nurses) per 100,000 population, and hospital beds per 100,000 population. Table 4.11 reports regional statistics on these two variables.

With 1,095 medical specialists and 627 hospital beds for every 100,000 residents, Beijing was obviously the most favored city in the nation. Shanghai residents were also very fortunate, as every 100,000 of them had 862 medical specialists and 554 hospital beds at their service. However, for people living in Guizhou, China's poorest province, the chance of seeing a doctor was quite slim, because, on average, medical specialists in Guizhou have to look after nearly 400 persons each, while their counterparts in Beijing only need to take care of around 90 persons. In terms of hospital beds, the gap between Beijing and Guizhou was also substantial. The situation in Guangxi, China's second-poorest province, was not much better than that in Guizhou. In general, it can be said that people's access to health services in poor provinces was more limited than the access available to those residing in richer areas. There were exceptions, however. Unlike Guangxi, China's four other autonomous regions (Inner Mongolia, Tibet, Xinjiang, and Ningxia) compared very favorably in the provision of health services with most of the other provinces, including such rich coastal provinces as Jiangsu, Zhejiang, Fujian, Shandong, and Guangdong. Only the three metropolises and the three provinces in the northeast supplied better health services. This could not be accidental. One possible explanation is that the central government might have earmarked health care funds for the autonomous regions. But if that were true, then how could we explain why Guangxi was different?

An alternative explanation is that something other than per capita GDP might have played an important role in determining the regional patterns in health care provision. Guizhou and Yunnan were not only the poorest provinces but also the least urbanized. In fact, the regional disparities in the provision of health services, as revealed by Table 4.11, can be better explained by the varying degrees of urbanization than by the per capita GDP differentials across provinces. The relative numbers of both medical personnel and hospital beds correlated highly with urbanization. The correlation coefficients were as high as 0.94 and 0.89, respectively. Such correlations unveil a strong urban bias in health care provision in China. Viewed from this angle, the cases of the four autonomous regions were by no means exceptional, because their degrees of urbanization were relatively high.

The number of medical personnel and hospital beds per person are measures of inputs into the health care system. However, what really interests us is the outcomes of the system, namely, the health conditions of the people. Therefore we use infant mortality and life expectancy as two proxies for health in the analysis that follows. The former can tell us to what extent mothers give birth under safe and healthy conditions, and the latter may indicate how likely a person is to avoid premature death.

Overall, China has done extraordinarily well in reducing infant mortality and in raising life expectancy.[48] But this does not mean that all its provinces have advanced side by side. Columns 3 and 4 in Table 4.11 reveal huge regional gaps in both areas.[49] The infant mortality rate in Tibet was as high as 95 per thousand, which was more than ten times the rates for Beijing and Tianjin, and nearly eight times the rate for Shanghai. Even excluding the three metropolises and only comparing Tibet with the other provinces, the infant mortality rate in Tibet still seems to be in a different order of magnitude altogether from such cases as Hebei, Shandong, Jiangsu, Guangdong, Zhejiang, and Liaoning. The infant mortality rate was high not only in Tibet but also in all the western provinces except Shaanxi. If we compare the western provinces and the coastal provinces as two groups, it immediately becomes clear that each of the former had an infant mortality rate that was two or three times higher than those prevailing in the latter economies. In Central China, the worst infant mortality rates were observed in Jiangxi and Hunan, whose mortality rates were no better than those of some western provinces.

Table 4.11

Selected Indicators of Health, 1994

Province	Medical personnel per 100,000 persons	Hospital beds per 100,000 persons	Infant mortality per 1,000 live births	Life expec-tancy at birth (years)	Birth rates per 1,000	Depend-ency ratio (%)
Beijing	1,095.3	627.2	8.7	73.6	9.0	38.4
Tianjin	793.7	436.0	10.6	72.7	11.0	43.7
Hebei	311.0	249.8	9.2	71.7	14.9	50.1
Shanxi	468.1	371.1	19.1	69.5	17.5	51.3
Inner Mongolia	460.0	302.2	28.8	66.8	19.0	44.1
Liaoning	581.4	509.1	18.6	70.8	12.3	40.5
Jilin	524.7	377.6	24.3	68.3	14.1	39.2
Heilongjiang	503.1	359.8	18.4	68.0	15.1	38.6
Shanghai	862.3	554.4	12.4	75.3	5.8	41.1
Jiangsu	352.8	254.7	15.0	72.2	13.8	44.5
Zhejiang	334.0	244.2	17.0	72.3	13.2	41.5
Anhui	249.2	200.4	26.0	69.9	16.7	49.2
Fujian	291.0	233.5	22.9	70.2	16.2	58.1
Jiangxi	310.8	241.4	42.6	66.7	19.4	52.0
Shandong	305.1	230.0	12.8	71.2	9.7	47.5
Henan	278.7	212.1	18.5	70.2	15.4	55.5
Hubei	403.1	284.6	25.0	67.5	18.2	52.8
Hunan	301.3	234.7	37.8	67.2	13.9	50.6
Guangdong	328.8	216.7	15.8	73.1	18.2	63.3
Guangxi	253.6	186.3	43.6	69.3	18.8	58.5
Sichuan	293.2	233.7	38.1	67.1	16.9	44.5
Guizhou	260.3	177.5	51.9	65.1	22.9	57.1
Yunnan	289.3	245.0	65.0	64.0	21.8	55.3
Tibet	344.9	258.6	94.6	59.1	25.6	62.0
Shaanxi	370.4	288.1	21.9	68.3	17.6	50.5
Gansu	344.3	238.1	31.2	67.5	20.8	48.9
Qinghai	443.4	376.9	65.4	61.8	22.1	52.6
Ningxia	416.8	258.0	37.0	68.2	19.7	55.2
Xinjiang	560.6	448.5	57.9	65.1	20.8	65.2
Hainan	448.4	332.7	29.0	72.2	20.8	63.5

[a]Data on infant mortality rate and life expectancy are for 1990.

In terms of life expectancy, the spatial differences were smaller, but nevertheless the same regional patterns were repeated. All the coastal provinces were able to raise their life expectancy above 70 years, and all the central provinces above 65. In the meantime, however, life expectancy figures lingered around the mid-60s in the western provinces. Tibet, again, lagged far behind all others. As a matter of fact, infant mortality and life expectancy were highly correlated ($r = 0.9$). This means that, generally speaking, the provinces with low infant mortality rates tended to have high life expectancy. Whether measured by infant mortality rates or life expectancy figures, the regional difference in health conditions between Coastal China and West China, to a large extent, resembled that between the high-income countries and the low- and middle-income countries in the world, which showed how large the gap was.[50]

A careful examination of Table 4.11 also reveals two additional points that are interesting. First, there does not appear to be any strong correlation between the inputs and outcomes of the provincial health care systems. Inner Mongolia, Xinjiang, Ningxia, and Tibet might have more medical personnel and hospital beds per 100,000 people than Jiangsu, Zhejiang, Fujian, Shandong, and Guangdong, but infant mortality rates were much higher and life expectancy figures much lower in the former than in the latter. More generally, correlating the infant mortality and life expectancy figures, on the one hand, with the numbers of medical personnel and hospital beds per 100,000 people, on the other, we find none of the coefficients to be higher than 0.4. This finding may not be as surprising as it first appears. The determinants of infant mortality and life expectancy are complex. In addition to the quantity of health care provision, the quality of such services, sanitation, access to safe water, food availability, education (particularly medical knowledge), shelter, the level and distribution of income, and the like may also directly or indirectly affect death rates among young children and adults. Since many of these variables tend to move in the same direction as per capita GDP, the level of per capita GDP is expected to have some influence on infant mortality and life expectancy rates. As it turns out, there did exist relatively strong polynomial relationships between infant mortality and per capita GDP ($r = 0.614$), and between life expectancy and per capita GDP ($r = 0.742$). This is the second interesting point mentioned above.

A low infant mortality rate is desirable not only because it indicates a high health standard, but also because it may bring about a positive change in the pattern of demographic development—a lower birth rate. Wherever the infant mortality rate is high, people are inclined to over-insure themselves against possible infant deaths. Consequently, the birth rate tends to be high. Fewer child deaths thus may lead people to desire smaller families. For this reason, we expect regions with low infant mortality rates to have low birth rates as well. This conjecture is confirmed by the data presented in Table 4.11, where the birth rate demonstrates a strong correlation with the infant mortality rate (r = 0.78). We thus find that two types of provinces coexisted in China in 1994. One had an inefficient demographic regime of high mortality and high fertility, while the other had a more efficient regime of low mortality and low fertility.[51] Examples of the former were Tibet, Qinghai, Xinjiang, Guizhou, and Yunnan, and examples of the latter were Beijing, Tianjin, Shanghai, Shandong, Jiangsu, and Zhejiang.

Persistent spatial differentiation in birth rates, in turn, is likely to produce spatial differentiation in dependency ratios.[52] Dependency ratio here refers to the proportion of the total population aged 0 to 14 and 65+, two age cohorts that are economically unproductive and therefore must be supported financially by others.[53] On the assumption that a higher birth rate will result in a larger proportion of youthful dependents in the total population, we may expect that the dependency ratio will be high in regions with high birth rates, and vice versa. As Table 4.11 shows, such a correlation did exist in 1994 (r = 0.71). In general, dependency burdens were heavier in less-developed than in more-developed provinces, because the former tended to have higher birth rates. For example, the dependency ratio was 62.02 percent in Tibet, 58.48 percent in Guangxi, 57.12 percent in Guizhou, and 55.31 percent in Yunnan. But the comparable figure was much lower in such wealthier provinces as Beijing (38.40 percent), Heilongjiang (38.67 percent), Jilin (39.22 percent), Liaoning (40.45 percent), Shanghai (41.1 percent), and Zhejiang (41.46 percent). Of course, the correlation was by no means perfect. Thus, we find that the dependency ratio was quite high in Hainan (63.47 percent), Guangdong (63.26 percent), and Fujian (58.08 percent). With relatively high per capita GDP, those living in the three southern coastal provinces might not view the high dependency ratios as a major challenge. However, for those living in poor provinces, heavy dependency burdens constituted an obstacle to future economic development.

Summary

This chapter provides a snapshot of China's problem of regional inequality at a specific point in time, 1994. Although China is a country that has been undergoing drastic change, there is no reason to believe that its

regional disparities today significantly deviate from the patterns identified in this chapter.[54] What are the main findings of this chapter? The
analysis of data presented here points to the following three conclusions.

First, regional inequality is indeed a multidimensional phenomenon.
Table 4.12 summarizes the arithmetic means, ranges (largest value
minus smallest value), standard deviations (SD, a measure of the absolute dispersion of a distribution in terms of the units of the original
data), and coefficients of variation (CV, a unitless measure of the
relative dispersion of distribution) for all the variables examined in the
previous pages. The table makes it abundantly clear that, no matter
which dimension we look at, there appear to be regional differences in
relative as well as absolute terms. In particular, human development
indicators are all significantly worse in poor provinces as compared
with rich ones. Although the coefficients of variation (CV) of social
indicators are normally not as high as that of per capita GDP (66.57),
there are nevertheless visible gaps between provinces. This is brought
out also in Table 4.13. Despite its relatively low GDP per head, China
as a whole has a remarkably low illiteracy rate and infant mortality
rate, and extraordinarily high mean years of schooling and life expectancy, all of which surpass the levels achieved in middle-income countries. However, in the same areas, regional differences among China's
thirty provinces are so large that they resemble the gaps between the
advanced industrial countries and the poorest countries in the world—
while China's most developed province follows closely after high-
income economies, its least-developed province is hardly much better
than low-income economies. In this sense, First World and Third
World coexist within China!

Second, the three dimensions of regional inequality examined here
all correlate roughly with disparities in output, though the directions of
causality may differ. Obviously, it is not plausible to say that disparities in per capita GDP cause a discrepancy in geographic conditions,
natural resource endowment, or transportation infrastructure. Conversely, output disparities must be regarded as one of the causes, not
the result, of regional gaps in such social indicators as disposable
income and infant mortality. The relationship between the level of a
region's per capita GDP and its economic structure may be more complicated. Two-way causation is possible. However, if we believe that
any economy will inevitably go through certain structural changes during its development process,[55] then structural differences across re-

Table 4.12

Multidimensional Facets of Regional Disparity, 1994

Variables (unit)	Mean	Range	SD	CV
Per Capita GDP (yuan)	4,310.40	13,652.00	2,869.24	66.57
Resource-endowment				
Land area below 500m as % of total land area (%)	51.71	100.00	38.44	74.33
Annual mean temperature (C°)	11.79	25.50	6.37	54.06
Annual mean precipitation (mm)	921.17	1,750.00	479.31	52.03
Arable land as % of total land (%)	20.07	46.16	13.75	68.49
Irrigated land as % of arable land (%)	56.57	87.78	23.72	41.94
Han as % of total population (%)	86.48	95.00	21.99	25.43
Waterway (km/sq km)	0.035	0.331	0.072	206.38
Railway (km/sq km)	0.020	0.098	0.024	118.90
Roadway (km/sq km)	0.239	0.669	0.156	64.96
Total of waterway, railroad, and roads (km/sq km)	0.295	0.963	0.214	72.61
Savings rates (%)	43.01	38.00	10.02	23.30
Investment rates (%)	46.95	53.60	11.51	24.52
Per capita investment (yuan)	2,202.09	8,418.19	2,016.14	91.56
Labor force as % of population (%)	51.12	20.90	5.17	10.10
Economic Structure				
Agriculture as % of GDP (%)	22.67	43.57	9.03	39.82
Industry as % of GDP (%)	44.47	40.70	8.57	19.28
Services as % of GDP (%)	32.86	19.77	4.54	13.81
Agriculture as % of labor force (%)	51.86	68.29	17.24	33.25
Industry as % of labor force (%)	24.71	52.39	11.70	47.34
Services as % of labor force (%)	23.44	36.09	7.27	31.01

(continued)

Light industry as % of total industrial output (%)	37.08	44.84	12.99	35.02
Heavy industry as % of total industrial output (%)	62.92	44.84	12.99	20.64
State sector as % of the total value of fixed assets in all industrial enterprises (%)	73.73	63.67	16.15	21.90
Collective sector as % of the total value of fixed assets in all industrial enterprises (%)	11.36	34.41	7.54	66.36
"Others" as % of the total value of fixed assets in all industrial enterprises (%)	14.92	51.14	12.97	86.90
State share of total industrial output by enterprises at the township level and above (%)	63.73	59.72	17.95	28.17
State share of total industrial output by all enterprises (%)	48.51	67.90	19.17	39.52
Total rural output (billion yuan)	194.65	816.79	208.50	107.12
Rural industrial output as % of total rural output (%)	41.16	88.17	23.10	56.11
Provincial rural industrial output as % of national total rural industrial output (%)	3.33	18.80	4.67	140.06
Rural labor force as % of total labor force (%)	66.25	59.60	17.97	27.13
Labor force in non-farming as % of the total rural labor force (%)	26.83	67.01	15.49	57.74
Labor force in rural industry as % of the total rural labor force (%)	30.49	52.34	12.61	41.34
Exports as % of provincial GDP (%)	15.83	104.62	20.19	127.54
Provincial exports as % of the total national exports (%)	3.33	44.00	7.97	239.04
Provincial foreign investment as % of the total national foreign investment (%)	3.33	43.48	7.95	238.46
Per capita foreign investment (US$)	36.34	181.87	52.99	145.82
Human well-being				
Level of urbanization (%)	27.49	56.78	15.10	54.93
Urban per capita disposable income (yuan)	3,528.47	3,873.96	979.96	27.77
Rural per capita disposable income (yuan)	1,314.08	2,712.88	603.13	45.90
Urban per capita consumption (yuan)	2,865.96	3,137.96	775.77	27.07
Rural per capita consumption (yuan)	1,061.94	2,151.01	450.49	42.42

(continued)

Table 4.12 (continued)

Variables (unit)	Mean	Range	SD	CV
Television sets per 100 rural households	74.69	110.05	24.99	33.46
Newspapers sold in 1994 (copies per person)	16.69	21.34	4.59	27.50
Telephones per 100 persons	2.84	11.63	2.66	93.89
Provincial rates of poverty (%)	9.15	28.32	8.02	87.65
Provincial share of total poverty (%)	3.33	11.92	3.61	108.33
Illiteracy rates (%)	13.30	33.62	7.21	54.21
Mean school years (year)	6.09	6.50	1.20	19.65
Engineers per 100,000 persons (no.)	632.39	2,844.70	609.44	96.37
Scientists per 100,000 persons (no.)	49.69	666.92	122.19	245.91
Engineers & scientists per 100,000 persons (no.)	682.08	3,503.72	718.66	105.37
Patents per 100,000 persons (no.)	4.14	36.51	6.72	162.24
Medical personnel per 100,000 persons (no.)	426.00	846.07	194.48	45.65
Hospital beds per 100,000 persons (no.)	306.09	449.75	112.79	36.85
Infant mortality per 1,000 live births	30.64	85.87	19.99	65.25
Life expectancy at birth (year)	68.83	16.20	3.58	5.19
Birth rates per 1,000	16.70	19.84	4.47	26.74
Dependency ratio (%)	50.50	26.79	7.85	15.54
Per capita budgetary revenue (yuan)	245.37	1,166.00	222.92	91.98
Per capita budgetary expenditure (yuan)	444.85	1,257.10	300.59	67.57
Per capita extrabudgetary revenue (yuan)	158.34	477.69	108.58	68.58
Per capita extrabudgetary expenditure (yuan)	147.99	457.87	100.77	68.09

Table 4.13

Selected Human Development Indicators: China and the World[a]

	China			World				
	Worst province	Average	Best province	Low-income economies	Lower-middle income economies	Middle-income economies	Upper-middle income economies	High-income economies
Urbanization (%)	13.3	27.5	70.1	27	54	60	71	78
Illiteracy Rates (%)	40.0	13.3	6.4	49	19	17	14	<5
Mean School Years (year)	2.2	6.1	8.7	1.6	3.9	5.3	8.8	11.1
Life Expectancy (year)	59.1	68.8	75.2	56	67	68	69	77
Infant Mortality (per 1,000 live births)	94.6	30.6	8.7	89	40	39	36	7

Source: World Development Report 1995, pp. 162–63, 214–15, 222–23; Mahbub ul Haq (1995), pp. 208, 218.
[a]Data on China are for 1994; data on other economies are for 1993.

Figure 4.10 **Resource Endowment and Per Capita GDP, 1994**

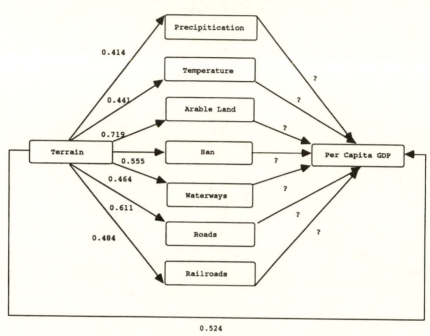

gions are more likely to be the results of regional disparities in development level than the other way around.

Figure 4.10 illustrates how resource endowment is related to per capita GDP. Here terrain (measured by the percentage of total land area below 500 m elevation above sea level) seems to be a key factor. The correlation between terrain and per capita GDP is fairly strong (r = 0.524). This means that the more mountainous a province, the less developed its economy. Of course, terrain as such does not directly affect the level of economic development. However, as discussed in the previous sections and indicated by Figure 4.10, a region's topography may have some impact on its climate, the availability of arable land, its ethnic makeup, and most importantly, its transportation infrastructure, all of which may condition the region's economic development in one way or another. Our regression analysis shows that the impacts on the per capita GDP level associated with precipitation, the availability of arable land, and the density of railroads are not really statistically significant.[56] Temperature and ethnic makeup (measured by the proportion of Han in the total population) do have some impact,

Figure 4.11 **Economic Structure and Per Capita GDP, 1994**

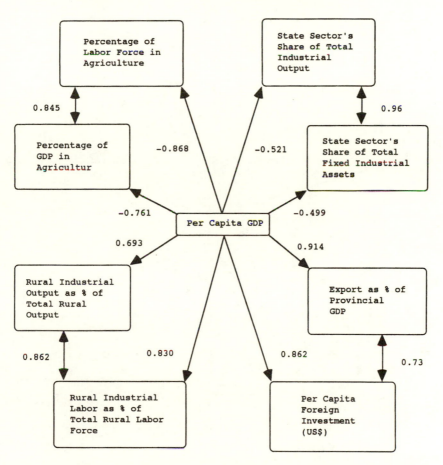

but negatively rather than positively.[57] The variable that explains the most variance in per capita GDP is the density of roads. The density of waterways explains the second-greatest amount of variance in the dependent variable. Thus, we may conclude from this analysis that transportation infrastructure is extremely important for economic development.

Figure 4.11 depicts the impact of per capita GDP on economic structures. In terms of economic structure, rich provinces can be easily distinguished from poor ones. The former are normally much less agrarian than the latter. Even their countryside is rapidly becoming industrialized. All provinces have mixed economies, featuring both

Figure 4.12 **Private and Public Consumption and Per Capita GDP, 1994**

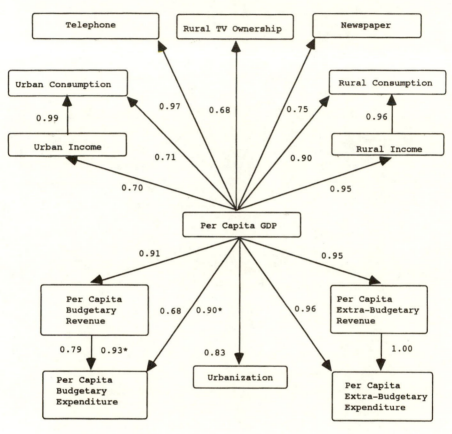

* Tibet is excluded.

state and non-state ownership. However, the division between the two and their relative importance seem to be mostly a function of the development level. That is, the more developed a province, the more diversified its ownership structure. The degree of openness is another important structural feature that differentiates the rich from the poor. Foreign trade plays a much bigger role in the former than in the latter, and foreign capital tends to bypass the latter and flow mainly into the former.

Figure 4.12 sets out findings on the relationship between per capita GDP, on the one hand, and private and public consumption, on the other. Since, in both the urban and rural sectors, the private consumption level correlates almost perfectly with the income level, our attention first focuses on how per capita GDP is related to income. Figure 4.12 reveals an extremely strong correlation between rural income and per capita GDP but not as strong a correlation between urban income and per capita GDP. This result suggests that state policy may have performed the function of income redistribution in the urban sector, but failed to do so in the rural sector. Even in the urban sector, however, the state's role as a redistributor is a rather weak one. Consequently, regional disparities in private consumption largely mirror regional disparities in output in both sectors.

Public consumption is supposed to be more evenly distributed. But this does not seem to be the case in China. As shown by Figure 4.12, per capita budgetary revenue is highly correlated with per capita GDP ($r = 0.91$), which means that the former is probably as unevenly distributed as the latter. At first glance, the coefficient for the correlation between per capita budgetary revenue and per capita budgetary expenditure does not appear to be very high ($r = 0.79$). This implies that the central government may have adopted some redistributive measures to reduce fiscal gaps between provinces. A close examination of the data, however, reveals that whatever these measures may be, Tibet is probably the only beneficiary of them. Were the case of Tibet to be dropped, the aforementioned coefficient would instantly increase to 0.93. Similarly, if Tibet is excluded, the correlation between per capita budgetary expenditure and per capita GDP becomes very high ($r = 0.90$), suggesting that there is little budgetary redistribution other than a special assistance program for Tibet alone.

In addition to budgetary funds, China's fiscal system also contains so-called extrabudgetary funds.[58] These are by no means small supplements to budgetary funds. In 1994, extrabudgetary funds were equivalent to about one-third of budgetary funds.[59] For this reason, many Chinese economists refer to extrabudgetary funds as China's "second budget." Unlike budgetary funds, however, these funds are almost entirely out of central budgetary control and thereby subject to no redistribution at all. This point is confirmed by Figure 4.12, which illustrates that both per capita extrabudgetary revenue and expenditure are almost perfectly correlated with per capita GDP.

Third, given the unequal distribution of both budgetary and extrabudgetary expenditure, it is impossible for the provision of key public goods to be standardized across the country, which may very well be one of the causes of the large regional disparities in human well-being.[60] Table 4.14 demonstrates this point by regressing six social indicators against two fiscal variables: per capita budgetary expenditure on health, education, and culture, and per capita extrabudgetary expenditure. The latter is included because "off-budget funds are commonly used to supplement salaries of teachers and public health workers, to meet other recurrent expenditures for providing these services, and to provide matching funds that are often required for obtaining capital construction grants [for new projects in health and education] from higher level governments."[61] Extrabudgetary funds are so critical in today's fiscal system in China that it is often impossible, without taking them into consideration, to explain regional disparities in human development. Unfortunately, we do not have any information about how large a proportion of extrabudgetary funds is used to finance health and education in the various provinces. Nor do we know much about the provincial breakdown of per capita budgetary expenditure on health, education, and culture. However, it is not unreasonable to assume that the higher the two broad categories of expenditure are in a province, the more will be spent to support education and public health there. The regression analyses presented in Table 4.14 show that the partial regression coefficients for both variables are statistically significant at the p .05 level in almost all models. In addition, the two variables can statistically explain more than 50 percent of the variations in nearly all the dependent variables.

Table 4.14

Impacts of Budgetary and Extrabudgetary Expenditures on Social Indicators

Independent variables	Illiteracy rates (%)	Mean school years	Medical personnel per 100,000 persons	Hospital beds per 100,000 persons	Infant mortality per 1,000 live births	Life expectancy at birth (year)
			Beta			
Per capita budgetary expenditure on health, education, and culture	0.78 (4.225)	−0.54 (3.487)	0.346 (2.21)	0.341 (1.949)	0.742 (3.829)	−0.581 (3.492)
Per capita extrabudgetary expenditure	−1.066 (5.749)	1.127 (7.305)	0.539 (3.441)	0.493 (2.819)	−1.026 (5.296)	1.107 (6.654)
Adj. R^2	0.517	0.67	0.655	0.571	0.473	0.612
F statistics	16.534	29.885	28.568	20.295	14.023	23.851

Note: t-statistics are in parentheses.

Notes

1. Mick Dunford, "Regional Disparities in the European Community," pp. 727–43.

2. Mahbub ul Haq, *Reflections on Human Development;* UNDP, *Human Development Report 1996,* pp. 66–85; Kai-yuen Tsui, "The Measurement of China's Regional Inequalities," pp. 413–30.

3. Sumner J. La Croix and Richard F. Garbaccio, "Convergence in Income and Consumption in China During the Maoist and Reform Regimes."

4. Simon Kuznets, *Economic Growth of Nations;* Hollis B. Chenery, *Structural Change and Development Policy;* Michael P. Todaro, *Economic Development.*

5. Thomas P. Lyons, "Interprovincial Disparities in China."

6. Zhao Songqiao, *Geography of China,* p. 5.

7. Albert Keidel, "China," p. 2.

8. Although no exact data on Hainan are available, from travel experience in the province, I believe that it belongs to this category.

9. Zhao, *Geography of China,* p. 10.

10. Ibid., p. 36.

11. Ibid., p. 4.

12. Ibid., pp. 10–11.

13. Angang Hu, Shaoguang Wang, and Xiaoguang Kang, *Zhongguo diqu chaju baogao,* p. 106.

14. Zhao, *Geography of China,* pp. 38–40.

15. Ibid., p. 34.

16. We agree with Albert Keidel that although Guangxi appears to be coastal, it should not be included in the coastal category. Two reasons may be used to support this argument. First, Guangxi's coastline is very short, and its only major seaport, Beihai, is rather small. Beihai's freight in 1992 accounted for less than 1 percent of the national total. See Hu, Wang, and Kang, *Zhongguo diqu chaju baogao,* pp. 108. Second, much of the province is cut off from the sea by hills and mountains. See Keidel, "China," p. 4.

17. Zhao, *Geography of China,* p. 116.

18. Ibid., p. 288.

19. Ibid., p. 307.

20. Ibid., p. 124.

21. Gunnar Myrdal, *Economic Theory and Under-Developed Regions.*

22. Ibid., pp. 108–10.

23. See Figure 6.1 in Zhao, *Geography of China,* p. 107.

24. Ibid., pp. 107–8.

25. Ibid., p. 108.

26. Ibid., p. 112.

27. Hebei has only one major port, Qinhuangdao.

28. See Table 3 in World Bank, *World Development Report, 1995,* pp. 166–67.

29. Hu, Wang, and Kang, *Zhongguo diqu chaju baogao,* p. 233.

30. Hiroyuki Kato, "Regional Development in the Reform Period," pp. 130–32.

31. State Statistical Bureau, *Zhongguo tongji nianjian 1996* (hereafter cited as *ZGTJNJ*), p. 426.

32. Scott Rozelle, "Rural Industrialization and Increasing Inequality," pp. 300–24; idem, "Stagnation Without Equity," pp. 63–92. Also see Tianlun Jian, "Inequality in Regional Economic Development and Tax Reforms in China."

33. Ibid.

34. Yusheng Peng, "Geographical Variations in China's Rural Industrial Output and Employment."

35. Ibid.

36. Agriculture has never been dominated by the state sector. The state's share of the service sector has always been lower than that of industry.

37. State Statistical Bureau, *A Statistical Survey of China, 1996*, p. 4.

38. Jun Ma and Yong Li, "China's Regional Economic Policy," p. 47.

39. Tiejun Cheng and Mark Selden, "The Origins and Social Consequences of China's *Hukou* System," pp. 644–68.

40. Thomas Rawski, "The Simple Arithmetic Of Chinese Income Distribution," pp. 21–36; Nicholas Lardy, "Consumption and Living Standards in China," pp. 849–65; Azizur Rahman Khan, Keith Griffin, Carl Riskin, and Zhao Renwei, "Household Income and Its Distribution in China," pp. 1029–61; Guonan Ma, "Income Distribution in the 1980s"; Martin King Whyte, "City Versus Countryside in China's Development," pp. 9–22.

41. For information about the degree of urbanization in other countries, see World Bank, *World Development Report, 1995*, pp. 222–23.

42. The figure presented here may underestimate average income in both rural and urban sectors. Urban income, in particular, may be substantially underestimated because incomes from implicit subsidies, welfare benefits, and transfers in kinds are not included here. See Khan et al., "Household Income and Its Distribution."

43. The poverty line in 1993 was officially defined as any rural household with a per capita income below 400 yuan. The figure of 80 million counts not only those registered in the 592 designated impoverished counties but also the rural poor residing outside the officially designated impoverished counties. See Zhu Fengqi et al., *Zhongguo fenpinkun yanjiu*, pp. 3–4, 28–29. Excluded from China's official statistics on poverty are an estimated 14 million urban poor. See Mark Selden, "China's Rural Welfare System."

44. Carl Riskin, "Chinese Rural Poverty," p. 281.

45. We do not have data for 1994.

46. Keidel, "China," pp. 21–22.

47. Alex Bowen and Ken Mayhew, *Reducing Regional Inequalities*, pp. 95–97.

48. Amartya Sen, "Food and Freedom," pp. 769–81; Peter Nolan and John Sender, "Death Rates, Life Expectancy and China's Economic Reforms," pp. 1279–1303.

49. No statistics on infant mortality and life expectancy are available for 1994. Therefore, columns 3 and 4 are based on the 1990 data, the most recent available to us.

50. For figures about other countries, see World Bank, *World Development Report, 1995*, pp. 162–63, 214–15.

51. The terminology is adopted from Skinner's "Differential Development in Lingnan," pp. 42–46.

52. Ibid., p. 46

53. Michael P. Todaro, *Economic Development*, p. 669.

54. We have compared the 1996 data with 1994 data on a number of key indicators used in this study; no visible difference can be identified as far as regional patterns are concerned.

55. See Simon Kuznets, "Modern Economic Growth," pp. 247–58; idem, "Modern Economic Growth and the Less Developed Countries"; Hollis B. Chenery, *Structural Change and Development Policy*.

56. This is not a surprising result. After all, precipitation and the availability of arable land can at best only have a marginal influence on agricultural production, but the level of per capita GDP now depends more on industry and service than on agriculture. As far as railroad density is concerned, its impact is insignificant, probably because the length of the railroads is too short compared to either waterways or roads.

57. Running a stepwise regression yields the following equation:

$$\text{Per capita GDP} = 4021 + \underset{(9.353)}{(17016)} \text{ Roadway} + \underset{(5.707)}{(17819)} \text{ Waterway}$$

$$- \underset{(4.875)}{(197)} \text{ Temperature} - \underset{(2.215)}{(25)} \text{ Han}$$

Adj. $R2 = 0.886$, $F = 46.392$

As is the case with precipitation, the annual average temperature of a region cannot be a very important determinant of its per capita GDP level. However, it is not clear why its sign is negative. Some scholars suspect that large numbers of minority nationalities in a region's population are associated with low levels of development. See Albert Keidel, "China," p. 20. This is certainly true if we only examine the relationship between the two variables. However, after controlling for the three variables in the equation, the relationship between the proportion of Han in the population and per capita GDP becomes negative, which suggests that the impact of ethnic makeup on development is not as straightforward as many have assumed.

58. For a discussion of China's extrabudgetary funds, see Shaoguang Wang, "The Rise of the Regions."

59. See Shaoguang Wang, "China's 1994 Fiscal Reform."

60. For a case study of Guizhou and Shandong, see Loraine A. West and Christine P.W. Wong, "Fiscal Decentralization and Growing Regional Disparities in Rural China."

61. Ibid.

5

The Economic Causes of Uneven Regional Development

As shown in Chapter 3, growth rates exhibited tremendous variance across China's thirty provinces during the post-Mao era. Varying rates of growth in themselves do not necessarily generate increasing regional inequality. Had the poorer provinces grown faster than their richer counterparts, regional disparities would have declined. But this was not the case. Throughout the period, the southeastern coastal provinces took the lead in economic growth. The western provinces grew, but at much lower rates. When provinces with per capita GDP higher than the national average grew faster than those below, divergence was inevitable. Why were some provinces able to grow faster than others? What were the factors underlying differential economic-growth performance among provinces? These are the questions we attempt to address in this chapter.

It goes without saying that economic growth is governed by many determinants—economic, social, political, cultural. However, if these diverse factors are to affect economic growth positively, they must somehow help either to increase the supply of factor inputs (mainly capital and labor) or to enhance factor productivity. Thus, to arrive at an understanding of the causes behind the growth of output, we must first identify the immediate economic sources of growth, which is what we intend to do in the first section of this chapter. The section's empirical framework is provided by a set of growth accounts that decompose the growth of output into the contributions made by each such source.

Our main finding is that the acceleration in capital investment has been the most important engine of growth for all Chinese provinces. But the rates of capital accumulation differ considerably from one province to another.

Although growth accounting can help to identify the immediate causes of uneven regional development, this technique by itself can hardly yield much information about the forces behind changes in these immediate determinants. One may even question how much useful understanding can be gained from a study that focuses on nothing but the immediate determinants of growth. For instance, it is good to know that the rate of capital accumulation is the most important factor in explaining growth variations. However, if we concluded this study with such an observation, our understanding of growth causality would still be very superficial. A satisfactory explanation of growth variations must probe further why some regions are able to mobilize greater capital resources than others. This is what the second section of this chapter intends to do. It will identify the main sources of capital accumulation for different provinces.

The Proximate Sources of Output Growth

The Method of Growth Accounting

A crude but robust method called growth accounting is the method employed here. This method is based on a simple notion: Growth in output is generated by growth in inputs (capital and labor), or by gains in the efficiency with which the inputs are used, or by some combination of the two. These factors may be called the proximate sources of growth. Whatever the ultimate causes of growth may be, whether they are governmental policy, religious beliefs, attitudes toward income and leisure, international environment, and so forth, they must work through these channels.[1] Growth accounting is a method that can break down the observed total output growth into the contributions of each of the following direct determinants of output:[2] (1) the contribution of capital, (2) the contribution of labor, (3) the contribution of human capital, and (4) the contribution of technical progress. A formal discussion of the method is presented in Appendix 5.1, "The Method of Growth Accounting." Although this method by itself cannot identify the fundamental causes of growth, it allows us to speculate in a disciplined way about what the fundamental causes of growth may be and how they operate.

Data for the Growth Accounts

We pursue the following five steps to allocate the growth rate of output to its contributing factors:[3]

1. Constructing an index of output and deriving its average annual growth rate from the indices so constructed.
2. Constructing a separate index for each of the factor inputs (capital, labor, and human capital) and deriving the average annual growth rates of various factor inputs from the indices so constructed.
3. Estimating the elasticities of output with respect to each of the factor inputs.
4. Calculating the contribution made by each factor input to the growth rate of output as the product of the growth rate of each factor input, on the one hand, and its production elasticity, on the other.
5. Subtracting from output growth the portion of this growth that is accounted for by the growth in measured factor inputs. The residual is treated as the contribution of technical progress.

Output

The basic output measure we use in this study (Y) is provincial gross domestic product (GDP), which can be obtained from various provincial statistical yearbooks. Then the implicit price deflators for provincial GDPs are employed to estimate real provincial GDPs in 1978 prices.

Capital Input

Capital input (K) is measured by the total fixed capital stock,[4] which is defined as "goods that are durable (lasting more than one year), tangible (intangible assets like patents and copyrights are excluded), fixed (inventories and work in process are excluded, though mobile transport equipment is included) and reproducible (natural forests, land and mineral deposits are excluded)."[5]

As in other developing countries, no data on capital stock are available in China. Time series data on provincial capital stocks are estimated by using the method presented in Appendix 5.2, "Estimating Provincial Capital Stocks."

Labor Input

Labor input (L) is simply measured as the total number of working persons. In measuring the contribution of labor input to output, the number of hours worked is probably a much better yardstick than the number of workers, but data for the former are difficult to obtain. In the kind of study we are doing, cross-regional comparisons, it may also not be imperative to estimate labor input in hours worked, because the average weekly hours worked per employee did not vary much across regions or between years in China during the period under discussion.

Human Capital

The measure we use to assess labor input has another problem: It does not take into account workers' diverse characteristics. Workers are, of course, not identical. They may differ in education, age, gender, skill, and occupation, and they may work in different economic sectors and geographic regions. All of these characteristics may influence their marginal productivity. Accordingly, improvements in labor quality and changes in labor composition may more or less increase the overall level of labor productivity. Growth accounting is supposed to capture changes in the quality components of the labor force. However, adjusting labor inputs for their qualitative differences requires detailed information about the characteristics of the workforce, which is hard enough for an individual case study, and nearly impossible for our type of study involving thirty cases. For this reason, we adjust labor inputs only for one crucial determinant of labor quality—education or human capital embodied in workers. Education is crucial because "it conditions both the types of work an individual is able to do and his efficiency in doing them."[6] A better-educated workforce is more productive and is expected to have a positive effect on growth.[7]

In this study, the average years of schooling in the population are used as a proxy for the stock of knowledge available for productive use or human capital (H). Ideally, education should be defined in a way that includes both formal education (schooling) and informal education (job training). The informal part is excluded because no such data are available. Even data on formal education are limited. That is why we cannot directly measure the attained educational level of the labor force. We can only hope that the educational distribution of the population is representative of the educational distribution of the labor force.

Factor Shares

In order to identify the separate contributions of the three factor inputs to output growth, our last task is to estimate the elasticities of output with respect to each of them. We give capital a weight of 0.45, which is slightly higher than the World Bank's estimate of 0.40.[8] Furthermore, the output elasticities of labor and human capital are assumed to be 0.30 and 0.25, respectively. The method used to obtain these values is discussed in Appendix 5.3, "Estimating Factor Shares."

Results

Table 5.1 shows the indices of output and factor inputs, including physical capital, labor, and human capital; and Table 5.2 shows their respective implicit annual average growth rates over the 1978–95 period. Clearly, during this period, each of China's thirty provinces experienced an extraordinary increase in its capital stock. In all but two provinces (Fujian and Hunan), capital stock rose faster than GDP, and in some provinces the difference between the growth of capital stock and the growth of GDP was very large.[9] A positive correlation between the growth rates of GDP and capital stock is evident in Table 5.2: it was the provinces with faster capital accumulation that had enjoyed more rapid economic growth.

The growth of labor and human capital was much slower. The annual growth rate of the labor force was seldom higher than 3.3 percent, and the growth rate of human capital was generally below 2.5 percent per annum.[10] Moreover, the growth rates of labor and human capital appeared less dispersed than capital input growth.

We are now in a position to allocate the growth of GDP among the various sources of growth. Table 5.3 presents the absolute contribution of each input to GDP growth, which is estimated as the product of its growth rate and its output elasticity. The first column shows the growth of GDP. The second, third, and fourth columns show the contributions of physical capital (with 0.45 weight), labor (with 0.3 weight), and human capital (with 0.25 weight), respectively. The last column shows the residual, namely, the difference between GDP

Table 5.1

Growth Indices of GDP and Production Factors, 1978–95 (1978 = 1.000)

Province	GDP	Capital	Labor	Human Capital
Beijing	4.932	8.929	2.282	1.230
Tianjin	4.264	7.511	1.405	1.202
Hebei	5.248	6.120	1.542	1.301
Shanxi	4.204	6.22	1.478	1.271
Inner Mongolia	4.982	6.897	1.578	1.365
Liaoning	4.153	5.546	1.617	1.200
Jilin	4.688	6.207	1.969	1.316
Heilongjiang	3.220	4.370	1.532	1.297
Shanghai	4.364	6.967	1.137	1.192
Jiangsu	7.693	9.038	1.314	1.409
Zhejiang	9.056	9.429	1.460	1.341
Anhui	5.158	5.909	1.712	1.536
Fujian	9.105	8.541	1.708	1.339
Jiangxi	5.518	5.609	1.675	1.335
Shandong	6.769	7.831	1.476	1.274
Henan	5.782	6.896	1.606	1.385
Hubei	5.425	5.594	1.353	1.245
Hunan	4.125	4.029	1.521	1.234
Guangdong	9.588	10.627	1.560	1.245
Guangxi	4.967	5.045	1.637	1.301
Hainan	7.201	13.302	1.580	1.316
Sichuan	4.586	5.419	1.494	1.303
Guizhou	4.369	6.273	1.720	1.565
Yunnan	4.953	6.625	1.636	1.560
Tibet	3.918	7.074	1.223	1.444
Shaanxi	4.407	6.109	1.622	1.320
Gansu	4.085	5.239	2.137	1.350
Qinghai	3.058	7.455	1.483	1.307
Ningxia	4.268	9.195	1.772	1.481
Xinjiang	5.993	11.017	1.377	1.382
Nation	4.965	7.115	1.692	1.313

growth and the growth explained by the increase in factor inputs. Table 5.4 translates the absolute contribution of each factor into its relative contribution.[11]

We may draw four principal conclusions from Table 5.4. First, physical capital was the most important source of economic growth for all the provinces with probably only one exception: Fujian. The contribution of capital averaged approximately 56 percent. This finding confirms the central importance of capital accumulation for growth at early stages of economic development, a position held by writers who have influenced thinking on the development process (Harrod-

Table 5.2

Average Annual Growth Rates of Output and Inputs (%), 1978–95

Province	GDP	Capital	Labor	Human Capital
Beijing	9.84	13.74	4.97	1.61
Tianjin	8.91	12.59	2.02	1.43
Hebei	10.24	11.24	2.58	2.04
Shanxi	8.81	11.35	2.32	1.86
Inner Mongolia	9.91	12.03	2.72	2.42
Liaoning	8.74	10.60	2.87	1.41
Jilin	9.51	11.34	4.07	2.13
Heilongjiang	7.12	9.06	2.54	2.02
Shanghai	9.05	12.10	0.76	1.36
Jiangsu	12.75	13.83	1.62	2.67
Zhejiang	13.84	14.11	2.25	2.28
Anhui	10.13	11.02	3.21	3.36
Fujian	13.87	13.45	3.20	2.27
Jiangxi	10.57	10.68	3.08	2.25
Shandong	11.91	12.87	2.32	1.88
Henan	10.87	12.03	2.83	2.54
Hubei	10.46	10.66	1.79	1.70
Hunan	8.69	8.54	2.50	1.63
Guangdong	14.22	14.92	2.65	1.70
Guangxi	9.89	9.99	2.94	2.04
Hainan	12.31	16.44	2.73	2.13
Sichuan	9.37	10.45	2.39	2.06
Guizhou	9.06	11.41	3.24	3.51
Yunnan	9.87	11.76	2.94	3.48
Tibet	8.36	12.20	1.19	2.87
Shaanxi	9.12	11.23	2.89	2.16
Gansu	8.63	10.23	4.57	2.34
Qinghai	6.80	12.54	2.35	2.08
Ningxia	8.91	13.94	3.42	3.07
Xinjiang	11.11	15.16	1.90	2.52
Nation	9.88	12.23	3.14	2.12

Domar model,[12] Arthur Lewis,[13] Rostow[14]). It is also consistent with the results of many empirical studies of economic growth. As a matter of fact, the role of capital in the explanation of growth in China was very similar to that found in other East Asian economies and in developing countries at large.[15]

Second, labor was a less important source of economic growth, contributing from 2.5 percent of output growth in Shanghai to 15.9 percent in Gansu. On average, only about 10 percent of output growth could be explained by the growth of the labor force. This is consistent

Table 5.3

Sources of Growth (%)

Province	GDP	Capital	Labor	Human Capital	Residual
Beijing	9.84	6.18	1.49	0.40	1.77
Tianjin	8.91	5.67	0.61	0.36	2.27
Hebei	10.24	5.06	0.77	0.51	3.90
Shanxi	8.81	5.11	0.70	0.47	2.53
Inner Mongolia	9.91	5.41	0.82	0.61	3.07
Liaoning	8.74	4.77	0.86	0.35	2.76
Jilin	9.51	5.10	1.22	0.53	2.66
Heilongjiang	7.12	4.08	0.76	0.51	1.77
Shanghai	9.05	5.44	0.23	0.34	3.04
Jiangsu	12.75	6.22	0.49	0.67	5.37
Zhejiang	13.84	6.35	0.68	0.57	6.24
Anhui	10.13	4.96	0.96	0.84	3.37
Fujian	13.87	6.05	0.96	0.57	6.29
Jiangxi	10.57	4.80	0.92	0.56	4.29
Shandong	11.91	5.79	0.69	0.47	4.96
Henan	10.87	5.41	0.85	0.63	3.98
Hubei	10.46	4.80	0.54	0.42	4.70
Hunan	8.69	3.84	0.75	0.41	3.69
Guangdong	14.22	6.71	0.80	0.42	6.29
Guangxi	9.89	4.49	0.88	0.51	4.01
Hainan	12.31	7.40	0.82	0.53	3.56
Sichuan	9.37	4.70	0.72	0.51	3.44
Guizhou	9.06	5.13	0.97	0.88	2.08
Yunnan	9.87	5.29	0.88	0.87	2.83
Tibet	8.36	5.49	0.36	0.72	1.79
Shaanxi	9.12	5.05	0.87	0.54	2.66
Gansu	8.63	4.60	1.37	0.58	1.81
Qinghai	6.80	5.64	0.70	0.52	−0.06
Ningxia	8.91	6.27	1.03	0.77	0.84
Xinjiang	11.11	6.82	0.57	0.63	3.09
Nation	9.88	5.51	0.94	0.53	2.90

with the finding of a World Bank study that attributes about 17 percent of growth to improvements in both quantity and quality of the labor force in the Chinese economy as a whole.[16] The abundant labor supply may explain the relatively small contribution of labor in China. It is intuitively plausible that, in a capital-scarce and labor-abundant economy, the injection of more manpower would not increase output very significantly or rapidly.

Third, human capital played little role in economic growth for all provinces, accounting for barely 5 percent. One would expect that

Table 5.4

Relative Contributions to Output Growth (%)

Province	Capital	Labor	Human capital	TFP
Beijing	62.85	15.16	4.08	17.92
Tianjin	63.64	6.81	4.00	25.56
Hebei	49.40	7.56	4.99	38.05
Shanxi	57.97	7.91	5.28	28.84
Inner Mongolia	54.64	8.24	6.11	31.01
Liaoning	54.61	9.85	4.04	31.50
Jilin	53.62	12.82	5.61	27.95
Heilongjiang	57.27	10.71	7.09	24.93
Shanghai	60.12	2.51	3.76	33.61
Jiangsu	48.79	3.81	5.24	42.16
Zhejiang	45.88	4.88	4.12	45.12
Anhui	48.93	9.51	8.28	33.28
Fujian	43.61	6.92	4.09	45.38
Jiangxi	45.45	8.74	5.32	40.49
Shandong	48.64	5.84	3.95	41.57
Henan	49.78	7.80	5.83	36.59
Hubei	45.86	5.15	4.06	44.93
Hunan	44.22	8.62	4.69	42.47
Guangdong	47.19	5.59	2.99	44.23
Guangxi	45.46	8.93	5.17	40.45
Hainan	60.09	6.64	4.33	28.93
Sichuan	50.18	7.65	5.49	36.68
Guizhou	56.65	10.73	9.67	22.95
Yunnan	53.65	8.93	8.82	28.61
Tibet	65.62	4.27	8.57	21.54
Shaanxi	55.45	9.50	5.92	29.14
Gansu	53.35	15.88	6.76	24.01
Qinghai	83.06	10.35	7.65	−1.06
Ningxia	70.40	11.52	8.60	9.47
Xinjiang	61.41	5.13	5.67	27.78
Nation	55.70	9.54	5.35	29.41

improvement in human capital would accelerate the speed of economic growth. But that does not appear to be the case in China for the period covered by this study. We have no explanation for this phenomenon. Odd behavior of the schooling variables has also been observed in other empirical studies.[17]

Finally, the contrast between provinces in the relative importance of the contribution of technical progress is most striking. While technical progress played no role in the economic growth of Qinghai, gains from this source accounted for more than 40 percent of growth in nine provinces. The real surprise is that technical progress appeared to have contributed more to output growth in China than in East Asian and Latin American NIEs.[18]

There are strong reasons to believe that our growth accounts may have overstated the contribution of technological progress and underestimated the contributions of input growth, particularly the contribution of capital accumulation. We have to remember that unobservable technical progress is measured as the "residual," namely, the growth in output after the effects of the growth in measured inputs have been taken into account. The residual no doubt covers technological advance. But it may also reflect the effects of "miscellaneous output determinants for which separate estimates have not been made."[19] In addition, the residual may pick up the net error in the measurements. For these reasons, it is probably better to call the residual a "grab-bag" or "some sort of measure of our ignorance," as Abramovitz does,[20] than to call it "the contribution of technical progress."

Besides technological advance, what other sources of growth may be included in this grab-bag?

Changes in the composition of the labor force. In this study, labor input is measured only by the total number of working persons. We do not take into account the age and gender composition of the labor force. Were those elements of labor quality included in our measurements, the size of the residual might turn out to be somehow different.[21]

Improvement in human capital. Only the average years of schooling is used to measure human capital in this study. On-the-job training and improving health are neglected. Both are very likely to contribute to economic growth.[22]

External effects of capital input. The residual may also include external effects of physical capital of the type studied by Romer[23] and Lucas.[24] In particular, investment in infrastructure is likely to generate strong positive externalities.[25] Assuming that the provinces that experienced greater capital accumulation also invested more in infrastructure, we would expect those provinces to benefit more than others from such externality-generating activities.

Increasing returns. We assume constant returns to scale in this study. This means that the actual size of the growth residual would be much smaller if there are, in fact, increasing returns to capital or/and labor, especially to the former.[26]

Structural change. Another major factor that might have inflated the size of the measured growth residual and underestimated the contribution of factor inputs, especially labor, is the reallocation of resources from less- to more-productive activities. In postreform China, for instance, we have witnessed a massive movement of surplus labor from the countryside to urban areas and from the state sector to the non-state sector. A number of authors have attributed a large part of the growth residual observed in studying the Chinese case to "efficiency gains obtained from the process of reallocation of labor both across sectors and across ownership forms."[27]

Embodied technologies. Our method assumes that additions to the capital stock mean more of the same, and that technical progress is exogenous, arising independently of expenditure on capital. Neither assumption is true. In reality, capital accumulation and technological progress are interdependent. Most technological progress requires a substantial investment of resources. In other words, capital investment increases not only the stock of physical capital but the level of technology.[28] For this reason, we would expect that an acceleration of the pace of capital accumulation, by reducing the age of the capital stock, speeds the rate at which embodied technical progress is incorporated into production.[29] Moreover, foreign investment may embody more advanced production technology and management practice than domestic investment.[30] Countless studies have established that investment in physical capital is the principal means by which new technology enters the production process.[31] To the extent that there cannot be embodied technical progress without new fixed investment, the contribution of embodied technical progress to growth should probably also be attributed to capital. If this is done, the contribution of capital accumulation would be substantially greater than our rough growth accounts suggest.[32]

Based upon the preceding discussion, we may arrive at two conclusions about the proximate sources of growth. First, the growth residual is not as large as it appears to be, because, due to data limitations, some important growth determinants are not included in our growth accounting calculations. Second, if we take into consideration both direct and indirect beneficial effects of rapid capital accumulation, then growth of the physical capital stock alone can account for a very substantial part of GDP growth for each and every province of China.

The Sources of Capital Accumulation

Since capital accumulation is the key to economic growth, regions with greater capital mobilization capacity are expected to grow faster. Therefore we have to ask why gross investment has increased at much faster rates in some provinces than in others. This section sets out to identify the factors behind capital accumulation.

By China's official definition, capital investment is financed from one or another of the following five sources of funds or from some combination of these sources: state budgetary appropriations, domestic bank loans, self-raised funds, other domestic funds, and foreign capital.[33] We reclassify the sources of capital investment into three large categories: local capital, capital imports from or exports to other provinces, and foreign capital. The question is why some provinces were more capable than others of mobilizing these funds.

Local Capital

If the nation is the unit of analysis, a high level of investment is possible only when the country enjoys a commensurately high level of domestic savings. For the regions within a country, however, such a relationship is expected to be much weaker, because capital movement between regions faces many fewer barriers in the context of a national economy than in an international context. Moreover, the central government may play a strong redistributive role, allocating funds across regions through fiscal transfers. Thus, it is possible for a region with a relatively low level of savings to invest at a much higher level as long as it is able to obtain capital inflows from other regions.

In China just as in other countries, there were certainly instances of capital moving from one region to another. But, as will be discussed in a moment, such interregional capital flows shrank substantially during the course of reform. As Figure 5.1 shows, local domestic investment (i.e., total investment minus foreign investment) and local savings were highly correlated in China's thirty provinces for the period from 1985 to 1995 (the Pearson correlation coefficient is as high as 0.965).[34] Such a high correlation suggests that domestic investment in most provinces was predominantly financed by local savings. The higher local savings were, the higher local domestic investment. To put it

Figure 5.1 **Local Savings and Local Domestic Investment, 1985–95**

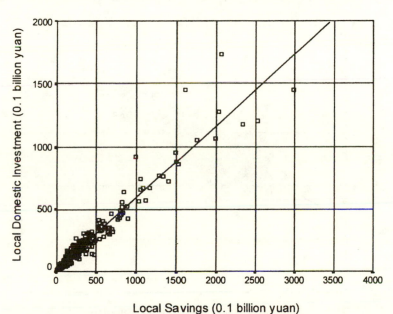

Local Savings (0.1 billion yuan)

differently, a high level of provincial domestic investment was not possible unless the province was able to achieve a higher level of local savings.

What were the determinants of local savings? Figure 5.2 implies that the income level was a major predictor.[35] There appears to be a strong correlation between the savings rate (savings/GDP) and per capita GDP for the thirty provinces during the 1978–95 period (the Spearman correlation coefficient is 0.72). On the one hand, as per capita GDP grew, the savings rates increased in almost all provinces.[36] On the other hand, at any given moment, provinces with higher per capita GDP tended to enjoy higher savings rates. With both higher per capita GDP and higher savings rates, rich provinces were obviously in a much better position to mobilize funds and to invest in their local economies.

Foreign Capital

Whereas foreign capital was completely absent from China's pre-reform economy, its role has become increasingly visible after 1978. In the early years of reform, foreign capital came mainly in the forms of grants and loans from foreign governments, international organiza-

Figure 5.2 **Savings Rate and Per Capita GDP, 1978–95**

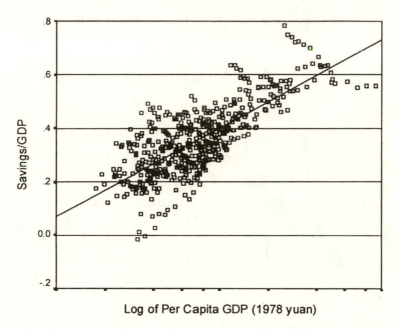

Log of Per Capita GDP (1978 yuan)

tions, and international capital markets. At that time, the central government played a dominant role in allocating foreign capital. Since the promulgation of the Provisions for the Encouragement of Foreign Investment in late 1986, foreign direct investment (FDI) has been growing continuously. Especially after 1991, China has become the largest recipient of FDI among all developing countries. As FDI inflows surpassed the combination of foreign grants and loans, the share of foreign capital channeled regionally has increased sharply in recent years. By 1994, less than 20 percent of foreign capital was still channeled through the central ministries (see Figure 5.3).

All provinces welcomed foreign investment, because it would augment their capital and investment stocks. But not all of them were equally successful in attracting foreign investors. As Figure 5.4 shows, the spatial distribution of foreign capital in China was highly uneven. Of the total accumulated amount of foreign capital that China's thirty provinces received between 1983 and 1995, Guangdong alone took one-third. Jiangsu, Fujian, and Shanghai were also able to attract substantial amounts of foreign capital. On the other hand, the record of the

Figure 5.3 **Share of Centrally and Locally Channeled Foreign Investment, 1983–95**

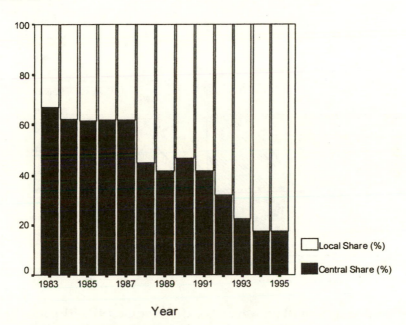

Year

inland provinces was rather poor. Among the provinces that received more than 3 percent of the total, none was an inland province.

What were the determinants of the spatial distribution of foreign capital in China? If the provincial accumulated stock of foreign capital for 1983–95 is used as the dependent variable, we have reason to believe that the following five factors are the most important explanatory variables.

Market size. Other things being equal, the greater the local market, the greater the opportunity for making profit and the incentive to invest.[37] This variable is measured by provincial GDP for 1991, because more than two-thirds of the total accumulated foreign capital for the entire period from 1983 to 1995 came to China after 1991. The market size variable is expected to be positively related to foreign capital inflows.

Rate of economic growth. "Other things being equal, a more rapid growing economy provides greater profit opportunities than an economy that is growing slowly."[38] Foreign investors may find it attractive to invest in rapidly growing economies. The growth can be measured

Figure 5.4 **Provincial Shares of Accumulated Foreign Investment, 1983–95**

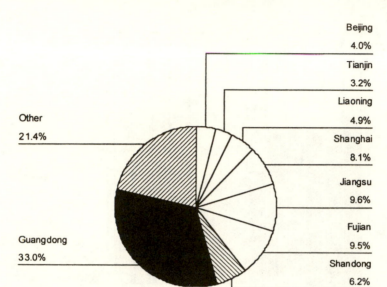

by the average annual growth rate of GDP for the 1978–91 period and is expected to be positively related to foreign capital inflows.

Infrastructure. Better infrastructure facilities can substantially lower transaction costs. Therefore, investors are likely to take into consideration the infrastructure conditions in different regions when making location choices. We use the density of transportation routes (including navigable inland waterways, railroads, and roads) in 1990 as an approximation of a province's infrastructure conditions. This variable is expected to be positively related to foreign capital inflows.

Human capital. Because better human capital can make physical capital more productive and more profitable, investors may base their decisions on a host region's labor quality. Adult illiteracy for 1990 is therefore included as an indicator of labor quality in the provinces.[39] It is expected to have a negative relationship to foreign capital inflows.

Preferential Policy. It is generally believed that the availability of fiscal incentives stimulates foreign investment. A more generous incentive program is expected to attract more foreign investors. We will discuss why China's foreign investment regime has been heavily slanted in favor of cities along the coast in the next chapter.[40] For the moment, suffice it to say that some of the coastal provinces enjoyed more generous packages of incentives than others. For this reason, we use an ordinal variable to reflect the degree of preferential policy with its construction based on (1) the size of the economy that enjoyed preferential treatment, (2) the generosity of the incentive package, and (3) the length of time in which preferential policies were applicable. The indices of preferential policy are listed in Table 5.5. It is important to note that, in the period under review, only coastal provinces were allowed to provide fiscal incentives for foreign investors. Therefore, this policy variable may also reflect a province's geographical location. The variable is expected to be positively related to the level of foreign capital stock.

We use OLS regression methods to test four models containing economic and policy variables. Table 5.6 summarizes the results.

We begin by estimating a baseline economic model that includes economic variables that are believed to have important effects on a region's foreign capital inflows. GDP91 and Growth78–91 are found to be significant determinants of foreign capital accumulation. Infrastructure has the expected sign but is not significant. The coefficient of illiteracy appears with a totally unexpected positive sign and is statistically not significant. Overall, this baseline economic model performs well, accounting for 42 percent of the variation in the spatial distribution of foreign capital.

Model 2 in Table 5.6 regresses the foreign capital stock on a constant and the policy variable alone. As expected, preferential policy is a significant predictor of foreign capital inflows and has the expected sign. More importantly, this single-variable model performs very well, accounting for 72 percent of the variance in foreign capital accumulation.

The two models suggest that foreign capital stocks are best understood as a consequence of both economic and policy factors, for each may explain aspects of foreign capital accumulation that the other cannot. What happens when we combine the economic model with the policy model? The results of this experiment are contained in Model 3. Beginning with the economic variables, adding the policy variable significantly alters the parameter estimates and t values on the previous growth record and infrastructure. In fact, the coefficient on the growth variable changes dramatically. It decreases from 0.348 in Model 1 to 0.023 in Model 3. While this coefficient still

Table 5.5

Indices of Preferential Policy

Region	SEZ 1980-88	COC 1984	ETDZ 1984-95	CEOZ 1985-88	TFZ 1990-93	Index of Preferential Policy[a]
Beijing						2
Tianjin		1	1	5	1	3
Hebei		1	1	14		2
Liaoning		1	3	23	1	3
Shanghai[b]	1	1	3	6	1	4
Jiangsu		2	3	47	1	3
Zhejiang		2	4	34	1	3
Fujian	1	1	3	37	2	4
Shandong		2	3	31	1	3
Guangdong	3	2	3	57	4	5
Guangxi		1	1	6		2
Hainan	1				1	3
Others			5[c]			1
Total	6	14	30	260	13	

Note: SEZ, Special Economic Zone; COC, Coastal Open City; ETDZ, Economic and Technological Development Zone; CEOZ Coastal Economic Open Zone; TFZ, Customs-Free Zone.

[a]Policy Index (the degree of preferential policies) × (the size of open economy) × (the length of open period).

[b]Shanghai's Pudong was granted special privileges similar to those of the SEZs in 1990.

[c]Five additional ETDZs are not located in these coastal provinces but in Changchun (Jilin), Harbin (Heilongjiang), Wuhan (Hubei), Wuhu (Anhui), and Chongqing (Sichuan).

has the expected sign, it is now far from significant. Meanwhile, both infrastructure and illiteracy now bear unexpected signs and are statistically insignificant. The odd behavior of the infrastructure and human capital variables is puzzling, and we have no explanation for these findings.[41]

Table 5.6 contains an additional specification, Model 4, which excludes the three insignificant variables from Model 3—those for growth, infrastructure, and illiteracy. Model 4 appears to be the most parsimonious and efficient model, explaining almost three-fourths of the variance in foreign capital inflows with only two variables—GDP in 1991 and preferential policy. We also find that these two variables are rather stable across all the models.

Table 5.6

Explaining Foreign Investment Flows

	(1) Economic Model		(2) Policy Model		(3) Political Economy Model		(4) Reduced PE Model	
	β	t	β	t	β	t	β	t
Constant		-2.259		-4.096		-1.577		-4.726
GDP91	0.383	2.258[b]			0.239	2.092[b]	0.217	1.962[a]
Growth78–91	0.348	2.259[b]			0.023	0.203		
Infrastructure 90	0.292	1.709			-0.208	-1.477		
Illiteracy 90	0.037	0.226			0.025	0.235		
Policy			0.853	8.643[c]	0.858	5.827[c]	0.739	6.695[c]
F	6.302		74.707		18.480		43.082	
Adj. R^2	0.422		0.718		0.751		0.744	

Note: β is beta coefficient

[a]Significant at 10 percent level, two tails.
[b]Significant at 5 percent level, two tails.
[c]Significant at 1 percent level, two tails.

Thus, we conclude that market size and preferential policies are the two most important determinants of the spatial distribution of foreign capital.

Interregional Movement of Capital

As pointed out above, for China's thirty provinces, domestic investment may include not only funds originating from within the province but capital imported from other provinces. In this sense, a province's capital investment actually depends on its ability (1) to mobilize local capital, (2) to attract foreign capital, and (3) to obtain capital imports from other provinces.

Which provinces were exporters of capital? Which provinces were recipients of capital imports? Unfortunately, no direct data on interregional movement of capital are available. However, we may be able to gauge the direction of capital flows by examining data on net exports, which are defined as the difference between a province's total savings and the total investment in the province.[42] If a province saves more than it invests locally, it is investing outside of the province. Conversely, if the total amount of investment in a province exceeds its total savings, it must have received capital imports from somewhere else. This method would not allow us to obtain the exact amount of capital that a province exports to, or receives from, other provinces, partly because the figure on investment in a province includes capital from foreign countries,[43] and partly because it is also possible for the province to export capital to (invest in) foreign countries. But this does not bother us much, because what we are really interested in is the direction and trend, not the exact amount, of interregional capital flows.[44]

Capital is expected to flow from relatively advanced provinces to less-developed provinces. This was found to be the case in the early years of reform. Between 1978 and 1984, the provinces' ratios of net exports to GDP had fairly strong correlations with their per capita GDPs (the Pearson correlation coefficients ranged from 0.67 to 0.72), which meant that rich provinces were exporting capital to poor provinces during this period. After reform programs were introduced into urban areas in 1984, however, the correlation between the two variables significantly weakened. By 1994 and 1995, there was virtually no correlation between the two variables at all. In other words, although there were still capital-surplus and capital-deficit provinces, the

Table 5.7

Provincial Average Net Export/GDP (%)

Region	1978–80	1981–85	1986–90	1991–93
Beijing	29.44	17.00	−6.11	1.10
Tianjin	28.83	24.50	5.55	−0.66
Hebei	10.86	11.78	1.79	6.78
Shanxi	NA	NA	NA	−3.91
Inner Mongolia	−15.58	−22.54	−9.27	−10.55
Liaoning	23.15	16.51	4.88	−2.52
Jilin	−7.87	−6.10	−6.31	−4.14
Heilongjiang	17.24	8.96	1.71	0.72
Shanghai	57.75	43.09	13.31	12.77
Jiangsu	16.13	8.06	5.93	4.92
Zhejiang	15.01	10.17	3.92	10.10
Anhui	−1.39	−0.82	0.67	−0.14
Fujian	−11.60	−2.51	−2.36	0.78
Jiangxi	−3.61	−5.48	−6.15	−3.34
Shandong	3.63	8.14	5.19	4.28
Henan	2.37	3.54	4.54	6.02
Hubei	21.64	11.90	3.11	3.48
Hunan	3.45	2.69	0.56	−2.09
Guangdong	4.97	1.21	3.60	5.13
Guangxi	−10.51	−9.02	−10.02	−3.87
Hainan	−17.75	−14.52	−17.63	−17.81
Sichuan	−1.52	−0.11	−2.46	−0.40
Guizhou	−21.93	−13.58	−9.80	4.89
Yunnan	−14.00	−5.81	0.86	−7.29
Tibet	NA	NA	NA	−18.72
Shaanxi	NA	NA	−20.78	−12.34
Gansu	−11.10	−9.44	−14.29	−12.77
Qinghai	−40.71	−29.25	−23.13	−18.88
Ningxia	−39.15	−38.77	−40.25	−29.70
Xinjiang	−27.97	−27.34	−24.89	−23.26

level of development could no longer serve as a predictor of whether a province was a capital exporter or a capital recipient.

The trend can be clearly seen in Table 5.7, which reports the provincial average ratios of net exports to GDP for four subperiods. The table may also enable us to estimate the rough magnitude of interregional capital flows in different phases of reform. When China's reform started in the late 1970s, there appeared to be a massive interregional movement of capital. Capital outflow from Shanghai, for instance, amounted to nearly 60 percent of its GDP for the period of 1978–80. Meanwhile, Qinghai and Ningxia received capital inflows that were equivalent to about 40 percent of their GDPs. Interregional movement of capital began to slow down in the 1980s. Proportionally, capital-surplus provinces exported much less than they had done in the earlier period. Consequently, capital-deficit provinces were no longer able to obtain as much help from other provinces as before. By the first half of the 1990s, capital seemed to have become very "sticky," tending to stay where it was originally generated. Except for Shanghai, no province now exported more than 10 percent of its GDP to other provinces. At the same time, only five provinces were now able to obtain capital imports that amounted to more than 15 percent of their GDPs. Four of them (Tibet, Qinghai, Ningxia, and Xinjiang) happened to be minority-concentrated autonomous regions.

As far as interregional capital movement is concerned, the most important change during the reform era, especially after the mid-1980s, seemed to be that all provinces had become financially more independent. On the one hand, rich provinces now did not have to transfer much of their locally generated savings to other provinces. Several rich provinces, such as Beijing and Tianjin, occasionally became net recipients of capital from other provinces. With more capital left at their disposal, these provinces' ability to increase local investment was undoubtedly strengthened. On the other hand, poor provinces were forced to become financially more self-reliant. As capital inflows from other provinces dwindled, they had to rely increasingly upon local savings to finance local investment. Given their relatively low per capita GDP and low savings rates (and thereby per capita savings), poor provinces were unlikely to achieve as high rates of capital accumulation as rich provinces were.

Summary

To summarize, in China, a province's investment depended on three sources of capital: local savings, capital inflows from (or capital outflows to) other provinces, and foreign savings. Local savings were primarily determined by the province's level of economic development. Therefore, advanced provinces had a decisive edge over other provinces in mobilizing local savings. This advantage was discounted in the early years of reform, because at that time advanced provinces had to export substantial proportions of their local savings to relatively poor provinces. However, as reform proceeded, they were allowed to keep more and more local savings to themselves. As a result, their ability to increase local investment was strengthened at the expense of the poor provinces that used to benefit from their capital exports. As for foreign investment, its destination was, to a large extent, determined by the size of the provincial economy and by preferential policy. Here again, it was precisely the provinces with relatively strong ability to mobilize local savings that were in foreign investors' good graces.

The findings that the level of development is an important determinant of local savings and that the size of the provincial economy is an important determinant of foreign investment have rather limited value, because there is little that can be done to change these facts. For our purpose, that is, to explain what enabled certain provinces to achieve and maintain high rates of capital accumulation, it is more interesting to know why interregional capital flows slumped and why coastal provinces were blessed with preferential policies. To answer these questions, we now turn to the political factors that affected the direction of capital flow.

Notes

1. Nancy L. Stokey, "Comments on Barro and Lee," p. 47.
2. There are many approaches to the study of economic growth. An alternative to growth accounting is growth regression. A weakness of the growth-regression approach, however, is that such studies often suffer from simultaneity, multicollinearity, and limited degrees of freedom. Thus, their results must be interpreted with great caution. See Stokey, "Comments on Barro and Lee," p. 47.
3. Bakul H. Dholakia, *The Sources of Economic Growth in India*, p. 6.
4. Inventories are also necessary for production. In China, increases in inventory stocks typically represent from one-third to one-fifth as much capital as investment in fixed assets. See State Statistical Bureau, *Zhongguo tongji nianjian 1996* (hereafter cited as *ZGTJNJ*), p. 47. We exclude inventories, partly because data on inventories for a number of key provinces are not available, and partly because we are convinced that fixed capital is far more important for production and growth than inventories. See J. Bradford De Long and Lawrence H. Summers, "Equipment Investment and Economic Growth," pp. 445–502.
5. Derek W. Blades, "Comparing Capital Stocks," p. 400. In standard growth accounting, residential assets are normally excluded. However, due to data limitations, we cannot separate residential construction from the total stock of fixed assets. There is reason to believe that excluding residential housing from the total would not substantially alter the overall picture of rapid growth in capital stock. For an effort to adjust capital stock data for Chinese state industry only, see Kuan Chen, Gary H. Jefferson, Thomas G. Rawski, Hongchang Wang, and Yuxin Zheng, "New Estimates of Fixed Investment and Capital Stock for Chinese State Industry," pp. 243–66.

6. Edward F. Denison, *Why Growth Rates Differ,* p. 78.

7. Some economists have argued that human capital accumulation is the most important factor in economic growth. See Paul Romer, "Increasing Returns and Long-Run Growth," pp. 1002–37; and Robert E. Lucas, "On the Mechanics of Economic Development," pp. 3–42. According to them, knowledge-driven growth can lead to a constant or even an increasing rate of return. Empirical studies have also found a positive relationship between education and growth. See Robert J. Barro and Xavier Sala-i-Martin, "Convergence across States and Regions," pp. 107–58; Ross Levine and David Renelt, "A Sensitivity Analysis of Cross-Country Growth Regression," pp. 942–63; Alwyn Young, "A Tale of Two Cities," pp. 13–54.

8. World Bank, *China 2020,* pp. 106–8. We are fully aware that the contribution of physical capital is somehow sensitive to the choice of its output elasticity; either overestimation or underestimation of the capital share would create serious distortions in the estimation, not only of capital's contribution to output growth, but also of the other two factors' contributions.

9. Consequently, the capital-output ratio must have risen substantially in many provinces.

10. The relatively faster growth of capital stock must have produced an important increase in the capital-labor ratio in all regions.

11. This is done by dividing the absolute contribution by the growth rate of GDP.

12. Roy F. Harrod, *Towards a Dynamic Economics*; E. Domar, "Expansion and Employment," pp. 34–55.

13. Arthur Lewis, "Economic Development with Unlimited Supplies of Labor," pp. 131–91, and *The Theory of Economic Growth.*

14. W. W. Rostow, *The Stages of Economic Growth.*

15. Pilat estimated that in Japan, 43 percent of growth in the period from 1953 to 1990 was explained by increases in the capital stock, and in Korea, for the period from 1963 to 1990, this figure was almost 45 percent. See Pilat, *The Economics of Rapid Growth,* p. 87. Kim and Lau concluded that the most important source of economic growth in all East Asian NIEs was capital accumulation, accounting for between 48 and 72 percent of their economic growth. See Kim and Lau, "The Sources of Economic Growth of the East Asian Newly Industrialized Countries." Young's study of East Asian NIEs came to the same conclusion. See Young, "The Tyranny of Numbers." Maddison's study of twenty-two developing countries in the period from 1950 to 1965 found that for all countries capital accumulation was the most important source of output growth (55 percent). See Maddison, *Economic Progress and Policy in Developing Countries,* p. 53. The World Bank studied sixty-eight countries for the period from 1960 to 1987. Growth in capital was found to have accounted for 65 percent of the growth in output. See World Bank, *World Development Report, 1991.*

16. World Bank, *China 2020,* p. 4. Collins and Bosworth made the same observation. See Susan M. Collins and Barry P. Bosworth, "Economic Growth in East Asia," p. 158.

17. Robert J. Barro and Jong-Wha Lee, "Sources of Economic Growth," pp. 1–46.

18. Kim and Lau, "Sources of Economic Growth"; Young, "Tyranny of Num-

bers"; Elias, *Sources of Growth.* Several other scholars have come to the same conclusion. For instance, Collins finds that the gain in TFP in China is so large that it is out of line with that experienced by the other East Asian economies at similar stages of their development. See Collins and Bosworth, "Economic Growth in East Asia," p. 161. Also see World Bank, *China 2020,* and *The Chinese Economy.*

19. Edward F. Denison, *Trends in American Economic Growth,* p. 44.

20. Moses Abramovitz, "The Search for the Sources of Growth," p. 218.

21. Edward F. Denison, *The Sources of Economic Growth in the United States and the Alternatives Before Us.*

22. Robert J. Barro, *Determinants of Economic Growth.*

23. Romer, "Increasing Returns and Long-Run Growth," pp. 1002–37.

24. Robert E. Lucas, "On the Mechanics of Economic Development," pp. 3–42.

25. Numerous studies have found that infrastructure is consistently correlated with growth. See Andrei Shleifer, "Externalities and Economic Growth"; and William Easterly and Sergio Rebelo, "Fiscal Policy and Economic Growth," pp. 431–33.

26. Collins and Bosworth, "Economic Growth in East Asia," pp. 142–43; Lim, *Explaining Economic Growth,* pp. 51–57. Endogenous-growth theories stress increasing returns to physical capital investment. For instance, Romer argues that the elasticity of output with respect to capital is near one, not the 0.5 or 0.3 that normal constant-returns models suggest. See Romer, "Increasing Returns and Long-Run Growth." In their empirical study of four East Asian NIEs, Kim and Lau found evidence of increasing returns. See Kim and Lau, "Sources of Economic Growth."

27. The World Bank believes that such structural transformation can explain some of China's unusually large growth residual. See World Bank, *China 2020,* and *The Chinese Economy.* Also see Eduardo Borensztein and Jonathan D. Ostry, "Accounting for China's Growth Performance," pp. 225–27.

28. The influence of capital accumulation on technological progress is the heart of the "new growth theories" associated with Robert Lucas and Paul Romer. Paul M. Romer, "The Origins of Endogenous Growth," p. 7. Also see Abramovitz, "Search for the Sources of Growth."

29. According to vintage theory, the assets created by investment at any one time are superior to the assets created in earlier times, and inferior to those created later. See Maurice F. Scott, *A New View of Economic Growth,* pp. 81–83.

30. Technology acquisition and absorption from abroad has been seen as the best way for developing countries to achieve rapid growth and catch up with industrial countries. Technology may be transferred to developing countries through a variety of channels, one of which is the flow of foreign direct investment. Findlay postulates that FDI increases the rate of technical progress in the host country through a "contagion" effect from the more-advanced technology, management practice, etc., used by the foreign firms. See Ronald Findlay, "Relative Backwardness, Direct Foreign Investment, and the Transfer of Technology," pp. 1–16; and Eduardo Borensztein, Jong-Wha Lee, and Jose De Gregorio, "How Does Foreign Direct Investment Affect Economic Growth?"

31. Lau concludes: "Technical progress, when it exists, is mostly, but not

exclusively, embodied in new capital goods." See Lau, "Sources of Long-Term Economic Growth," pp. 80–81. Also see Paul Romer, "Endogenous Technological Change"; Gene Grossman and Elhanan Helpman, *Innovation and Growth in the Global Economy*; and Robert Barro and Xavier Sala-i-Martin, *Economic Growth*.

32. Lau, "Sources of Long-Term Economic Growth," p. 68.

33. State Statistical Bureau, *ZGTJNJ 1996*, pp. 196–97.

34. For the 1978–84 period, no data on domestic investment were available for many provinces.

35. This is largely consistent with Keynes's absolute income hypothesis. J. M. Keynes, *The General Theory of Employment, Interest and Money*.

36. Shanghai was a notable exception. Its savings rate declined from nearly 80 percent in 1978 to below 60 percent in 1995. The slide is captured by a descending curve in the upper-right corner of Figure 5.2. Were Shanghai removed from the sample, the correlation between savings rate and per capita GDP would be stronger.

37. Lim, *Explaining Economic Growth*, p. 126.

38. Ibid.

39. Alternatively, we may use average years of schooling to measure human capital. But in experiments substituting adult illiteracy by the average year of schooling we found that using another indicator of human capital would not change the basic findings of this exercise.

40. Harry G. Broadman and Xiaolun Sun, "The Distribution of Foreign Direct Investment in China," p. 8.

41. In this regard, our results contradict the findings of Broadman and Sun.

42. Please note that we are using the concept of total investment rather than fixed investment. The former includes not only investment in fixed assets but also goods in stock.

43. We have data on provincial savings and investment for the entire period of 1978–95 and data on foreign investment for 1983–95. While the former are presented in Chinese RMB, the latter are given in U.S. dollars. We do not know what is the best method to convert foreign investment figures from U.S. dollars into Chinese RMB. Judging from cases for which figures on foreign investment are available in both U.S. dollars and Chinese RMB, it is clear that using the average exchange rate is not a good method.

44. Foreign capital only accounted for a very small proportion of total investment for most provinces prior to 1992–93. After 1992, as the share of foreign capital increased, net exports may not be as close an approximation to the volume of capital flowing from a province as for the previous period.

6

The Political Causes of
Uneven Regional Development

Since beneath the growth-accounting sources lie deeper causes that govern the proximate causes of economic growth, this chapter attempts to examine some of the links between proximate and ultimate growth causality. In particular, we analyze how the central government's regional preferences and extractive capacity affect the spatial distribution of investment resources and ultimately affect the growth potential of different regions.[1]

The Analytical Framework

In a world where government intervention was absent, capital would presumably move across regions to seek no objective other than maximization of return. And the direction of capital movement would be determined only by such economic factors as regional climate and terrain, endowment in natural resources, geographic location, infrastructure, quality of the labor force, market size, and so on. However, no such world exists. In few countries are capital mobilization and allocation completely left to the free play of economic forces. Every government in the world pursues some sort of regional development policy by guiding or inducing capital investment to move in a certain direction.[2] This is especially true in China, a country where central planning once prevailed. Since government plays an important role in facilitating or restraining capital mobility, any story about regional disparities in capital accumulation would be seriously incomplete without taking into consideration the role of government policies or political factors.

Although many have argued that government intervention is essential for narrowing regional disparities, it should be made clear at the outset that government intervention as such does not necessarily help to achieve that goal. In fact, government policies can result in regional divergence rather than convergence. Whether government intervention will alleviate spatial inequality depends on two variables: (1) the government's willingness to keep regional gaps from growing, and (2) its ability to influence the movement of capital flows in a direction that would benefit poor regions.

Strictly speaking, all governments want to see regional gaps narrowed, as long as it does not involve any cost. If it is believed that regional policies would somehow lower overall economic efficiency, however, some governments may be less willing to trade more equality for less efficiency. Especially if a government subscribes to the logic of the trickle-down thesis, it will favor maximal aggregate economic growth and tolerate regional inequality. When the political will to promote balanced regional development is lacking, it is not likely that the government will allocate capital investment to areas where conditions are deemed not to be most suitable for high growth.

Even if a government has a strong commitment to egalitarianism, it may still not be able to reduce regional inequality unless it is capable of mobilizing, aggregating, and directing the requisite resources to fulfill the goal. In any society, in order to advance its chosen goals, regardless of what those goals may be, the state must overcome the resistance of various groups with competing priorities. Since revenue is an absolute requirement for formulating and implementing any policy, the bottom line is whether the government is able to extract enough resources from the population and allocate these resources according to its preferences in the face of societal resistance. Without such resources, governments simply cannot govern.[3] Only with adequate resources at its disposal can the government function. The more resources available to a state, the more options it will have and the more capable it will become. A capable government can resolve the challenges associated with development far more effectively than a less-capable government under similar circumstances.[4]

As far as regional development is concerned, the role of the central government should be emphasized. Provincial governments may be able to reduce regional disparities in territories within their jurisdictions, but they cannot be entrusted with the task of narrowing regional gaps between provinces. Because of their divergent interests, if decision-making were left to provincial governments, the only possible result would be a pattern of resource allocation that simply reflects existing economic disparities. Only the central government may have sufficient incentive to change the pattern by redistributing resources between rich and poor regions.[5] But the central government's ability to perform the function of redistribution depends crucially on its ability to generate revenue. The center's financial strength is the economic base for it to implement regional policy. If there are severe fiscal constraints on the amount of transfers that the central government is able to direct, its regional policy caonot be very effective, no matter how strong its commitment to egalitarianism may be.

The relationship between state preference and ability is depicted in Figure 2.1. Here "state" refers to the central state. Obviously, it is not possible to narrow regional gaps in Regimes I and II, because the government's desire to do so is weak. Regardless of how strong its ability is, policy-induced capital flows would not be used to help poor regions. The goal cannot be achieved in Regime III either because, despite a strong desire, the ability is lacking. Only in Regime IV, which features both strong desire and strong ability, can a government resolve the problem of widening regional disparities.

Mao's China

Let us briefly examine how alternative policy regimes affected regional disparities during the era of Mao Zedong.

In 1949, the Chinese Communists inherited an economy in which regional gaps were already very large by international standards.[6] Throughout Mao's era, the Chinese leadership was strongly committed to egalitarianism. This fundamental philosophical belief motivated the government to give high priority to balance in the distribution of productive capacity and equity in the distribution of income.[7] Since there is little doubt about the government's resolve to reverse the lopsided economic development, the question then is whether it had the ability to pursue the goal through redistributive policies.

By and large, the central government enjoyed considerable control over the distribution of resources during Mao's era. The fiscal system was so arranged that rich provinces were required to remit large proportions of their revenues to the central government and poor provinces were allowed to "retain all their revenues and receive additional direct subsidies from the central government."[8] Acting as a redistributor between the richer and poorer provinces, the central government could use fiscal transfers to influence the interregional flows of resources.

But this "strong state" image for the entire pre-reform period disguises the vicissitudes of central extractive capacity in these years. In fact, four different subperiods can be identified.

1. In the early years of the People's Republic (between 1949 and 1956), the Chinese central government greatly strengthened its extractive capacity.[9]
2. Between 1957 and 1960, Mao introduced his first decentralization drive, which resulted in a sharp decline in central extractive capacity.
3. The period 1961–66 was one of recovery, during which Beijing recentralized fiscal power and strengthened its extractive capacity.
4. In the first two years of the Cultural Revolution (from late 1966 to the end of 1968), China was in total chaos. While Mao enjoyed absolute personal power, the state lacked the basic ability to maintain social control, much less to direct economic development. Public authority was restored in 1969. But soon after, Mao initiated yet another decentralization drive, which again weakened the center's extractive capacity.[10]

Since the leadership's commitment to balanced regional development was a constant factor throughout the Maoist era, the variations in central capacity become the key in determining whether the policy regime in a given subperiod fits Regime III or Regime IV in our model.

In Regimes III and IV, the expansion and contraction of the central government's extractive capacity are expected to have a direct bearing on regional gaps. This was indeed the case in Mao's China. Many other studies in addition to our own (See Figure 6.1) have established that regional disparities in China narrowed somewhat between 1953 and 1957 and in the early 1960s, but widened during the Great Leap Forward (1958–60) and the Cultural Revolution (1966–76).[11] In other

Figure 6.1 **Dispersion of Provincial Per Capita National Income, 1953–77**

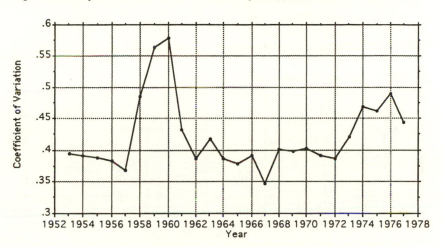

Note: Beijing, Shanghai, and Tianjin are excluded from the data set.

words, regional inequality and central capacity were moving in precisely opposite directions: increasing disparities coincided with declining extractive capacity, while decreasing disparities were associated
with growing state capacity. Figure 6.2 captures the significant negative correlation between the two variables. Such a relationship is by no
means surprising. During the Maoist era, the central government pursued its regional objectives mainly through interregional transfers of
investment resources. Only with stronger central capacity was greater
flow of fiscal transfers from richer to poorer regions possible, as was
essential to reduce the variations in development across provinces.
Conversely, the decline in the center's financial strength was unfavorable for controlling regional disparities.

The late Mao era, namely, the period from the mid-1960s to the
mid-1970s, was characterized by two seemingly contrasting trends: At
the same time that the state was becoming increasingly repressive, its
organizational structure was gradually becoming fragmented, with
lower levels of government gaining at the expense of the center.[12]
With fewer resources under its control, the center's redistributive ability fell far short of its egalitarian desire, which resulted in an upsurge
in regional disparities in the period. In the end, despite continuous
efforts on the part of the central government, regional inequality was in
fact greater in 1977 than in 1953.

Figure 6.2 **Central Capacity and Regional Disparities, 1953–77**

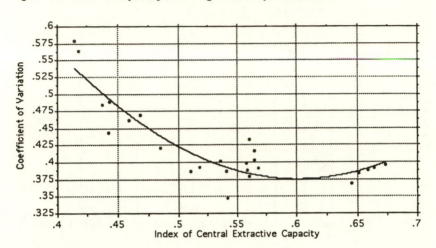

Note: The index is calculated as the ratio of central revenue to the sum of total budgetary funds and extrabudgetary funds.

The Policy Preference in the Reform Era

After Mao's death in 1976, his regional development strategy was criticized as having been too costly in terms of comparative advantage, production efficiency, and national growth forgone. Underlying the reform that followed was a fundamental transformation of development philosophy. Now, Chinese policymakers placed their top priority on rapid aggregate growth. This predominant concern with growth made them no longer willing to sacrifice growth for such goals as balance and equity. Instead, they were ready to tolerate a certain degree of inequality or widened disparity. It was their belief that if certain regions were allowed to prosper first, their affluence would eventually trickle down to other regions.[13]

While in the West, adherents of the trickle-down theory generally hold that government should not intervene in the course of economic development, their Chinese counterparts advocated government intervention on behalf of the more-developed regions. In their view, China, as a developing country, had to make the best use of extremely scarce capital. Therefore, it was necessary for the government to concentrate investment resources where conditions were most suitable for growth.[14]

Which regions should have the blessings of the center? The coastal provinces, of course. These provinces enjoyed considerable advantages at the beginning of reform, because they possessed a large number of skilled workers, a high level of technology and managerial sophistication, and a relatively well developed infrastructure. Being coastal, they also had much easier access to foreign trade and the closest ties to the overseas Chinese, an important source of capital and business know-how. Concentrating investment resources in these areas clearly offered the prospect of much more rapid aggregate growth than spreading resources thinly or investing in interior areas where the preconditions for modern growth were still lacking.

For these reasons, a so-called gradient theory (*tidu lilun*) dominated the thinking of Chinese policymakers for much of the 1980s. The theory divided China into three large geographic regions—eastern (coastal), central, and western—and likened them to rungs on a ladder. According to the theory, the government should capitalize on the advantages of the coast first. Only after the coast had become sufficiently developed should attention be turned to the central region. The western region, however, would have to wait patiently for its turn to receive attention. To counter this strategy's unfavorable implications for equity, its advocates advised people to think of its long-term effects. In the long term, the theory promised, the fruits of development would eventually come down to everyone in the country.

The central government's new non-even development strategy manifested itself in two key policy areas: shifting the focus of state investment from the interior to coastal regions, and granting the latter preferential treatment.[15]

Table 6.1 presents data on state investment in capital construction in both the pre-reform and post-reform periods. This is a category of investment over which central control has been relatively tight.[16] For this reason, we may use it to show whether the central government actually shifted its investment priorities from the interior to the coast. In the pre-reform period, nearly two-thirds of the state's capital investment went to the central and western provinces, whereas the coastal provinces received only 36 percent. Since 1979, the center of gravity in state capital investment has obviously shifted from the interior to the coast. During this period, the coastal region as a whole accounted for about half of all state capital investment, while the interior's share shrank to about 43 percent. The western region suffered the greatest loss, with its share falling more than 7 percent. At the provincial level,

Table 6.1

State Investment in Capital Construction by Periods

Region	Investment (100 million yuan)		% of Total		
	1953–78	1979–91	1953–78	1979–91	Change in %
Nation	6,216.26	13,957.34	100.00	100.00	0.00
Coast	2,233.87	6,862.78	35.94	49.17	13.23
Beijing	252.10	655.07	4.06	4.69	0.64
Tianjin	129.79	400.17	2.09	2.87	0.78
Hebei	277.47	615.84	4.46	4.41	−0.05
Liaoning	418.94	839.09	6.74	6.01	−0.73
Shanghai	186.38	846.13	3.00	6.06	3.06
Jiangsu	180.51	624.73	2.90	4.48	1.57
Zhejiang	98.90	341.37	1.59	2.45	0.85
Fujian	91.48	370.60	1.47	2.66	1.18
Shandong	243.92	824.48	3.92	5.91	1.98
Guangdong	240.34	1,061.58	3.87	7.61	3.74
Guangxi[a]	114.04	206.47	1.83	1.48	−0.36
Hainan					
Central	1,921.30	3,624.18	30.91	25.97	4.94
Shanxi	213.99	511.25	3.44	3.66	0.22
Inner Mongolia	124.19	300.81	2.00	2.16	0.16
Jilin	171.58	286.40	2.76	2.05	−0.71
Heilongjiang	313.97	625.36	5.05	4.48	−0.57
Anhui	165.49	338.89	2.66	2.43	−0.23
Jiangxi	118.52	221.57	1.91	1.59	−0.32
Henan	217.53	493.94	3.50	3.54	0.04
Hubei	340.25	509.47	5.47	3.65	−1.82
Hunan	201.78	336.49	3.25	2.41	−0.84
West	1,496.39	2,336.25	24.07	16.74	−7.33
Sichuan	464.88	701.51	7.48	5.03	−2.45
Guizhou	150.89	176.93	2.43	1.27	−1.16
Yunnan	174.15	242.08	2.80	1.73	−1.07
Tibet	13.45	52.71	0.22	0.38	0.16
Shaanxi	236.05	348.20	3.80	2.49	−1.30
Gansu	212.26	237,78	3.41	1,70	−1.71
Qinghai	73.35	150.01	1.18	1.07	−0.11
Ningxia	44.52	87.73	0.72	0.63	−0.09
Xinjiang	126.84	339.30	2.04	2.43	0.39
Nonregional	564.70	1,069.07	9.08	7.66	−1.42

Source: Li Boxi (1995), p. 89.
[a]Note that Guangxi is listed in the category of coastal provinces.

on the one hand, the shares of all but three coastal provinces went up; on the other hand, the shares of all but six interior provinces declined. Among the six interior provinces whose shares did not drop, three were minority-concentrated autonomous regions for which the central government might have offered special assistance.

As one may imagine, competition for central investment among the Chinese provinces was extremely keen as the pressure for rapid growth built up during the reform period. The emerging distribution pattern of state capital investment, however, no longer showed an egalitarian strand that would narrow the gap in investment resources between needy provinces and their richer counterparts. Instead, provinces that already had greater resource-mobilization capacity were placed in advantageous positions in the race for central investment. The locational bias of central investment can be explained only by the central government's policy preference.

The new leadership's growth-first strategy was also reflected in its decisions to open up certain areas along the coast to foreign investors and grant them preferential treatment in varying degrees:[17]

Special Economic Zones (SEZ). In 1980, four SEZs were created in Shenzhen, Zhuhai, and Shantou in Guangdong province and Xiamen in Fujian province. In 1988, Hainan Island was separated from Guangdong province and the entire island was designated the fifth SEZ. Starting from 1990, Shanghai's Pudong was also granted special privileges similar to those the SEZs enjoyed.

Coastal Open Cities (COC). In 1984, the government decided to open fourteen coastal cities to foreign investors. These included nearly all the major port cities along China's coast, stretching from Dalian in Liaoning to the north to Beihai in Guangxi to the south.

Economic and Technological Development Zones (ETDZ). From 1984 to 1988, twelve ETDZs were established near some of the open cities. After 1992, an additional eighteen ETDZs were set up. All thirty of these ETDZs were located in coastal provinces except one each in Jilin, Heilongjiang, Hubei, Anhui, and Sichuan.

Coastal Economic Open Zones (CEOZ). Between 1985 and 1988, five huge CEOZs were created in the Yangzi, Pearl, and Yellow River deltas, southern Fujian, and the Liaodong Peninsula. Altogether, they covered 260 cities and counties.

Customs-Free Zones (CFZ). From 1990 to 1993, the government approved the establishment of thirteen CFZs in Liaoning, Tianjin, Shanghai, Jiangsu, Zhejiang, Fujian, Shandong, Hainan, and Guangdong.

As Table 6.2 shows, to encourage foreign investment on the coast, the central government gave coastal areas special autonomy in a wide range of economic decisions, including the authority to approve large-scale investment projects, the freedom to grant tax concessions to foreign investors, and the right to retain a higher proportion of earned foreign exchange. These privileges enabled the coastal areas to offer more incentives to potential investors than the interior areas could. Combined with the coast's naturally and historically advantaged position, these policies ensured that much of China's foreign investment took place along the coast.[18]

In sum, the bias of central policymakers explains why the central government poured an increasing proportion of its investment resources into the coastal provinces, and why it went out of its way to help the same provinces to lure foreign investment. The large influx of investment resources in turn made it possible for the coastal provinces to grow at faster rates than did the others. There is little doubt that the central government's pro-coastal bias was an important factor contributing to the worsening of regional inequality.

Indeed, the central government's policy preference seems to be a fairly good predictor of changes in regional disparities in the 1980s.

Although the growth-first philosophy has served as China's guiding principle for development since 1978, the central government's policy has not been hard-and-fast. Rather, there have been several minor and major changes in the government's development strategy, which, as Figure 6.3 shows, somehow coincided with changes in regional disparities.

The shift of regional development priority began as soon as Deng Xiaoping consolidated his power in 1978. In the last three years (1978–80) of China's Fifth Five-Year Plan, the coastal provinces' shares of state investment steadily increased.[19] During the Sixth Five-Year Plan period (1981–85), China officially adopted a pro-coastal policy program. Yet old ideas died hard, and the remnants of the former balanced-development strategy could still be seen in the new plan. Although its main goal was to accelerate the development of the coastal region, the importance of bringing along the interior provinces was not entirely ignored.[20] Nevertheless, the coastal provinces' share of state investment continued to grow in the period.[21] The same period also witnessed the introduction and expansion of the open-door policy,

Figure 6.3 **Changes in Regional Disparity, 1978–94**

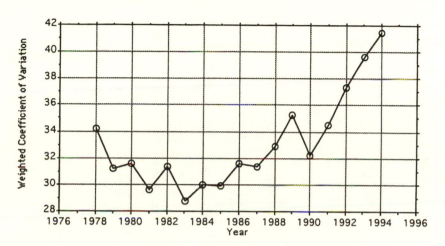

Source: Reproduced from data presented in Figure 3.7.

which primarily benefited the southern coastal provinces.[22] The fast growth of these provinces rapidly narrowed the gaps between the southern coastal (e.g., Guangdong and Fujian) and eastern coastal provinces (e.g., Shanghai, Jiangsu, and Zhejiang), thus leading to the reduction of overall regional disparities in the early 1980s.[23]

In the second half of the 1980s, the central policymakers' pro-coastal policy orientation became more pronounced. The gradient theory discussed above became the cornerstone of China's Seventh Five-Year Plan (1986–90). For the first time, the government divided China into three regions: the eastern coastal region, the central region, and the western region. According to the plan, investment priorities for the rest of the twentieth century would be placed on the coast. The central region might be allocated investment resources in energy and raw materials insofar as they were necessary for supporting the development of the coast. As far as the western region was concerned, its development would have to be postponed, at least for the time being.[24]

The Chinese government's pro-coastal policy orientation was further strengthened in 1988 when it announced an explicit coastal-development strategy. To speed up the country's aggregate growth, the government now decided to open the whole coastal strip to foreign investors. The coastal provinces were even encouraged to seek their raw materials

Table 6.2

Preferential Policies by Types of Zones

	Standard	SEZ	COC	ETDZ	CEOZ	CFZ
National income tax	30% (joint ventures); 20–40% (foreign companies)	15% 1– to 3-year tax holidays	24%	15%	24%	
Local income tax	10% of above	Reduction or exemption	Reduction or exemption	Reduction or exemption	Reduction or exemption	
Industrial & commercial; consolidated tax on exports		Exemption	Exemption	Exemption	Exemption	Exemption
Industrial & commercial consolidated tax and custom duties on FDIs' imported equipment		Exemption	Exemption	Exemption	Exemption	Exemption

Industrial & commercial consolidated tax and custom duties on imports						Exemption
Right to approve foreign investment		Much greater freedom	Greater freedom	Much greater freedom	Greater freedom	Much greater freedom
Right to retain and use own foreign exchange earnings	25%	100%	50%			

Source: Li Boxi (1995), pp. 47–48; Robert Kleinberg (1990), p. 213.
Note: SEZ, Special Economic Zone; COC, Coastal Open City; ETDZ, Economic and Technological Development Zone; CEOZ, Coastal Economic Open Zone; CFZ, Customs-Free Zones.

from foreign sources and sell their products to the world market, though doing so might run a risk of severing their links with the interior provinces.[25] As is clearly shown in Figure 6.3, the central government's strong pro-coastal bias in the latter part of the 1980s resulted in the worsening of regional disparities.

The widening regional gaps gave rise to criticism of the government's pro-coastal bias in the late 1980s and early 1990s, which forced the government to adjust its policies when preparing the Eighth Five-Year Plan (1991–95). The gradient theory was quietly abandoned. While the government vowed to continue its pro-coastal development strategy, it nevertheless began to recognize the importance of preventing regional gaps from becoming excessively large.[26] As a result, numerous interior development zones were established and dozens of interior cities designated as open cities in the early 1990s.[27] Another major adjustment was to switch the focus of coastal development from the south coast (Guangdong and Fujian) to the east coast (Shanghai and the Yangzi River Delta).

Deng Xiaoping endorsed the second change, but viewed the first as unnecessary. During his famous 1992 tour to South China, for instance, he warned: "Do not throw obstacles in the way of areas that can grow fast. Areas with the potential for fast growth should be encouraged to develop as rapidly as they can." In his view, it was unwise to tackle the issue of regional disparities too early. He suggested that China should wait until the end of the century before it put this issue on the agenda.[28]

However, the regions that had been left behind could not wait any longer. At the annual sessions of the National People's Congress in 1993 and 1994, representatives from the interior provinces, especially those from the west, began to pour out their grievances against the center's bias. In 1994, a report by the State Planning Commission sounded a serious warning that if problems caused by the growing regional gaps were not settled properly, they might one day become a threat to China's social stability and national unity.[29]

Facing growing pressure from the interior provinces, the central government finally decided to reverse its coastal-development strategy in 1995. The new guiding principle was to "create conditions for gradually narrowing down regional gaps."[30] This principle was embodied in China's Ninth Five-Year Plan (1996–2000), which promised to increase central support to the less-developed regions in the central and western parts of the country.

It is clear from the preceding discussion that when the central government lacks interest in reducing regional inequality, state intervention in resource allocation would only worsen the existing regional disparities. Then, an interesting question arises: Why, despite the reorientation of the central development strategy, has regional inequality in China gone from bad to worse in the early 1990s (see Figure 6.3)? To answer this question, we have to look at the other key factor that affects spatial distribution of resources, namely, central capacity.

Central Extractive Capacity in the Reform Era

Central extractive capacity is relevant and important in this context because, as the only institution responsible for redistributing resources between regions, the central government must control an adequate amount of revenue before it can conduct any redistributive policy. Strong central extractive capacity may not be a sufficient condition for interregional redistribution, as there are cases where governments with strong extractive capacity do not do much redistribution. But it is a necessary condition, for no other institution, provincial governments included, has an incentive to pursue interregional redistributive policies.

However, the Chinese central government's extractive capacity has been critically enfeebled during the course of the economic reforms. At the core of Deng Xiaoping's reform program was decentralization. While no one denies that the decentralization of decision-making has been instrumental in generating high economic growth in China over the past two decades, many agree that it has probably gone too far, to the point of significantly weakening the central government's capacity to perform functions it is expected to perform, including the movement of investment resources from rich to poor provinces.[31]

Figure 6.4 may help demonstrate how decentralization works to weaken state capacity in general and central capacity in particular. What Figure 6.4 displays is the ratio of budgetary revenue to GDP for thirty provinces from 1978 to 1995. Inspection of Figure 6.4 reveals two clear trends. First, the ratio declined in almost all provinces. Second, provinces that had started with higher ratios in 1978 experienced greater drops in the ensuing years. By 1995, in no province did government revenue account for more than 10 percent of GDP.[32]

Since the growth of government revenue lagged far behind that of GDP in all the provinces, it was not possible for the country as a whole

Figure 6.4 **Decline of Tax Effort in Provinces, 1978–95**

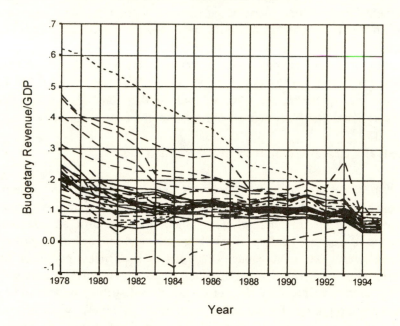

Year

to prevent its aggregate revenue to GDP ratio from falling. Thus, the first trend explains why China's overall government revenue to GDP ratio decreased from 31 percent in 1978 to less then 11 percent in 1995, despite its "miraculous" record of GDP growth (see Table 6.3).

As Figure 6.5 shows, there was a strong and positive correlation between the state's share of national income and the budgetary share of investment. As its share of national income shrank, the government did not have much to spare for capital investment. In the pre-reform era, the government budget used to finance the bulk of capital investments. Not any more. In fact, the deepest cut in the government budget in the reform era was made in capital investment.[33] Between 1981 and 1995, the share of China's total fixed investment financed by the state budget declined sharply, from nearly 30 percent to an almost negligible 3 percent (see Figure 6.6).

Of the 3 percent of investment financed by the government budget in 1994 and 1995, the central share was unknown. However, no matter how high the center's share might be, it could at best account for only a tiny portion of total investment. Of course, it does not follow that the central government had no control over investments financed by other

Figure 6.5 **State Capacity and Budgetary Investment, 1981–95**

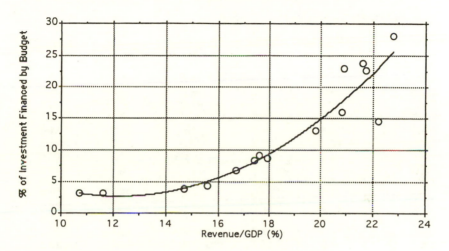

Figure 6.6 **Sources of Fixed Investment Funds**

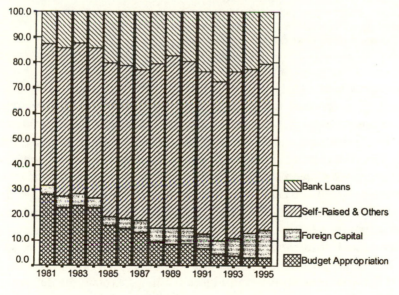

Table 6.3

Selected Fiscal Indices of China, 1978–96

Year	GDP Growth %	GGR/GDP %	CGR/GGR %	Deficit (billions)	Debt/CGR %
1978	11.7	30.9	45.8	−1.0	0.0
1979	7.62	27.6	46.8	20.7	5.5
1980	7.9	24.0	51.2	17.0	6.6
1981	4.5	22.8	57.2	9.9	12.1
1982	8.5	21.7	NA	11.3	14.6
1983	10.2	21.6	53.0	12.3	12.3
1984	14.5	20.9	56.0	12.2	10.5
1985	12.9	20.8	52.7	6.8	10.7
1986	8.5	22.2	NA	20.9	14.4
1987	11.1	19.8	48.8	25.0	16.4
1988	11.3	17.6	47.0	34.9	25.5
1989	4.3	17.4	NA	37.4	25.6
1990	3.9	17.9	48.5(45.1)	51.6	27.3
1991	8.0	16.7	45.0(40.3)	66.4	30.8
1992	13.6	15.6	45.6(38.6)	90.5	36.8
1993	13.5	14.7	NA (33.4)	89.9	35.5
1994	11.8	11.6	?	63.8	40.7
1995	10.2	10.7	?	NA	52.8
1996	9.7	10.9	?	54.8	NA

Source: Adopted from Shaoguang Wang (1997), p. 810.

Notes: GDP: Gross domestic product; GGR: General government revenue; CGR: Central government revenue; CGE: Central government expenditure.

Figures in parentheses exclude debt incomes.

means, such as bank loans, self-raised funds, and so on. Economic planning, investment quotas, project review and approval were some of the instruments that the central government might use to influence the level, structure, and direction of investment.[34] But even if we take into consideration all the projects under the center's supervision (so-called central projects), central control over investment still appears to have been small and declining (see Figure 6.7). By the mid-1990s, the central government could directly (through budgetary appropriation) and indirectly (through other means) deploy no more than 15 percent of total fixed investment funds, which meant that there was less leeway for the central government to redistribute resources between regions.

If the first trend observed in Figure 6.4 helps explain the decline of overall state capacity, the second trend further explains how decentralization has specifically impaired central extractive capacity. As Figure

Figure 6.7 **Decline of Central Investment Control, 1981–95**

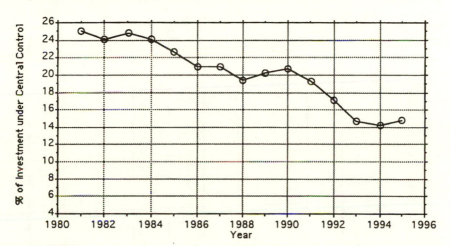

6.4 shows, in 1978 there was great variation in terms of the provincial revenue to GDP ratios. Shanghai had the highest ratio, which was more than 60 percent. The ratio was also very high in other developed provinces, such as Beijing, Tianjin, and Liaoning. In less-developed provinces, the ratio was substantially lower, ranging from less than 10 percent to 20 percent. If we use per capita GDP as the indicator of revenue potential and the ratio of revenue to GDP as the measure of the tax burden, we find that there was a very strong positive correlation between the two in 1978 (see Figure 6.8–A). Of course, this finding is by no means surprising. The level of development is expected to have a positive effect on levels of taxation because the larger the economic output per capita, the more a government can potentially extract.[35] In any event, the fiscal system in 1978 allowed the central government to play a strong role in redistribution by transferring surpluses extracted from more-developed provinces to less-developed provinces.

In the following years, as fiscal decentralization proceeded, the link between revenue potential and tax burden weakened. By 1993, the positive correlation between them disappeared altogether. If anything, the two appeared to be slightly negatively correlated (see Figure 6.8–B). China's defective revenue-sharing system, as practiced between 1980 and 1993, was to blame, because it gave those provinces that had to remit significant proportions of their revenues to the central government both incentives and opportunities to slack off in the collection of

Figure 6.8 **Level of Development and Tax Burden**

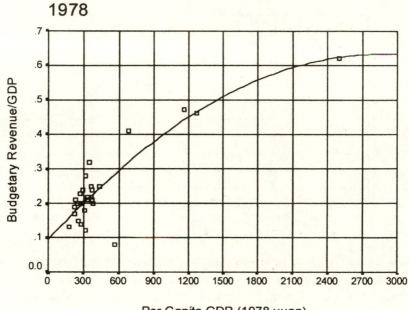

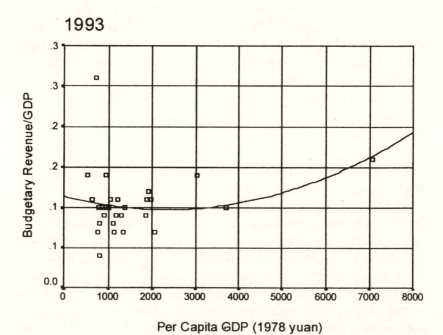

formal taxes so as to shield local resources from being shared with others.[36] The consequence is the trend revealed by Figure 6.4: the richer the province, the steeper the decline of the revenue to GDP ratio in the period 1978–95. Where did money go? A considerable portion went into extrabudgetary funds that were not subject to interregional (nor even to interunit) redistribution. In other words, huge financial resources that would have been appropriated by the state budget fell into the hands of local governments in other forms.[37] Rich provinces used to be big contributors to the central coffers. They were now the ones that greatly reduced their tax efforts during the period under study. Such opportunism was probably the most important cause of the decline both in total government revenue (formal taxes) relative to national income and in central relative to total government revenue (see Table 6.3).[38]

The decline of central extractive capacity has undermined the central government's redistributive ability. Table 6.4 reports average fiscal surplus/GDP (or fiscal deficit/GDP) for China's thirty provinces in four periods. Let us suppose that those provinces that run fiscal surpluses remit all the surpluses to the central government, and that those running fiscal deficits receive central subsidies to balance their budgets. Then Table 6.4 can tell us how fiscal transfers drained off in the age of decentralization. In the 1978–80 period, one-half of China's provincial units had financial surpluses. During this period, Shanghai had to turn over to the center a fiscal surplus equivalent to more than 50 percent of its GDP; the other most-developed provinces at the time, such as Beijing, Tianjin, Liaoning, Jiangsu, and Shandong, had to do the same, though to lesser degrees. Meanwhile, for the fifteen deficit provinces, subsidies from the central government could be as high as one-fifth to one-quarter of their GDPs. But after 1980, as the provinces with fiscal surpluses strategically held back their tax efforts, their remittances to the central coffers rapidly dwindled. Correspondingly, for poor provinces, the relative size of central subsidies decreased sharply. By the period 1991–93, Shanghai, the richest provincial unit in China, submitted only about 8.5 percent of its GDP to the center. Other rich provinces were turning in even less. As a new rich province, Guangdong's contribution to the central coffers, for instance, was barely 0.4 percent of its GDP. Consequently, for most of the provinces that ran deficits in the initial 1978–80 period, the relative sizes of central subsidies in 1993 were much smaller. As surplus provinces

Table 6.4

Provincial Fiscal Surplus/GDP, 1978–93 (%)

Region	1978–80	1981–85	1986–90	1991–93
Beijing	25.63	14.29	3.54	1.05
Tianjin	26.33	16.20	5.83	3.85
Hebei	6.00	2.38	−0.21	0.10
Shanxi	−0.28	−0.95	−2.28	−0.82
Inner Mongolia	−20.77	−15.94	−11.12	−7.14
Liaoning	22.38	11.50	2.68	0.99
Jilin	−2.88	4.72	−5.74	−3.66
Heilongjiang	−7.33	−3.41	−2.51	−1.71
Shanghai	51.07	38.68	17.26	8.54
Jiangsu	11.26	9.09	3.34	1.37
Zhejiang	6.98	6.84	3.16	2.03
Anhui	3.17	1.19	−0.90	−2.30
Fujian	−1.38	−2.19	−2.47	−0.93
Jiangxi	4.48	−2.73	−3.51	−2.82
Shandong	10.18	4.39	−0.81	−0.01
Henan	2.65	1.45	−1.06	−0.61
Hubei	2.19	4.09	−0.09	−0.30
Hunan	3.23	2.01	−1.12	−0.56
Guangdong	4.76	1.38	−0.66	0.38
Guangxi	−7.97	4.20	−5.97	−2.25
Hainan	−3.14	−5.12	−7.75	−5.87
Sichuan	0.50	0.43	−1.50	−0.84
Guizhou	−11.70	−8.04	−6.30	−3.34
Yunnan	−9.71	−5.07	−5.89	−1.19
Tibet	NA	−61.60	−50.83	−49.84
Shaanxi	−1.24	−3.72	−3.85	−2.44
Gansu	6.56	−3.36	−5.61	−3.83
Qinghai	NA	−25.59	−16.20	−11.57
Ningxia	−22.01	−23.03	−17.57	−10.17
Xinjiang	−24.15	−18.17	−11.72	−7.02

remitted less to the center and deficit provinces received less from the center, the center could no longer act as an effective redistributive agent.

If Table 6.4 is compared with Table 5.7, it will immediately become clear that provincial fiscal surpluses and net exports of capital are strongly correlated. The Pearson coefficients range from 0.84 to 0.96 for the first three periods. For the period 1991–93, the relationship between the two variables weakens, but the coefficient is still as high as 0.6. Such a strong correlation between fiscal surplus and net export of capital indicates that fiscal transfers have indeed been a very import-

Figure 6.9 Dispersion of Provincial Budgetary and Extrabudgetary Expenditures

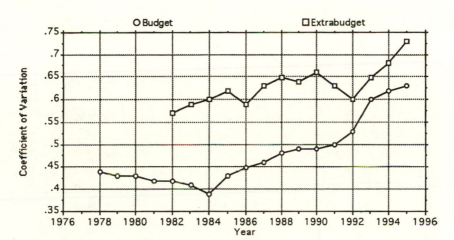

ant, if not the most important, mechanism for the central government to redistribute investment resources between regions. However, with fiscal surpluses from rich provinces draining off, what is available for the central government to transfer has become increasingly limited. A central government with weak extractive capacity cannot be expected to do much to counteract regional inequality, no matter how committed it is to achieving this goal.

Growing Regional Disparities in Resource Distribution

As the importance of fiscal transfers diminished, all the provinces were compelled to become financially more independent. The first result was growing fiscal gaps between provinces. In particular, before China's 1994 fiscal reform,[39] most taxes were collected and most expenditures undertaken on a jurisdiction-by-jurisdiction basis.[40] This meant that gaps in terms of economic development would directly translate into disparities in revenue collection and expenditure. As shown by Figure 6.9, the dispersion of provincial budgetary expenditures became more skewed after 1984. With larger tax bases, governments in rich provinces could afford to either directly invest more with their budgetary capital or offer more generous tax concessions to potential investors. The same fiscal autonomy, however, worked to the detriment of poor provinces, because, with smaller central subsidies, they were hard up even for resources to support daily government operations and to provide such basic services as health and education, not to speak of conducting productive investment.[41]

The resource differentials were even greater if extrabudgetary funds were included. By the late 1980s and early 1990s, almost as much public money was circulating outside the state budget as within it. Given their magnitude, many Chinese scholars and policymakers called extrabudgetary funds China's second budget. The spatial distribution of extrabudgetary funds was more unequal than budgetary revenues, because they were often levied on the same tax base as budgetary taxes, but were subject to no redistribution (see Figure 6.9).[42] The concentration of extrabudgetary funds in the hands of the richer provinces greatly expanded their allocative powers. To a large extent, the most important source of fixed investment, namely, the sum of self-raised funds and other funds in Figure 6.6, derived from the extrabudgetary funds. Local governments could channel those funds into their favored projects without being tightly monitored by the central government. Since poor provinces' access to extrabudgetary funds was just as limited as their access to budgetary funds, the growing reliance of the fiscal system on extrabudgetary funding amplified regional disparities in the distribution of resources.

Some believe that the fiscal disparities can be somewhat offset by greater interregional mobility of nonfiscal resources.[43] However, there is little evidence that nonfiscal resources were flowing from rich to poor provinces. The opposite was more likely to be the case. Take the case of bank loans. One of the goals of China's banking reform was to make banks operate more like profit-maximizing enterprises. Accordingly, a policy of "more deposits, more loans" (*duocun duodai*) was introduced in the early 1980s. Linking deposits and loans (*cundai guagou*) meant that the level of lending largely depended on the level of deposits attracted locally. As a result, all regions were forced to increase bank deposits as much as they could. Obviously, poor regions were in an inferior position to compete with their rich counterparts in such a fierce race.

If poor regions could not compete in mobilizing deposits, was it possible for them to attract bank loans from rich regions? It was possible but very unlikely. After 1986, an interbank money market (*tongye chaijie shichang*) was established that allowed money to flow "horizontally" between regions. But for two reasons, it was unlikely that poor provinces would benefit much from the new institution. First, interregional movement of bank savings was limited, as a result of local government preferences and ability to control banks in their jurisdictions. Given the general scarcity of funds, all local governments were motivated to retain as much local savings as possible instead of exporting funds to someplace else. They could do this by using their control rights over banks to dictate the banks' credit decisions.[44] Second, if there was any interregional flow of bank savings, its direction was more likely to be from poor to rich regions rather than the other way around. This was so because, when local government intervention was absent, banks themselves were looking for profitable projects, which were more likely to be located in developed than in less-developed regions. We do not have systematic data to back up our conjectures, but many well-informed Chinese scholars suggest that bank savings were indeed flowing from less-developed to more developed areas.[45]

Apart from bank credits, in the late 1980s and early 1990s, local governments could also use such new financial instruments as enterprise bonds, local government bonds, and stocks to mobilize investment funds. However, as shown by Table 6.5, the development of financial markets was uneven, with interior provinces lagging far behind coastal provinces. In other words, the new financial instruments worked better for rich provinces than for poor provinces. Moreover, just like bank credits, these funds tended either to stay where they had originated or to flow to places where there was the greatest chance of obtaining the highest returns in the short run, namely, fast-growing areas along the coast.[46]

In sum, China's decentralized development strategy has affected the mobility and direction of capital flow. By placing resource-allocation decisions at subnational levels of government, decentralization constrained rather than facilitated the geographic mobility of both fiscal and financial resources, which explains why interprovincial flows of capital declined and stagnated during the period under review (Table 5.7). If there was any voluntary movement of capital at all, its direction tended to be from less-developed to more-developed provinces.

Summary

The availability of investment resources may not be a sufficient factor for economic growth, but it is certainly a necessary factor. If government intervention is absent, a region's capacity to raise investment funds locally depends on the vitality of the local economy. Unless poor regions can attract a greater influx of capital from external sources than

Table 6.5

Financial Markets in the Chinese Provinces (100 million yuan)

Region	Volume of Stock Issue 1990	Volume of Bond Issue 1991	Volume of Interbank Transaction 1991
Beijing	0.2	14.8	107.0
Tianjin	0.0	2.1	257.0
Hebei	0.8	22.0	4.0
Shanxi	0.3	0.0	0.0
Inner Mongolia	0.07	0.0	0.0
Liaoning	1.3	20.6	650.0
Jilin	0.08	0.0	0.0
Heilongjiang	0.2	3.50	151.0
Shanghai	1.1	55.0	883.6
Jiangsu	1.3	48.8	328.0
Zhejiang	2.2	6.9	699.2
Anhui	0.2	12.3	80.0
Fujian	0.2	2.7	315.0
Jiangxi	0.4	5.0	195.8
Shandong	1.7	22.9	320.0
Henan	0.6	12.0	84.0
Hubei	0.2	15.2	16.0
Hunan	0.4	4.6	34.0
Guangdong	6.5	4.2	74.7
Guangxi	0.0	0.2	0.0
Hainan	0.3	2.0	168.2
Sichuan	3.5	16.4	311.0
Guizhou	0.3	0.0	0.0
Yunnan	0.4	5.4	119.6
Tibet	0.0	0.0	0.0
Shaanxi	0.3	1.3	45.0
Gansu	0.3	0.0	17.0
Qinghai	0.0	0.2	1.4
Ningxia	0.0	0.0	0.0
Xinjiang	0.3	2.6	0.0

Source: Li Boxi (1995), p. 80.

rich regions do, the latter would be in an advantageous position to stimulate growth, which in turn would strengthen their capacity for future
capital mobilization and thus perpetuate the gaps between the richer and
poorer regions. However, government intervention does not necessarily
narrow regional gaps. If the government lacks the political will to narrow
the existing regional gaps, or if its extractive capacity is severely circum-
scribed, poor regions cannot expect much help from the central government in their effort to catch up with the nation's rich regions.

This was what happened in China from 1978 to 1995. In the 1980s, the Chinese government was obsessed with a growth-first philosophy. Its pro-coastal development strategy led to growing regional dispari-ties, as expected. To the extent that the central government was very well aware of the trade-off between aggregate growth and regional inequality, it can be said that the increasing regional disparities during this period were part of a deliberate scheme by the central government.

In the early 1990s, the government reoriented its regional prefer-ences, hoping somehow to mitigate the tensions caused by the large regional gaps. However, regional disparities showed no sign of nar-rowing. This was so because the decentralization unleashed by the reforms had significantly eroded the capability of the central govern-ment to mobilize and redistribute resources. Unable to extract large surpluses from rich provinces, as it had done before, the central gov-ernment found it increasingly difficult to make large subsidies to poor provinces. With interprovincial fiscal transfers dwindling, all the prov-inces, rich and poor, were forced to become financially more self-reliant. Rich regions could draw on a wide array of instruments to ensure financing of their projects. But decisions made by local governments, banks, or enterprises naturally focused on immediate local concerns, such as profitability and employment, not on whether development was occurring in other regions.[47] Thus, the voluntary movement of capital from rich to poor regions was not very likely. While the con-centration of investment resources in economically prosperous areas allowed them to gain a good lead in growth, the lack of investment resources dampened the growth potential of the backward areas. The result was the worsening of regional inequality in the early 1990s, despite the reorientation of central preference. To the extent that the uneven spatial distribution of capital and other resources has led to an increase in growth differentials, decentralization may be viewed as one of the main causes of widening regional disparities. It is also a power-ful institutional obstacle to the rectification of regional disparities, be-cause it severely curtails the central government's ability to equalize resource distribution. Obviously, unless the center is able to regain control over the redistribution of resources, the trend of divergence observed in the last decade or so is unlikely to be reversed.

Notes

1. It is not feasible to cover all of the many potential factors influencing output growth. The explanation given in this study is to some extent selective, to

emphasize the point that the most important ultimate cause of growth differentials is probably government policy.

2. Donald J. Savoie, *Regional Economic Development*, p. 249.

3. Margaret Levi, *Of Rule and Revenue.*

4. Marina Arbetman and Jacek Kugler, *Political Capacity and Economic Behavior,* introduction.

5. Mark O. Rousseau and Raphael Zariski, *Regionalism and Regional Devolution in Comparative Perspective,* pp. 10–11.

6. Nicholas R. Lardy, "Regional Growth and Income Distribution in China," p. 170.

7. Thomas P. Lyons, "Interprovincial Disparities in China," p. 1.

8. Lardy, "Regional Growth and Income Distribution," pp. 172–73.

9. The ratio of government revenue to national income rose from below 10 percent in 1949 to 34 percent in 1957. See Ministry of Finance, *Zhongguo caizheng tongji,* p. 152. For the situation before 1949, see Nicholas R. Lardy, *Economic Growth and Distribution in China,* pp. 40–41. According to Lardy, "Under the somewhat more vigorous fiscal program of the Nationalist government after 1928, central government revenues were only about 3 percent of GDP. Even when provincial and local revenues are included, the total government revenue share of GDP was less than 5 percent." Of the rising proportion of national income captured by the budget, the central government's share accounted for 80 percent of the total revenue. See Liu Suinian and Wu Qungan, *China's Socialist Economy,* pp. 174–75.

10. We use two measures to gauge central extractive capacity. One is the central share of total budgetary revenues. The other is the size of so-called extrabudgetary funds relative to budgetary funds. For a detailed discussion of changes in central extractive capacity, see Shaoguang Wang, "The Rise of the Regions," pp. 87–113.

11. Lardy, "Regional Growth and Income Distribution"; Lyons, "Interprovincial Disparities"; Tianlun Jian, Jeffrey D. Sachs, and Andrew M. Warner, "Trends in Regional Inequality in China"; Kai-yuen Tsui, "China's Regional Inequality," pp. 1–21; Sumner J. La Croix and Richard F. Garbaccio, "Convergence in Income and Consumption in China During the Maoist and Reform Regimes."

12. Wang, "Rise of the Regions," p. 95.

13. Chen Huai, "Zhongguo 80 niandai yilai quyu jingji fazhan zhanlue de huigu yu qianzhan," pp. 3–12.

14. Dali Yang, "Patterns of China's Regional Development Strategy," pp. 230–57.

15. Wei Wei, *Zhongguo jingji fazhan zhong de quyu chayi yu quyu xietiao,* pp. 79–88.

16. State investment in capital construction included investment by local governments. But until 1991, more than one-half of total investment in this category involved central projects, over which the central government had nearly total control. Moreover, in this category, even investment financed by local governments was subject to review and approval by the central government.

17. Guo Kesha and Li Haijian, "Zhongguo diqu duiwai kaifang geju fenxi," pp. 20–22.

18. It needs to be noted that the coastal provinces did not all enjoy the same degree of preferential treatment. Judged by the size of the economy covered by

preferential policies, the generosity of approved incentive packages, and the length of time in which preferential policies were applicable, it is clear that southern coastal provinces like Guangdong and Fujian benefited most from central preferential policies. Little wonder that they were also the provinces that received the lion's share of China's total foreign investment. World Bank, *China: Regional Disparities,* pp. 34–35.

19. Liqun Jia and Clem Tisdell, "Resource Redistribution and Regional Income Inequality in China," pp. 57–58.

20. Chen Huai, "Zhongguo 80 niandai yilai quyu jingji fazhan zhanlue de huigu yu qianzhan."

21. Jia and Tisdell, "Resource Redistribution and Regional Income Inequality," pp. 57–58.

22. Jude Howell, *China Opens Its Doors,* pp. 44–80.

23. World Bank, *China: Regional Disparities,* p. 33. Jian, Sachs, and Warner also find that "most of the decline in the overall variance was driven by a decline in income dispersion within the coastal provinces." See Jian, Sachs, and Warner, "Trends in Regional Inequality," pp. 14–15.

24. Chen Huai, "Zhongguo 80 niandai yilai quyu jingji fazhan zhanlue de huigu yu qianzhan."

25. Ibid.

26. Document Research Office of the CPC Central Committee, *Selected Important Documents Since the 13th Party Congress,* pp. 1368–94.

27. Guo Kesha and Li Haijian, "Zhongguo diqu duiwai kaifang geju fenxi," pp. 22–24.

28. Deng Xiaoping, *Selected Works of Deng Xiaoping,* vol. 3, pp. 374–76.

29. Land Planning Institute of the State Planning Commission, "Study of the Coordinated Development of the Regional Economies in China."

30. Xinhua New Agency, Beijing, October 4, 1995.

31. Shaoguang Wang and Angang Hu, *Zhongguo guojia nengli baogao* (see Bibliography for English translation of this work).

32. In 1994 China introduced a new fiscal system—the tax-assignment system (*fenshuizhi*)—to replace the old discretion-based system of revenue-sharing. Unlike the old system, in which provincial governments remitted a negotiated percentage or amount of locally collected revenues to the central government, the new system divides all taxes into three distinct categories: central, local, and shared. Central taxes go into the central coffers, and local taxes into local budgets. Shared taxes are divided between the central and provincial governments according to established formulas. Thus, the sharp decline of the provincial revenue to GDP ratios in 1994–95 was largely due to this definitional change. Data for those two years are not quite comparable to data for the previous years. For a detailed discussion of the 1994 fiscal reform, see Shaoguang Wang, "China's 1994 Fiscal Reform," pp. 801–17.

33. The share of capital investment in the budget declined from 40.3 percent in 1978 to 11.6 percent in 1995. *ZGTJNJ* (1996), p. 229.

34. Yasheng Huang, *Inflation and Investment Controls in China,* pp. 63–88.

35. Jacek Kugler and Marina Arbetman, "Relative Political Capacity," pp. 11–45.

36. Under the revenue-sharing system, the more revenue a province was able to raise on its own, the more it would have to remit to the center if it was a surplus

province, or the less it might be eligible to receive from the center if it was a deficit province. In both cases, provinces would shirk their tax-raising effort. For a detailed analysis of defects associated with the revenue-sharing system, see Shaoguang Wang, "The Institutional Sources of Central-Local Rivalry."

37. For a discussion of the upsurge of extrabudgetary funds in the reform era, see Wang, "Rise of the Regions." Yasheng Huang suggested that extrabudgetary revenues be counted as part of government revenue. See his *Inflation and Investment Controls*, p. 47. However, the most important difference between budgetary and extrabudgetary revenues is that the former are subject to redistribution, but the latter are not. That is why local governments have been at pains to shift funds from budgetary to extrabudgetary categories. Otherwise, it is hard to understand why they have taken the trouble to move money around. In my understanding, funds that are not subject to redistribution should not be counted as budgetary revenues.

38. Many other studies have also verified that there was a wide variation in tax effort among the provinces. The World Bank, for instance, found that many of the richest provinces made a lower level of revenue effort than poor provinces. Zhejiang, Shandong, and Liaoning, for instance, all made below average efforts, and Shanghai was just above average. See World Bank, *China: Revenue Mobilization and Tax Policy*. Using data for 1981 to 1990, Zhu Min showed that while the tax effort dropped for all the provinces during this period, the speed of its dropping varied considerably across regions. In general, rates of decline were much faster in rich provinces. See Zhu, Min, "The Mechanics and Consequences of China's Revenue Contract System." Also see Lou Jiwei and Li Keping, "Guanyu jianli woguo caizheng zhuanyi zhifu xin zhidu de ruogan wenti," pp. 68–72.

39. See Wang, "China's 1994 Fiscal Reform."

40. See Wang, "Institutional Sources of Central-Local Rivalry."

41. The devastating effect of declining transfers on poor provinces can be seen in the case of Guizhou. In the early 1980s, central transfers financed nearly 60 percent of the province's total budgetary expenditures. By 1993, this amount had dropped to less than 20 percent. Loraine A. West and Christine P. W. Wong, "Fiscal Decentralization and Growing Regional Disparities in Rural China"; Mark Selden, "China's Rural Welfare System: Crisis and Transformation."

42. West and Wong, "Fiscal Decentralization and Growing Regional Disparities."

43. Guonan Ma, "Income Distribution in the 1980s," p. 35.

44. For a discussion of local governments' control rights over banks, see Huang, *Inflation and Investment Controls*, pp. 43–44.

45. Hiroyuki Kato cited a case in his "Regional Development in the Reform Period," pp. 129–30. Also see Li Boxi, *Diqu zhengce yu xietiao fazhan*, p. 79. According to several authors, even poverty-relief loans allocated specifically for poor regions by the central government flowed back to the coastal provinces. See Qi Jingmei, "Diqu guding zichan tongji zhuangkuang de fenxi ji 1997 nian zhanwang," p. 7; Xu Fengxian et al., "Diqu jingji hongguan chaju yu weilai fazhan duice xuanze," p. 9; Yuan Gangming, "Diqu jingji chayi yu hongguan jingji bodong," p. 53.

46. Li Boxi, *Diqu zhengce yu xietiao fazhan*, pp. 80–81.

47. Penelope B. Prime, "China's Economic Reforms in Regional Perspective," pp. 9–27.

7

Confronting Inequality in China

In the first decade of the post-Mao era, when everyone was benefiting from the fast-growing economy and levels of spatial and class inequality were relatively low, the fairness issue rarely surfaced in China. However, concerns about the distributive effects of the post-Mao reforms began to emerge in the late-1980s.[1] By the mid-1990s, mounting inequality and its possible consequences both for social and economic instability and for continued growth have become central issues of policy debate and of scholarly research.

Challenges

This study focuses on one type of inequality—interregional inequality. It has examined changes in regional disparities and explored why these changes have occurred. Three broad conclusions can be drawn from the data presented in the preceding chapters. First, interprovincial inequality has been widening. Spatial inequality was reduced in the early years of the reforms, but the trend was soon reversed. The disparity in per capita GDP between China's coastal and interior provinces has been on the rise since 1983. And what is worse, the divergent trend accelerated after 1990.[2] Second, regional gaps in China are unusually large. Compared to seventeen countries for which data are available, China's degree of interregional inequality is the most acute (see Chapter 3). Third, regional inequality is a multidimensional phenomenon. No matter what dimension we examine, we find notable regional disparities. The rich and poor provinces differ not merely in per capita GDP. Rather, regional inequality manifests itself in almost every aspect of economic and social life. Measured by such human development indicators as education, life expectancy, and infant mortality, for instance, the difference between China's most developed and least-developed provinces is comparable to that between the Western industrial countries and the poorest countries in the world.[3]

Neoclassical economists predict that unfettered market forces and economic growth will lead to the convergence of regional income. Our study challenges this view. Were the neoclassical hypothesis correct, the marketization and high-speed growth produced by the post-Mao reforms would have greatly reduced regional gaps. Such blind faith in the magical power of markets has proven illusory. Production factors have not moved in the directions predicted by neoclassical economics. Instead, market forces have led to the clustering of scarce resources (e.g., capital, high-human-capital labor, information, technology, and the like) in advanced areas. This build-up may prove to be self-sustaining because of increasing internal and external economies at these centers of agglomeration. The limited advantages of backward regions (e.g., cheap labor) have been insufficient to offset these agglomeration advantages. As a result, a rising tide fails to lift all boats: Despite rapid aggregate growth, regional gaps have widened and poor areas have stagnated. We are not saying that convergence is not possible. What this study conclusively demonstrates is that convergence is by no means automatic.

Interprovincial inequality is only part of the story concerning China's income distribution. While regional disparities measured in terms of per capita GDP were worsening, gaps were also expanding between urban and rural populations,[4] and between rich and poor households in both urban and rural China,[5] as well as between men and women.[6] These inequalities are overlapping and interrelated. Growing interregional and rural-urban income differentials make China's overall income distribution far more unequal today than ever before in the history of the People's Republic.[7] In the early 1980s, China was among the world's most egalitarian societies, with income inequality substantially below the world average.[8] By 1995, although the degree of income inequality was still lower in China than in most Latin American and Sub-Saharan African countries, "there [was] no room for complacency."[9] Even by a conservative estimate, the inequality of income distribution in China already exceeded the inequality found in most of the transition economies of Eastern Europe and in the high-income countries of Western Europe and North America, and even more striking, in some of China's large Asian neighbors, such as India, Pakistan, and Indonesia, countries that have often been treated in the development literature as classic cases of substantial income inequality.[10]

Income inequality has grown in many, but not all, countries in the 1980s. In China it has increased more rapidly and gone further than almost anywhere else. The World Bank reports that the increase in China's overall inequality was "by far the largest of all countries for which comparable data are available."[11] So steep a rise in inequality in such a short time is highly unusual in both the historical and the comparative perspective.[12] Unless the trend of increasing polarization can be halted or reversed, the glaring inequalities prevailing in Latin America and Sub-Saharan Africa are soon likely to emerge in China.

Should China's policymakers be concerned about this ominous trend? Absolutely. As long as building a socialist market economy is still their professed goal, and stability (*wending*) and development (*fazhan*) remain their top priorities, they should handle the issue of income inequality with great caution and acumen. No society is free of inequality. But high levels of inequality can be dangerous and damaging. For a regime whose claim to legitimacy has long been based upon egalitarian principles, it is impossible to justify rapid growth in levels of inequality. The government may be able to persuade people that some must get rich first so that everyone will eventually get rich. But if it persists in failing to distribute the gains from reforms more or less evenly, and if the gap between those who flourish and those who stagnate becomes unacceptably large, the moral foundations of the regime will be shaken.

Moreover, if the benefits of market transition and growth become even more concentrated and no redistributional adjustments take place, people's frustration with the growing inequality will eventually reach a crisis point. Experience elsewhere suggests that few nations have succeeded in maintaining political stability under conditions of severe economic disparity. China's own history is full of uprisings, rebellions, and revolutions sparked by economic injustice. Even if the crisis does not reach the point of revolution, social tension and instability are harmful to economic growth. Thus, there is a great danger that growing inequality will derail China's reforms and imperil its future growth.

This conclusion is supported by numerous empirical comparative studies showing that greater inequality is often associated with slower growth.[13]

In this context, a few words about the possible political consequences of regional disparities are in order. Geographical imbalance is a politically divisive issue that can undermine national unity, particularly if people conclude that the state has systematically favored some regions over others. On the one hand, there is apt to be a widespread sense of frustration and deprivation in regions where incomes are strikingly low. Residents of those regions may readily believe that an insufficiently sympathetic central government is partly responsible for their plight. On the other hand, more-developed regions frequently perceive central redistributive intervention of any kind as unfair siphoning off of their resources. All regions desire policy changes favorable to their own interests. By virtue of their dominant positions in the national economy, however, the prosperous regions tend to have greater political leverage in dealing both with the central government and with other regions. Thus, the center may be "captured" by the rich regions and become a tool for advancing their interests. That would exacerbate the regional inequality and further enrage poorer regions. Otherwise, rich regions may be attracted to the idea that their interests would be better served by an independent development path. Especially when such regions are more closely integrated with the world economy than with other regions in the same country, or when ethnic, religious, or linguistic differences coincide with economic differences, separatist temptations are more likely to emerge. Examples of this sort are abundant, including the Punjab in India, Slovenia in the former Yugoslavia, the Baltic states (Lithuania, Estonia, and Latvia) in the former Soviet Union, Bougainville in Papua New Guinea, Lombardy in Italy, Katanga in Zaire, and Biafra in Nigeria. Each of these is or was the highest-income region within its nation, and all considered secession a solution to the interregional conflict in which they were involved.[14]

We are not suggesting that China is already on the brink of national disintegration. Far from it. In our view, disintegrating forces are kept firmly at bay in today's China.[15] Nevertheless, Chinese leaders should never treat this danger lightly. Instead, they should make every effort to prevent this worst-case scenario from becoming a reality. It is time for China to make the reduction of income inequality in general, and of regional disparities in particular, a top national priority.

Rising Inequality Is Not Inevitable

Few deny that inequality has widened in China.[16] The debate is over whether anything can be done about it, and over whether anything should be done about it. Some argue that growing inequality is inevitable. Because of differences in natural endowments, because of the nature of market transition, and because of the nature of modern economic growth, certain individuals, social groups, and regions will naturally prosper. Since such inequality is determined by natural forces or the inner laws of economic forces, governmental intervention to moderate it is at best wrongheaded and at worst destructive.[17]

We reject this philosophy. Besides being morally repugnant, it is a doctrine without empirical foundation. A number of conclusions can be drawn from the findings in the previous chapters and from other recent studies.

1. Inequality may be unavoidable, but a rise in inequality is by no means natural.

Take regional inequality. As discussed in Chapter 4, the observed regional level of development is associated with the local physical environment. In China, resource endowments vary widely from region to region. Many lagging interior provinces are characterized by rough terrain, limited arable land, cold dry weather, remoteness from lucrative urban and international markets, poor infrastructure, and the like. In consequence, higher production and transaction costs disadvantage these provinces in pursuing economic development as compared with the more generously endowed coastal provinces. In this sense, income variations across provinces can be attributed to natural conditions and are unavoidable.

However, these factors cannot explain changes in regional disparities. Natural endowments are constant variables; they do not change much in the short or even the medium term. But systems of regional inequality are changeable. We showed in Chapter 3 how the degree of regional inequality changed over time: contracting in the early years of reforms, expanding in the mid- and late-1980s, and accelerating in the 1990s. Clearly, such fluidity cannot be explained by changes in natural conditions, whether geographic location or resource endowments. Rather, the changing degree of inequality must have been a result of changes in policy decisions that the Chinese government made—or chose not to make.

In any event, increasing inequality is not fated. Policy matters. If the degree of inequality has changed in the past, it can be altered in one direction or another in the future, depending on what kind of policy is adopted.

2. Rising inequality is not inevitable during a market transition.

Income distribution has worsened in the course of China's transition to a market economy. But this does not mean that increasing inequality is inevitable during the market transition. Certainly, the degree of inequality need not increase as much or as rapidly as it did in China. Many countries underwent profound system transitions in the 1980s and 1990s. While few grew as rapidly as China, none registered increases in inequality as large as those observed in China. Some countries (e.g., South Korea, Malaysia, and Indonesia) actually experienced declining inequality during this period.[18] The variability in outcomes across these countries suggests that market transition does not necessarily lead to growing inequality.

No two market systems in the world are identical. All actually existing market systems are socially embedded and politically constructed.[19] As Amartya Sen points out, "Different social, political and economic arrangements can be combined with basically market economies."[20] Depending on the market-state mix, market systems may select winners and losers in very different ways. Consequently, some market systems may be more friendly than others to the less fortunate.[21] The growing inequality in China in recent decades was, therefore, not an inevitable by-product of market transition. Instead, its causes have to be sought in particular institutional arrangements made and particular public policies pursued during this period. Viewed from this angle, it is clear that our concern about increased inequality is not an attack on the goal of market-oriented reform. We only propose an overhaul of the institutional arrangements and public policies responsible for the growing inequality in general and the widening regional disparity in particular.

3. Rising inequality is not a necessary trade-off for economic growth.

Some argue that rising inequality is a price China has to pay for rapid economic growth. In their view, there is an inevitable efficiency-equity trade-off. Any attempt to secure greater equality through redistributive policies would impair China's growth potential, thus reducing income and producing a less-favorable outcome for all or most people.

Recent research, however, suggests that the trade-off between efficiency and equity may not be inevitable. The two values are only in opposition when either is pushed to an extreme. Otherwise, as the experience of, for example, Japan, Taiwan, and South Korea shows, egalitarian outcomes are not necessarily incompatible with rapid economic growth. There are institutional and policy choices conducive both to greater economic equality and to improved economic performance.[22]

On the other hand, inequality may be an impediment to economic growth. There is ample empirical evidence that inequality is negatively correlated with subsequent economic growth: societies that are more unequal tend to grow less quickly than societies that are more equal.[23]

Must China tolerate gross inequality in order to achieve higher overall growth? If the assumption that the pursuit of equality necessarily impairs economic performance proves false, if greater equity helps, or at least does not harm, economic growth, then China need not make a morally wrenching choice between higher growth and more equality; it can and should have both.

4. State preference matters.

If the growing inequality in China is not an inevitable consequence of natural endowment, market transition, or economic growth, then how do we explain it? To a large extent, growing inequality has been the result of a deliberate state policy.

Underlying China's reform was a fundamental transformation of the leadership's development philosophy. Deng Xiaoping's famous remark, "Let some prosper first so that others may follow," reflected this change, marking a notable departure from Mao's egalitarian goals and policies. With the shift in ideology, Chinese leaders paid far less attention to the reduction of income inequality. On the contrary, under pressure to generate faster growth, they tolerated widening income gaps. The socialist ideal of equality was explicitly set aside to achieve faster growth, at least in the short run. Chinese leaders seemed to subscribe to the trickle-down theory: Market forces and economic growth, in the long run, would bring prosperity to all.

Indeed, from the beginning of the 1980s to the early 1990s, little attention was paid to issues of distributive justice. It was during this period that China adopted the coastal-led development strategy discussed in Chapter 6. As part of this strategy, the Chinese government shifted its investment priority from the interior to the coast. In addition, coastal regions were granted a wide range of preferential provisions that were not uniformly implemented across the country. These special policies reinforced the coastal regions' advantages in natural endowment, consequently exacerbating the gulf between the coastal and interior provinces. In this sense, the increasing regional inequality may be viewed as a deliberate scheme from the outset.

Realizing that intentional policies were responsible for much of China's expanding inequality in the 1980s is not only more accurate than theories of natural inequality; it is also more optimistic. "A more enlightened public policy could significantly ameliorate the polarizing tendencies while still reaping the rewards of greater efficiency and rapid growth."[24]

5. State capacity matters.

A state's commitment to distributive justice is certainly a necessary condition for narrowing income gaps, but alone may be insufficient to bring about real changes. For a government to achieve desired policy goals, it must be able to mobilize and redistribute resources in the face of resistance by groups with competing priorities. Without such resources at its disposal, the state may be unable to fulfill its policy objectives.[25] In general, governments with strong extractive capacity are able to pursue their policy goals far more effectively than are less-capable governments under similar circumstances. For this reason, we believe that state capacity matters greatly with regard to income distribution as well as the provision of social benefits.

In Chapter 6, we explored how the changing extractive capacity of the central government affected patterns of regional development in China. In the pre-reform period, the central government played a pivotal redistributive role, extracting large surpluses from rich provinces and making large transfers to poor provinces. The massive fiscal decentralization introduced after 1978, however, significantly reduced the central government's extractive capacities. Under the fiscal contract system (*caizheng baoganzhi*) as practiced between 1980 and 1993, taxes were collected and expenditures undertaken on a jurisdiction-by-jurisdiction basis, to a great extent. Consequently, the ratio of central revenue to GDP quickly shrunk to a level far lower than in most countries. Under severe fiscal strain, the central government was no longer able to redistribute resources across the country as it preferred.[26] As the central capacity to affect equalization declined, regional dispari- ties worsened.

Obviously, just as with the commitment to distributive justice, strong central extractive capacity alone is not a sufficient condition for reducing the levels of inequality. Only when a government has both the commitment and the resources is it possible to achieve equitable growth.

Policy Goals

As a socialist country, China cannot face increasing inequality with indifference. The socialist system is a system that commits itself to the idea of equity. After the collapse of the communist systems in the former Soviet Union and Eastern Europe, many have declared, once again, that socialism is dead. But the inequalities and deprivation that socialists condemn still exist in much of the world. The need for deal- ing with inequality and deprivation remains as strong as ever. Sen is eloquent when he points out that "even though socialist economies have been riddled with economic and political problems, the aims and objectives that made socialism appeal to people remain just as relevant today as they were half a century ago."[27] This is especially true in China, a country that still professes to uphold socialist principles. Un- less the Chinese government makes equality one of its top policy goals, the system will lose legitimacy.

But how equal do we want China to be? Consider the following four criteria of equality:[28]

1. *The minimax criterion.* Here "minimax" stands for minimizing the maximum. By this criterion, achieving equality means reduc- ing the incomes of the richest to the level of the poor.
2. *The maximin criterion.* Here "maximin" stands for maximizing the minimum. By this criterion, achieving equality means im- proving the position of the poorest.
3. *The ratio criterion.* By this criterion, achieving equality means decreasing the income ratio between the rich and the poor (reduc- ing relative inequality).

4. *The least-difference criterion.* By this criterion, achieving equality means narrowing the absolute income differences between the rich and the poor (reducing absolute inequality).

Which criterion is most appropriate for today's China? First of all, we do not recommend the minimax criterion. When pursuing the goal of equality, one has to remember that equality is not the only value about which society cares. Efficiency and prosperity are other desirable goals. Although equality and efficiency are not necessarily incompatible, they may become so if either is carried to an extreme. As Douglas Rae points out, the minimax criterion represents "the hard edge of egalitarianism."[29] If dragging the rich down to the level of the poor sacrifices overall efficiency, this may damage the interests of all, including the poor. Even if that does not happen, leveling down will at best reduce inequality, but will not ease the hardships of the poor.

The maximin criterion focuses on improving the welfare of the poorest. Any reallocation of resources that improves the prospects of the least fortunate is viewed as more equal. Certainly government should consider the welfare of the poorest. But the maximin criterion is a very weak form of equality. A country can satisfy this criterion while allowing the gaps between the rich and the poorest to worsen. China itself is a case in point: At the same time that the number of people living in poverty declined, inequality was growing. For this reason, any government that is serious about equality should establish the maximin criterion as its minimum goal, but should also strive to go beyond this minimum to reduce relative and absolute inequalities.

It needs to be noted that the income ratio between rich and poor may decline while the absolute differences between them expand (see Chapter 3). In people's everyday lives, absolute differences are central. Therefore, the most desirable goal is to eliminate absolute inequality (the least-difference criterion); narrowing relative inequality (the ratio criterion) may serve as the second-best choice. However, a policy recommendation must be contingent on feasibility. Since inequality is a phenomenon that may have been produced over a long period of time, there is no reason to believe that income gaps, in both the relative and absolute senses, can be closed in the near future. Drastic measures may help to achieve forced equalization, but they are inappropriate and counter-productive when seen in the context of other aggregate concerns, such as overall efficiency. Thus, in the short term, the best

China can do is to mitigate the trend of growing inequality, both relative and absolute. Only in the medium term may China expect to reduce relative inequality. Eliminating absolute inequality can only be a long-term goal.

Applying the above analysis to the issue of regional development, we do not propose that China's regional policy seek to restrain the growth of rich provinces. Rather, the focus should be on how to help the poor regions to speed up their growth rates. Only by doing so may the growth in regional gaps be halted and poor regions be offered the opportunity to catch up with richer regions. As far as the rich provinces are concerned, there is only one thing that needs to be done, which is to eliminate the policy preferences granted to the coastal regions. With all their advantages in natural endowment, geographic location, infrastructure, human capital, and so on, these regions are already better positioned than others to develop their economies even without preferential policies. The coastal bias in China's regional development strategy amounts to "maximizing the maximum," which violates all the criteria of equity discussed above. As Chapter 6 showed, this bias has exacerbated the gap between the rich and poor regions. Removing these preferential policies would help reduce regional inequality.

Three Important Relationships

To create an institutional environment that can ensure that the above policy goals will be achieved in the area of regional development, the Chinese government has to carefully handle the following three sets of relationships.

1. Market Forces and Government Intervention

In recent years, government intervention to promote equity has fallen into ill repute. Market forces are seen as the more natural way of resolving social problems. Many in China now believe, despite the large and growing income gaps, that all regions will eventually gain from the greater efficiency of the free play of market forces. The reason such wider benefits have yet to be delivered, in this view, is that the market has not been freed up enough. If China further diminishes the role of government, then the wealth will automatically flow from rich to poor regions in due course.

Market fetishism of this kind is very harmful for a country that urgently needs to arrest growing regional inequalities. Markets may be able to bring about many wonderful things, but allocating resources in conformity with distributive justice is simply not a market construct.[30] Countless studies have demonstrated that market forces, if left to themselves, normally tend to increase rather than decrease regional inequalities. Even if we accept the neoclassical assumption that market forces will eventually reduce the gaps between regions, such an outcome will not surface for a very long time—so long that the growing inequality, in the interim, may generate serious social conflicts and give rise to political instability. That is why few countries leave regional growth to the free play of market forces.

From the time when nation-states emerged, governments have almost always exerted a certain amount of countervailing power against the tendency toward regional inequality. In North America and Western Europe, government policies are often initiated to offset market forces resulting in backwash effects and support those resulting in spread effects. If regional development appears to be relatively balanced in today's industrial countries, this is not a balance brought about by natural forces in the market. Rather, it is to a large extent a created balance, brought about by government mediation of market forces which, if left to themselves, might lead to imbalance.[31] Government intervention is also prevalent in the development of backward areas in many Third World countries.[32] The important point here is that government intervention is indispensable for promoting balanced regional development. China is no exception. To reduce regional disparities, the Chinese government should actively pursue a balanced-development strategy, even though some economists advise it to wait patiently for market forces to perform miracles.

2. The Central Government and Provincial Governments

In the context of growing skepticism about the efficacy of central power and central decision-making, we have recently witnessed the rise of an ideology that sees local initiatives as an economic panacea. Today, there is hardly any country that is not talking about decentralization. In this worldwide trend, China seems to have been marching in the vanguard, with decentralization surpassing that in any other country. However, while some governmental functions are better performed by lower levels of government, it is often forgotten that others have to be carried out by the central government.[33] Regional policy is one such function. Regional policy is largely concerned with accommodating differences of interest between regions. If provinces are allowed to autonomously formulate and implement their own regional plans, the result would be a colossal coordination failure: their plans are unlikely to be consistent with one another, and the patterns of regional development resulting in the nation as a whole are unlikely to be even. Only the central government has the will and capacity to redistribute resources between provinces and thereby bring about a more egalitarian distribution of resources across all parts of the country.

We are not suggesting that provincial governments have no role to play in regional development. While funds may have to be coordinated by the central government, action can be locally planned. In some cases, the center should merely provide funding and leave everything else to locally initiated activities. In addition, provincial governments should be encouraged, and indeed required, to solve regional disparities within their own jurisdictions, in which they act as the "central" government.

3. Policy Changes and Institutional Changes

To confront the growing regional disparities, the Chinese government certainly has to change its skewed regional policies. If intentional policies have significantly constructed the inequalities China faces today, a different set of deliberate policies are needed to change them. We will present some policy suggestions in the following section. However, getting the policies right is not enough. A strategy for reducing regional disparities must focus not only on what type of policies are needed, but also on how to ensure that such policies will be enacted and implemented. Attempts to change regional policies without altering the basic political structure cannot guarantee that new policies will be implemented and that they will not be reversed.

Solving a problem as far-reaching as the regional disparity requires a central government empowered to intervene effectively in the economy. As pointed out above, if there are severe fiscal constraints on the amount of transfers that the central government can afford to offer, its regional policy will not be effective. Some scholars have recognized the absence of a fiscally strong central government as a key factor behind the growing regional inequality.[34] For the Chinese government to be able to effect equalization across regions, it has to rebuild its extractive capacity by overhauling the country's excessively decentralized fiscal system.[35]

But a strong central government is capable of enforcing all kinds of policies, including those exacerbating interprovincial income differences. Therefore it is extremely important to create an institutional environment in which state policies would not be biased in favor of the rich and powerful. This cannot be achieved unless all provinces, rich and poor, are given an equal opportunity to participate in the central decision-making process. As shown in Chapter 6, the claims of rich provinces outweighed those of their poor counterparts in central decision-making during much of the 1980s.[36] To achieve balanced regional development, the central government should balance conflicting claims between provinces rather than favor the rich. Thus, in the central decision-making process, "participation of the different groups involved in these conflicting claims is a basic necessity."[37] A system of decision-making that allows broad participation can best resist pressure from the economically powerful. Moreover, when the voices of all those involved are heard in the corridors of power, the government will become more accountable and transparent, and policies will be less likely to undergo sudden and precipitous changes.[38]

Six Essential Actions

As this study finds, the growing regional inequality in China is not the inevitable result of economic forces operating on natural conditions, but the aftermath of biased state policies and enfeebled state capacity. Since these can be altered, China has no reason to fatalistically let inequalities mount. Equitable growth is not merely desirable, but it is also an attainable goal. What can be done to accomplish equitable growth in China? Based on the discussion in the preceding sections, this chapter concludes with six policy suggestions.

1. Redressing the Coastal Bias

The development bias favoring the coastal regions is based upon the mistaken gradient theory (*tidu lilun*), which is morally more outrageous than the infamous trickle-down theory. While the trickle-down theory only opposes government intervention on behalf of the poor, this theory actually advocates government intervention on behalf of the rich. To achieve the goal of maximal aggregate economic growth, it advises the government to deliberately concentrate resources that could be targeted to more needy regions in the areas already developed.

Unless this development bias is removed, the interior provinces will have no chance to catch up with the coastal provinces that enjoy such tremendous natural and human capital advantages to begin with.

2. Rebuilding a System of Interregional Fiscal Transfers

As Chapter 5 showed, weaker ability to mobilize resources was the most important reason why China's poor provinces lagged behind its rich provinces. Thus, if the Chinese government aims at reducing regional inequality, it has to make efforts to mitigate resource differentials across provinces. Directed by the center, fiscal transfers from richer to poorer regions have been used as an important mechanism to reduce regional disparities in many countries. In the early decades of the People's Republic, China also addressed the issue of regional inequality with some success through interregional transfers.[39] In recent years, however, such transfers shrank, because the central government, unable to mobilize enough resources under an excessively decentralized fiscal system, simply had little to spare. With all regions moving toward a higher level of self-financing, regional disparities were further aggravated. To iron out some of the variations in economic development levels across provinces, the Chinese government must rebuild its extractive capacity so that it can again play a significant redistributive role in the economy. Only when the central government is able to command large surpluses from rich regions and make substantial transfers to poor regions can the effects of the initial unequal distribution of resources be offset.

3. Eradicating Poverty

The socialist promise implies the right of all human beings to lead a long and healthy life and to enjoy a decent standard of living. However, poverty denies such opportunities to some people. It deprives them not only of the minimum needed for material well-being, but also of human dignity and self-respect.[40] For this reason, no socialist government can relinquish its responsibility to eradicate poverty ("maxi-min").[41] China has done a great deal to reduce poverty in the last two decades. Over 200 million people have been lifted out of poverty since 1978. However, by 1998, there were still some 50 million people living below the government's absolute poverty line. If the "near poor," those who survived on less than $1.00 of income a day (measured in 1985 purchasing power parity dollars) are included, the number of people considered poor by international standards would amount to about 150 million, or 12.5 percent of the population.[42]

The Chinese government should keep poverty reduction as a top priority of its national economic policy. Poverty in China is not entirely a regional phenomenon. Even in the coastal provinces, Guangdong, Hebei, Zhejiang, Jiangsu, Shandong, and Hainan, there are people struggling with poverty (see Chapter 4). Nevertheless, "human poverty is far more pervasive in the remote interior provinces of the western regions than in the coastal region."[43] Therefore, in drawing up its regional-development strategy, the Chinese government should pay special attention to the poorest citizens living in the country's poorest areas. And in making interregional fiscal transfers, it should earmark special funds to alleviate the hardships that uneven growth has imposed on the poorest.[44]

4. Ensuring a Minimum Level of Essential Public Services

In China, a poor region is not only an area where people's average income is low; it is also a place where the public services, including education, health care, and welfare security, are inferior (see Chapter 4). The central government has the responsibility to ensure a minimum level of essential public services to all of the country's citizens. This can be done by using fiscal transfers to bring the fiscal capacity of poor regions up to their minimum expenditure needs.

Among all public services, basic education and health care are most crucial. Increased availability of such services would help poor regions in two ways. First, it would improve the quality of life for people living in those regions. Second, and more important in the long run, it would help poor regions to upgrade the quality of their labor force. Studies have repeatedly shown that investment in human capital is the most powerful engine for modern economic growth. Only with a healthier and better-educated workforce can the poor regions hope to be part of the mainstream forces of growth. Viewed from this angle, transfers used to ensure greater equality in access to education and health care should not be treated as charity. Rather, they are investments that will yield rich dividends for the poor regions as well as for the country as a whole.

5. Improving Infrastructure in Poor Regions

Good infrastructure facilities are fundamental to regional development. In China, poor regions are poor in part because the preconditions for modern growth, such as transportation and communications facilities, power and water supply, and so on, are lacking. Serious deficiencies in infrastructure constrain the growth potential of these regions in a number of ways: Links with lucrative markets along the coast and overseas are weak; production and transport costs are higher; external funds, technology, and human capital are reluctant to flow in; and local surplus laborers are ill-informed about income opportunities elsewhere. In sum, with inferior infrastructure, poor regions are at a disadvantage in competing with rich regions.

From the point of view of equitable growth, the Chinese government should at least create a level playing field so that all regions can compete with one another on an equal footing. Using central transfers to upgrade the physical infrastructure of poor regions would be a first step toward reinstating equal opportunities to all regions.

6. Facilitating Factor Mobility

In the final analysis, any regional policy that cannot generate a process of self-sustaining economic growth in lagging areas should be regarded as a failure. However, indigenous development is possible only if backward regions are able to attract new economic activities. The improvement of human capital and infrastructure will certainly create conditions more likely to attract such activities than otherwise, but such a change alone is hardly sufficient. External capital, for instance, will not flock to less-developed regions simply because infrastructural facilities are as good as those available in the developed areas. Therefore, it is important for public services and infrastructure subsidies to be supplemented by policies that will facilitate the mobility of production factors (capital, technology, labor, and talent) in ways beneficial to backward regions.

What can the government do to persuade business establishments to set up or relocate plants in the lagging regions of the economy rather than in the prosperous regions? Since it is recognized that location in the former is unlikely to be the first choice of firms, various types of inducements are necessary. Measures that have proved effective elsewhere include:[45]

- Assistance in providing information with regard to investment opportunities in backward regions to reduce uncertainty.
- Business relocation subsidies to defray the higher risks attached to investment in lagging regions.
- The provision of industrial development services, such as industrial parks, to lower investment costs.
- Subsidies for natural resource development.
- Locating central projects in backward regions to serve as a generator of expansion.[46]
- Transfer payments to prop up demand in lagging areas.

In addition to inducing capital to locate in depressed areas, a strategy designed to reduce regional inequality also needs to stimulate an increase in labor mobility so that surplus labor in depressed areas will move to areas where jobs are available. This policy suggestion is consistent with the neoclassical view that efforts should be made to remove impediments to factor mobility, and that convergence will occur if capital flows to poor regions and labor to rich regions. However, we doubt that capital and labor, if left to unfettered market forces, will necessarily move in the direction we deem desirable. That is why we suggest that the mobility of factors be "lubricated" by government.

Summary

China is in transition from a planned economy to a market economy. During the process, it should not give up the socialist goal of distributive justice, though some of its old institutional remedies for inequality may have to be replaced by new ones. In the preceding sections, we have proposed a number of ways to reduce regional disparities. Our proposals, while broadly compatible with the basic principles of the market system, address issues of human concern that transcend the market.

The pith and marrow of the above proposals can be summarized in one word: *empowerment*. The central government has to first empower itself so that it can effectively enforce its policies, including regional policies. Then the government is advised to focus on empowering backward regions rather than on restraining advanced regions. How should China empower the backward regions? Purely income subsidies are not recommended, except for those living in absolute poverty. Instead, the emphasis should be placed on enhancing the long-term development capabilities of backward regions. This is to be done by investing in human capital, upgrading infrastructure, and offering investment incentives. By pushing and pulling production factors into areas where they can be more fully and efficiently utilized, the empowerment approach makes it possible to reduce regional disparities and accelerate national development at the same time.

Notes

1. Such concerns were a cause of the 1989 protest movement. See Shaoguang Wang, "From a Pillar of Continuity to a Force for Change" and "Deng Xiaoping's Economic Reform and the Chinese Workers' Participation in the Protest Movement of 1989."

2. The World Bank arrives at an essentially similar conclusion in its *Sharing Rising Incomes*, p. 21.

3. UNDP, *Human Development Report, 1995*, pp. 139–41.

4. The World Bank finds that China's rural-urban gaps are very high by international standards. In other countries, the ratio of urban to rural income is normally below 1.5 and rarely exceeds 2.0. But in China, real urban incomes are as much as four times real rural incomes. World Bank, *Sharing Rising Incomes*, pp. 7–8.

5. By using unadjusted State Statistical Bureau (SSB) data, the World Bank concludes that the rural Gini coefficient (a measure of relative inequality ranging from 0, absolute equality, to 1, absolute inequality) increased from 0.242 in 1981 to 0.333 in 1995, and the urban Gini from 0.176 in 1983 to 0.275 in 1995. See World Bank, *Sharing Rising Incomes*, p. 17. Khan and Riskin adjust the SSB data and arrive at higher estimations. According to them, there was a sharp rise in both rural and urban inequalities between 1988 and 1995. The Gini ratio of rural income increased from 0.338 to 0.416, and the urban Gini ratio from 0.23 to 0.33. See Azizur Rahman Khan and Carl Riskin, "Income and Inequality in China," pp. 238 and 241.

6. World Bank, *Sharing Rising Incomes*, pp. 38–41. For other recent works on inequality in China, see Keith Griffin and Zhao Renwei, *The Distribution of Income in China*; and Terry McKinley, *The Distribution of Wealth in Rural China*.

7. The World Bank estimates that the Gini ratio for China as whole increased from a low 0.288 in the early 1980s to 0.388 in 1995. See World Bank, *Sharing Rising Incomes*, p. 7. Again, the Gini ratios estimated by Khan and Riskin were

higher. They believe that China's overall Gini coefficient increased sharply between 1988 and 1995, from 0.382 in 1988 to 0.452 in 1995. See Khan and Riskin, "Income and Inequality in China," pp. 246–47.

8. World Bank, *China 2020,* p. 8.

9. World Bank, *Sharing Rising Incomes,* p. 2.

10. Ibid., pp. 1–2, 7–8.

11. Ibid., pp. 7–8.

12. World Bank, *China 2020,* p. 8.

13. World Bank, *World Development Report;* Alberto Alesina and Dani Rodrik, "Distribution, Political Conflict, and Economic Growth," pp. 23–50; Torsten Persson and Guido Tabellini, "Is Inequality Harmful for Growth?" pp. 600–621; Roberto Perotti, "Growth, Income Distribution, and Democracy," pp. 149–87; United Nations Conference on Trade and Development, "Income Distribution, Capital Accumulation, and Growth," pp. 61–80.

14. Milica Zarkovic Bookman, *The Political Economy of Discontinuous Development,* pp. 2 and 27–33.

15. See Yasheng Huang, "Why China Will Not Collapse," pp. 54–68.

16. Even a study finding that "regional convergence is strongly associated with the extent of marketization and openness" concludes that China is "on a path of divergence." See Tianlun Jian, Jeffrey D. Sachs, and Andrew M. Warner, "Trends in Regional Inequality in China."

17. Dayuan Hu, "Zhuangui jingji zhong de diqu chaju," pp. 35–41.

18. World Bank, *Sharing Rising Incomes,* p. 8.

19. Claude S. Fischer et al., *Inequality by Design,* pp. 129–57.

20. Amartya Sen, "Social Commitment and Democracy," p. 19.

21. Victor Nee and Raymond V. Liedka, "Markets and Inequality in the Transition from State Socialism," pp. 202–24.

22. For instance, after the end of World War II, advanced capitalist countries were able to grow at fast rates while substantially reducing poverty and inequality. The period between 1945 and 1973 has been called the golden age of capitalism. See Stephen Marglin and Juliet B. Schor, *The Golden Age of Capitalism;* Gary S. Fields, *Poverty, Inequality, and Development;* Samuel Bowles and Herbert Gintis, "Efficient Redistribution," pp. 307–42; Joseph Stiglitz, "Distribution, Efficiency and Voice."

23. Persson and Tabellini, "Is Inequality Harmful for Growth?" pp. 600–21; Roberto Chang, "Income Inequality and Economic Growth," pp. 1–10; Alberto Alesina and Dani Rodrik, "Distributive Politics and Economic Growth," pp. 465–90; George R. G. Clarke, "More Evidence on Income Distribution and Growth," pp. 403–27.

24. Khan and Riskin, "Income and Inequality in China," p. 253.

25. Margaret Levi, *Of Rule and Revenue.*

26. Shaoguang Wang, "The Institutional Roots of Central-Local Rivalry: China, 1980–1996."

27. Sen, "Social Commitment and Democracy," p. 17.

28. These four criteria are drawn from Douglas Rae, *Equalities,* pp. 110–12.

29. Ibid., p. 112.

30. Shaoguang Wang, "The Roles of the State in the Transition to Market Economy."

31. Gunnar Myrdal, *Economic Theory and Under-Developed Regions,* pp. 39–49.

32. Albert O. Hirschman, *The Strategy of Economic Development,* p. 194.

33. Shaoguang Wang, *Fenquan de dixian.* Also see Remy Prud'homme, "On the Dangers of Decentralization."

34. Angang Hu, Shaoguang Wang, and Xiaoguang Kang, *Zhongguo diqu chaju baogao.* Also see Mark Selden, "China's Rural Welfare System"; Loraine A. West and Christine P.W. Wong, "Fiscal Decentralization and Growing Regional Disparities in Rural China."

35. Efforts have been made since 1994. See Shaoguang Wang, "China's 1994 Fiscal Reform."

36. This was so because the central decision-making process was characterized by a peculiar bargaining formula: the center separately conducted negotiations with individual provinces on a one-to-one basis. Under such an institutional arrangement, an economically advanced province could use its strategic importance in the national economy to drive a hard bargain in dealing with the central government, while a poor province could not. That difference in bargaining capacity was part of the reason why rich provinces generally found favor with the center in that decade. See Shaoguang Wang, "The Institutional Sources of Central-Local Rivalry: 1980–1993."

37. Sen, "Social Commitment and Democracy," pp. 21–22.

38. Joseph Stiglitz, "Distribution, Efficiency and Voice."

39. Nicholas R. Lardy, "Regional Growth and Income Distribution in China."

40. UNDP, *Human Development Report, 1997,* pp. 15–23.

41. Ibid., pp. 6–7.

42. World Bank, *Sharing Rising Incomes,* p. 4.

43. UNDP, *Human Development Report, 1997,* p. 23.

44. In China, there are 592 nationally designated poor counties (on the basis of average per capita income in 1992). They are the targets of poverty-reduction programs coordinated by central government agencies.

45. Stuart Holland, *Capital versus the Region;* A. J. Brown and E. M. Burrows, *Regional Economic Problems;* R. L. Mathews, *Regional Disparities and Economic Development;* Harvey Armstrong and Jim Taylor, *Regional Economics and Policy;* Douglas E. Booth, *Regional Long Waves, Uneven Growth, and the Cooperative Alternative;* Hal Hill, *Unity and Diversity;* David Smith, *North and South;* Alex Bowen and Ken Mayhew, *Reducing Regional Inequalities;* Huib Ernste and Verena Meier, *Regional Development and Contemporary Response;* Donald J. Savoie, *Regional Economic Development.*

46. In the United States, for instance, this policy often takes the form of targeted defense spending.

APPENDICES

Appendix 3.1

The Data

Our original body of data was somewhat tediously compiled from *China Statistical Yearbook* (1991–1996) and the statistical yearbooks of China's thirty provinces for 1993–1996. After we had largely finished data processing, China's State Statistical Bureau (SSB) published two volumes on the country's regional economy *China Regional Economy: A Profile of 17 Years of Reform and Opening Up* in 1996 and *The Gross Domestic Product of China, 1952–1995* in 1997. Most of the data used in this book are available in these two convenient volumes.[1] Unless indicated otherwise, all tables and figures are based on these sources.[2]

We use data from official sources not because they are flawless, but because there are no better alternatives. In fact, Chinese central and provincial officials are often among the first to point out the dubious quality of the data reported from below, particularly from grassroots units.[3] Raw data (*yuanshi shuju*) are unreliable primarily for two reasons. First, many small firms, especially township and village enterprises (TVEs), do not have even a basic idea of bookkeeping. Keeping accounts is something foreign and laborious to them. Whenever they are asked to report on their performance, the best they can do is to provide rough estimates, which can be extremely misleading.[4]

Second, and more important, self-interested enterprise managers and government officials have incentives to misrepresent their "accomplishments" in areas where pressures from above are strong. According to the SSB, data inflation is most severe in four areas: TVE output, rural per capita income, foreign investment, and exports. In the meantime, underreporting is rampant in such areas as wages, arable land acreage, rural birth rates, and any activity that is subject to taxation.[5]

How serious is the problem of statistical falsification in today's China? Some believe that it is even worse than in the notorious Great Leap Forward period.[6] A recent nationwide auditing campaign, for instance, uncovered more than 30,000 cases of overstatement, understatement, or some other sort of data manipulation.[7] These were surely just the tip of the iceberg.

Does this mean that Chinese official data are useless? The answer is no. It is important to bear in mind that SSB statistics are not simple arithmetical sums of raw data. Rather, they are the product of rigorous statistical treatment by the SSB. Can we trust the SSB? We have no reason to doubt its veracity. As pointed out by John Wong, there is no evidence of the Chinese central government having deliberately falsified or fabricated statistics.[8] In the former Soviet Union and East European communist countries, statistics were often distorted for propaganda purposes by central planners. In China, ironically, when the government was most ideological under Mao, no systematic economic data were ever released between 1959 and 1981, and this, as Yasheng Huang points out, ensured a degree of statistical accuracy for the period.[9] In the post-Mao era, accurate economic data became vital for macroeconomic management. The central government thus has no reason to cheat itself. If anything, it has a strong incentive to reduce data inaccuracy as much as possible. If this were not so, why would the central government have taken the trouble to enact the Statistical Law in 1983, to amend it in 1996, and to crack down on data falsification on a regular basis throughout the last fifteen years.

Is the SSB capable of improving data quality? Increasingly so. For a long time, the SSB's only source of information was the periodic reporting of raw data in a bottom-up fashion. This has been changed in recent years. Although China's statistical system still collects miscellaneous report forms from below, level by level, the range of such reporting has been substantially narrowed and its importance greatly reduced. Coordinated by the SSB and conducted by statistical bureaus at lower levels, periodic general surveys (*pucha*) and regular sampling surveys (*chouyang diaocha*) are now the two pillars of China's statistical system, whereas raw data reporting (*tongji baobiao*) plays at best a supplementary role.[10] Moreover, manifold statistical techniques have come into wide use at SSB's provincial bureaus and its national headquarters, further enhancing the system's ability to control data quality.[11]

One example may help illustrate our point. Fully aware of the acuteness of data inflation in the area of TVE output, the SSB makes substantial adjustments to what are reported to the bureau in this category every year. Its published figures for 1994 (4,258.85 billion yuan) and 1995 (6,891.52 billion yuan), for instance, represent the results of downward revisions by as much as 1,000 billion yuan and 1,800 billion yuan in those two years, respectively.[12] All data published by the SSB, including those contained in provincial yearbooks, have passed such statistical treatments.

In the final analysis, what really matters for us is the quality of data released by the SSB. How accurate are the numbers and figures we cite from the SSB's publications? Despite the bureau's unremitting efforts to purge distortions from its statistics, the quality of Chinese official data probably still leaves much to be desired. However, awareness that data may be inaccurate is no reason to ignore them. For our purpose, as long as data can correctly reflect trends and patterns of development, using them is justifiable. It is safe to say that SSB data are largely reliable. Even if they may not perfectly mirror reality, the world they depict is a close approximation to reality. Liu Hong, the current director of the SSB, insists that China's "macroeconomical data are on the whole reliable."[13] His confidence is based upon a simple fact: In retrospect, SSB statistics have proven to be quite consistent with major movements and changes in the real economy. Because the SSB is the best source available on China, its data are widely used by scholars, the World Bank, etc. We are confident that, based on the SSB data, our analysis of patterns and changes in regional development is suggestive of broad trends.

One source of bias in our data set, however, needs to be noted at this point. China has in recent years been experiencing interregional migration on an unprecedentedly large scale. It is now estimated that some 80–100 million people have left their hometowns. Although 70 to 80 percent of this "floating population" move mainly within their respective provinces, 20 to 30 percent have migrated to other provinces, especially to coastal areas.[14] Because most of these migrants are unregistered in their new residences, the population of the coastal regions may be underestimated, and the population of interior regions overestimated. Thus, we have to remember that regional differences in per capita GDP are probably in fact smaller than what our data seem to suggest.

Notes

1. For Hainan, which did not become a province until 1988, earlier data are unavailable.
2. Chapters 3 and 4 cover the period of 1978–94, and Chapters 5 and 6 the period of 1978–95. The difference is due to the availability of up-to-date data when these chapters were in preparation.
3. For a recent example, see Chen Zhongli, "Gansu shengwei shuji nuci tongji xujia" [Gansu Provincial Party Secretary Denounces Falsified Statistics], *Guangming Daily,* July 25, 1998.
4. Jin Zhanxiu, "Bajiushi niandai fukua toushi" [An Analysis of the Proneness to Boasting and Exaggeration in the 1980s and 1990s], *Zhongguo tongji* [China Statistics], no. 10 (1995): 20.
5. "1997 nian quanguo tongji zhifa dajiancha chengguo xianzhu" [The Achievements of the 1997 Auditorial Check-up of Statistical Work], *Zhongguo tongji,* no. 3 (1998): 15–16. Moreover, poverty counties often understate their output in order to keep central subsidies. See Chen Zhongli, "Gansu shengwei shuji nuci tongji xujia."
6. Jin Zhanxiu, "Bajiushi niandai fukua toushi." Also see Lu Baozhen, "Quanguo renda changweihui weiyuan tan zonghe zhili xubao fukua" [Comments on Statistical Falsification by Members of the Standing Committee of the National People's Congress], *Zhongguo tongji,* no. 10 (1995): 22–25; Qiong Sheng, "Tongji buneng chengwei shuzi youxi" [Statistics Should Not Be a Numbers Game], *Liaowang* [Outlook], no. 15 (1998): 10–15.
7. Lu Xianru, "Jianjie shazhu longxuzuojia waifeng" [Stop the Evil Trend of Cooking Accounts], *Guangming Daily,* July 24, 1998.
8. John Wong, *Understanding China's Socialist Market Economy* (Singapore: Times Academic Press, 1993), pp. 8–12.
9. Yasheng Huang, "The Statistical Agency in China's Bureaucratic System." *Communist and Post-Communist Studies,* vol. 29, no. 1 (1996): 59–75.
10. Ye Changlin, "Tongjifa xiugai de zhuyao fangmian" [Major Revisions of the Statistical Law], *Zhongguo tongji,* no. 6 (1996): 8–10.
11. Henan Provincial Statistical Bureau, "Hezhun tongji shuju cujin xiangzhen qiye fazhan" [Check Statistical Data, Promote TVE Development], *Zhongguo tongji,* no. 8 (1996): 6; Tang Wei, "Cong gongye pucha kan dishi shuju chuli zhiliang kongzhi de zhongyaoxing" [The Importance of Data Quality Control at the Prefecture/City Level: The Case of the Third Nationwide General Industrial Survey], *Zhongguo tongji,* no. 9 (1996): 16–17; Zhang Benqing, "Tongji shuju zhiliang kongzhi de duice" [Methods of Statistical Data Quality Control], *Zhongguo tongji,* no. 11 (1997): 18–19.
12. Lu Baozhen, "Quanguo renda changweihui weiyuan tan zonghe zhili

xubao fukua," p. 25; Qiong Sheng, "Tongji buneng chengwei shuzi youxi," p. 12.

13. Liu Hong, "Zai quanguo tongji gongzuo huiyi shang de jianghua" [Speech at the National Statistical Conference], *Tongji yanjiu* [Statistical Research], no. 2 (1998): 3–10. His judgment was shared by Zhao Yanyun, a leading statistics professor at People's University. See Qiong Sheng, "Tongji buneng chengwei shuzi youxi," p. 14.

14. Cai Fang, "An Economic Analysis of Labor Migration and Mobility in China."

Appendix 5.1

The Method of Growth Accounting

The underlying growth model used in growth accounting is an aggregate production function in which output is a simple function of factor inputs:

$$Y = AF(K,L,H),^1 \tag{1}$$

where
    Y = output
    K = a measure of physical capital input
    L = a measure of labor input
    H = a measure of human-capital input
    A = an index of the level of technology[2]

The identification of the immediate sources of output growth can be achieved by taking the logarithms of the variables on both sides and differentiating with respect to time, to produce the following discrete approximation:

$$G(Y) = G(A) + \alpha G(K) + \beta G(L) + \gamma G(H) \tag{2}$$

where G() represents the growth rate of any variable specified inside the parentheses, e.g. $G(Y) = \delta Y/Y$. The constant α measures the elasticity of output with respect to capital, when the supply of labor and the level of human capital are held constant: a 1 percent increase in capital will increase output by α percent, if the supply of labor and the level of human capital remain the same. Similarly, the constants β and γ measure the elasticities of output with respect to labor and human capital respectively, presenting percentage increases in output relative to 1 percent increase in labor and human capital respectively. If physical capital, labor, and human capital are all increased by 1 percent, then output will expand by $(\alpha + \beta + \gamma)$ percent. If increasing returns to scale are assumed, the sum of α, β, and γ would be greater than 1. If decreasing returns are assumed, then it is less than 1, and when constant returns are assumed, it is equal to 1.[3]

In principle, growth in Y, K, L, and H is observable and can be measured. As long as the constants α, β, γ can be obtained, we should be able to decompose the growth of output into the following four elements:

1. the contribution of capital = $\alpha G(K)$;
2. the contribution of labor = $\beta G(L)$;
3. the contribution of human capital = $\gamma G(H)$; and
4. the contribution of technical progress = $G(A)$

Although growth in A is not observable, we can measure $G(A)$ by reorganizing equation (2) to get (3):

$$G(A) = G(Y) - \alpha G(K) - \beta G(L) - \gamma G(H) \qquad (3)$$

In other words, the contribution of technical progress can be measured as a residual.[4]

Under the assumption of constant returns, we can further identify the sources of growth in per capita output by subtracting the growth rate of population $G(N)$ from the left-hand side of equation (2) and $(\alpha + \beta + \gamma)G(N)$ from the right-hand side $(\alpha + \beta + \gamma = 1)$ as follows:[5]

$$G(Y) - G(N) = G(A) + \alpha[G(K) - G(N)] \\ + \beta[G(L) - G(N)] + \gamma[G(H) - G(N)] \qquad (4)$$

But this exercise will not be necessary in our case, because, as Figure 5.1.1 shows, the provincial growth rates of GDP and the provincial growth rates of per capita GDP are highly correlated ($r = 0.9666$). What explains the growth of output may also be applied to the growth of per capita output. For the sake of simplicity, this chapter focuses on explaining the former rather than the latter.

Notes

1. It is assumed here that technical progress is neutral in the Hicksian sense. That is, changes in technology are assumed not to affect the factor-intensity of production. Accordingly, F(L,K) is supposed to increase A-times with technological progress.

2. In this literature, A is often called "total factor productivity" (TFP).

3. In this study, we adopt a simplifying assumption of linear homogeneity or constant returns to scale. Therefore, the sum of elasticities is equal to one ($\alpha + \beta + \gamma = 1$).

4. Since G(A) is a residual in the growth of Y after the effect of K, L, and H are subtracted, it measures the growth in output that is unexplained by the increase in measured factors of production. Although this residual is often narrowly interpreted as productivity growth, it should in fact be regarded as a measure of our ignorance.

5. Yujiro Hayami, *Development Economics,* pp. 117–19.

Figure A5.1.1 **Average Growth Rates of Provincial GDP and Per Capita GDP**

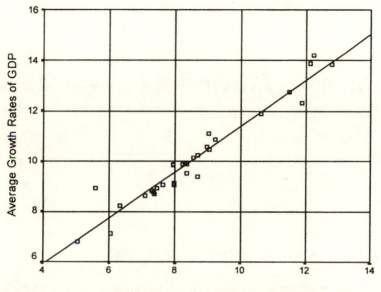

Average Growth Rate of Per Capita GDP

Appendix 5.2

Estimating Provincial Capital Stocks

As in other developing countries, no data on capital stock are available in China. Fortunately, however, Chinese statistical publications provide separate series for nominal fixed investment and the overall depreciation rate. In order to obtain the series of net capital stock, then we only need (1) to estimate the initial capital stock for the base year, which in our case is 1978, and (2) to derive a new time series of fixed investment valued at 1978 constant prices.[1] The latter can easily be done by using the implicit price deflators for provincial GDPs to estimate real fixed investments in 1978 prices.[2]

The initial capital stock in each of China's thirty provinces is estimated in two steps. We first estimate the 1978 national capital stock at 550 billion yuan. Any province's capital stock in that year can then be obtained by assuming its share of the national capital stock to be in the same proportion as its share of the total GDP.

Where does the estimate of 550 billion come from? The value of fixed assets in the state sector in 1978 is known (320.14 billion). To come up with an estimate of the total value of the national capital stock, we only need to estimate the 1978 value of fixed assets in the non-state sector. To do so, we first estimate the share of national income produced by the non-state sector in 1978, which was 49.7 percent (see Table 5.2.1). For the sake of simplification, let us suppose that a half of the national income was produced by the non-state sector in 1978. Obviously, if the capital-output ratio were the same in both sectors, the value of the non-state fixed assets would be equal to the value of the state fixed assets. This, of course, was not the case in reality. Given the state's domination of industry, construction, and transportation, the capital-output ratio must be much lower in the non-state sector, concentrated in agriculture and commerce. Suppose that the ratio in the non-state sector was 70 percent of that in the state sector, then the value of fixed assets in the former would be 224.10 billion yuan (320.14 × 70 percent). Adding this figure to 320.14 billion, we obtain a figure close to 550 billion yuan (544.24 billion yuan to be exact).

Another way to estimate the value of total fixed assets (state plus non-state) is to assume that the 1978 fixed capital stock in China was one and a half times as high as its GDP (362.41 billion yuan).[3] This method leads us to a similar result: 543.62 billion yuan. Thus, we have reason to believe that our estimate is not too far off the mark.

With all the necessary raw data, we are now in a position to form a time series on provincial capital stocks. This can be done by using the perpetual-inventory method.[4] The method involves adding new investment to an initial stock estimate and subtracting assets when they reach the end of their service lives. More specifically, following the inventory method, the value of capital stock in a given year is equal to the value of the capital stock of the previous year, plus the real gross investment during that year, minus the depreciation of the initial capital during that year:

$$K(t) = K(t-1) + I(t) - \delta K(t-1) = (1-\delta)K(t-1) + I(t)$$

where t indicates time, $K(t)$ is the stock of physical capital at time t, $I(t)$ is the gross investment corrected for price changes during period t, and δ is the depreciation rate.

Clearly, this procedure is fraught with error. In particular, the estimated capital stocks during the first few years would be sensitive to the estimate of the initial capital stock and therefore not quite reliable. However, because subsequent investment rates were extremely high in all thirty of China's provinces, error in our estimate of any province's initial capital stock would constitute only a very small portion of the stock available for the following years, and the estimated stocks thus would become progressively more accurate.[5]

Table A5.2.1

Non-State Share of National Income, 1978

	Agriculture	Industry	Construction	Transport	Commerce	Total
National Income (billion yuan)	98.6	148.7	12.5	11.8	29.4	301.0
Non-state share of each industry (%)	97.0	22.4	36.3	24.5	45.4	149.7
Value produced by non-state sector (billion yuan)	95.6	33.3	4.5	2.9	13.4	
Overall non-state share of national income (%)						49.7

Notes

1. Some argue that to measure what has been called embodied technical progress, it is better to measure capital stock at current prices rather than at constant prices, because, in their view, the price variable captures the embodied technical change. See David Lim, *Explaining Economic Growth*, p. 59.

2. No data on provincial deflators of capital goods are available. In the event that they are somewhat higher than the GDP deflators, the estimated stocks of capital would be lower.

3. For a discussion of this method, see Angus Maddison, *Economic Progress and Policy in Developing Countries*, pp. 38–40.

4. The method was pioneered by Dr. Goldsmith in the United States. See his "A Perpetual Inventory of National Wealth."

5. Note that the capital variable used in this study is measured in the conventional way, without taking into account the actual level of capital utilization or adjusting for improvements in its quality. Ideally, the quantity of capital input should be measured by the amount of machine hours used in the production process, and the quality of capital input measured by the successive vintages of capital. However, available data allow us to do neither. Because improvements in the quality of capital are not captured, its contribution to output growth might more or less be understated.

Appendix 5.3

Estimating Factor Shares

Two methods can be used to obtain the values of the elasticities of output with respect to each of the three factor inputs (α, β, and γ). One approach is based on the assumptions of perfect competition and of constant returns to scale. Since, under these conditions, factors of production are supposed to be paid at the value of their marginal products, it is believed that the shares of total income paid to the factors are equal to their respective output elasticities. There are two problems with applying this method to our study. First, no reliable measures of factor income shares are available in China. Second, even if such data were available, perfect competition, the assumption behind the approach, does not exist, and thus the results obtained would still be unreliable.

An alternative approach is to estimate the output elasticities statistically without assuming either factor market equilibrium or constant returns to scale. With fewer restrictions on the form of the production function, the advantage of this approach is that the values for α, β, and γ are no longer presumed and the estimate for the residual A will not be biased.[1] However, the use of parametric estimates is subject to certain technical difficulties.[2] In particular, some of the right-hand-side variables in such a regression (e.g., K, L, and H) may be correlated with the residual term A (for example, we expect the capital stock to increase in response to improvements in productivity).[3] As a result, the coefficients (output elasticities) obtained by such multiple-regression analysis may not be very reliable.

In light of the above-mentioned difficulties, we use fixed-output elasticities in this study. Under the assumption of constant returns to scale, the key of this exercise is to determine the level of the capital elasticity. Since the sum of α, β, and γ is supposed to be 1, once the capital elasticity (α) is known, it is not difficult to come up with the estimates of β and γ.

Our estimate of China's capital elasticity is based on the following findings of the existing literature on growth accounting:

1. An economy's capital elasticity appears to be fairly stable over time.[4]
2. Over a long period of economic development, as the capital/labor ratio rises, capital elasticity tends to decline.[5]
3. Due to relative factor scarcities, capital elasticity tends to be higher in developing economies than in developed economies.
4. Capital elasticities in industrial economies range from 0.25 to 0.4 but generally cluster around 0.3.[6]
5. For developing economies, variations in capital elasticity are much greater, ranging from 0.3 to 0.65, and generally in excess of 0.4.[7] For this reason, several studies suggest that the partial elasticity of output with respect to capital should be set around 0.5.[8]
6. In the case of China, estimates of the capital share vary from 0.4 to 0.6.[9]

For these reasons, we give capital a weight of 0.45 in the case of China, which is slightly higher than the World Bank's estimate of 0.40.[10] Furthermore, the output elasticities of labor and human capital are assumed to be 0.30 and 0.25, respectively.[11]

Notes

1. If constant returns to scale are assumed or the sum of α, β and γ is assumed to be equal to 1, the production function estimated will allow increasing or decreasing returns to scale only to be captured by A, the index for technology. "This means that the measured contribution of technical progress to output growth will be overstated if there are increasing returns and understated if there are decreasing returns." David Lim, *Explaining Economic Growth*, pp. 51–57.

2. Lim, *Explaining Economic Growth*, pp. 51–57; Hayami, *Development Economics*, pp. 117–19.

3. World Bank, *China 2020*, pp. 106–8.

4. Susan M. Collins and Barry P. Bosworth, "Economic Growth in East Asia," pp. 154–56.

5. For instance, Kuznets found that the average capital elasticity in nine Western countries fell from about 0.45 to about 0.25 during the period between the mid-nineteenth century and the mid-twentieth century. See Simon Kuznets, *Economic Growth of Nations*, p. 71. Similarly, Kendrick found that the average capital share for the United States from 1890 to 1990 ranged from 0.416 in 1890–1915 to 0.306 in 1981–1990. See John W. Kendrick, "How Much Does Capital Explain?" p. 136.

6. World Bank, *World Development Report, 1991*, p. 43; Jong-il Kim and Lawrence J. Lau, "The Sources of Economic Growth of the East Asian Newly Industrialized Countries," pp. 235–71; Angus Maddison, "Growth and Slowdown in Advanced Capitalist Economies," pp. 649–98; Steven A. Englander and Andrew Gurney, "OECD Productivity Growth: Medium-Term Trends," pp. 111–29; Kendrick, "How Much Does Capital Explain?" p. 136.

7. World Bank, *World Development Report, 1991*; Kim and Lau, "Sources of Economic Growth." The capital share has been found to be especially high in Latin America. For instance, Argentina, Brazil, Chile, and Venezuela have a capital income share around 0.5, while Colombia, Mexico, and Peru have a value around 0.65. See Victor J. Elias, *Sources of Growth*, p. 36. The capital elasticities are also relatively high among East Asian NIEs (Hong Kong, Taiwan, South Korea, and Singapore). See Alwyn Young, "The Tyranny of Numbers," pp. 641–79; and Lawrence J. Lau, "Sources of Long-Term Economic Growth," pp. 63–91.

8. Maddison, *Economic Progress and Policy in Developing Countries*, pp. 51–52; Dirk Pilat, *The Economics of Rapid Growth*, p. 60.

9. Gregory C. Chow, "Capital Formation and Economic Growth in China," pp. 809–42; Wing Thye Woo, "Chinese Economic Growth"; Li Jingwen, "Productivity and China's Economic Growth," pp. 337–50; Eduardo Borensztein and Han Hong, "Regional Growth Differentials in Post-Reform China"; World Bank, *The Chinese Economy*, pp. 68–70; idem, *China 2020*, pp. 106–8.

10. World Bank, *China 2020*, pp. 106–8. We are fully aware that the contribution of physical capital is somehow sensitive to the choice of its output elasticity: either overestimation or underestimation of the capital share would create serious distortions in the estimation not only of capital's contribution to output growth but also of the other two factors' contributions.

11. We assume here that all provinces have the same aggregate production function. Considering that the capital share tends to be higher in less-developed economies than in more-developed economies, application of the same set of production elasticities to the analysis of economies in different stages of development may not be appropriate. Hayami, *Development Economics*, p. 131.

Bibliography

Abramovitz, Moses. "Catching Up, Forging Ahead, and Falling Behind." *Journal of Economic History* 46 (June 1986): 385–406.

———. "The Search for the Sources of Growth: Areas of Ignorance, Old and New." *Journal of Economic History* 53 (June 1993): 217–43.

Aguignier, P. "Regional Disparities Since 1978." In *Transforming China's Economy in the Eighties,* ed. Stephan Feuchtwang, Athar Hussain and Thierry Pairault, vol. I. Boulder: Westview Press, 1988.

Alesina, Alberto, and Dani Rodrik. "Distribution, Political Conflict, and Economic Growth." In *Political Economy, Growth, and Business Cycles,* ed. Alex Cukierman, Zvi Hercowitz, and Leonardo Leiderman, pp. 23–50. Cambridge: MIT Press, 1992.

———, and ———. "Distributive Politics and Economic Growth." *Quarterly Journal of Economics* 109 (1994): 465–90.

———, and Roberto Perotti. *Income Distribution, Political Instability, and Investment.* NBER Working Paper 4486. Cambridge, MA: National Bureau of Economic Research, 1993.

Arbetman, Marina, and Jacek Kugler, eds. *Political Capacity and Economic Behavior.* Boulder: Westview Press, 1997.

Armstrong, Harvey, and Jim Taylor. *Regional Economics and Policy,* 2d ed. New York: Harvester Wheatsheaf, 1993.

Baer, Werner. "Regional Inequality and Economic Growth in Brazil." *Economic Development and Cultural Change* 12, no. 3 (April 1964): 268–85.

Banerijee, Abhijit, and Andrew Newman. "Risk Bearing and the Theory of Income Distribution." *Review of Economic Studies* 58 (1991): 211–35.

Barro, Robert J. *Determinants of Economic Growth: A Cross-Country Empirical Study.* Cambridge: MIT Press, 1997.

———, and Jong-Wha Lee. "Sources of Economic Growth." *Carnegie-Rochester Conference Series on Public Policy,* June 1994, pp. 1–46.

———, and Xavier Sala-i-Martin. "Convergence across States and Regions." *Brookings Papers on Economic Activity,* no. 1 (1991): 107–58.

————, and Xavier Sala-i-Martin. *Economic Growth.* New York: McGraw-Hill, 1995.

————, and Xavier Sala-i-Martin. "Regional Growth and Migration: A Japan-United States Comparison." *Journal of the Japanese and International Economies* 6 (1992): 312–46.

Baumol, William J. "Productivity Growth, Convergence, and Welfare: What the Long-Run Data Show." *American Economic Review* 76 (1986): 1072–85.

————, and Edward N. Wolff. "Productivity, Growth, Convergence, and Welfare: Reply." *American Economic Review* 78 (December 1988): 1155–59.

Berry, B. J. L. "Hierarchical Diffusion: The Basis of Development Filtering and Spread in a System of Growth Center." In *Growth Centers in Regional Economic Development,* ed. Niles M. Hansen. New York: Free Press, 1974.

Bhat, L. S. et al., eds. *Regional Inequalities in India: An Inter-State and Intra-State Analysis.* New Delhi: Aruna Printing Press, 1982.

Blades, Derek W. "Comparing Capital Stocks." In Szirmai, Van Ark, and Pilat, eds., *Explaining Economic Growth.*

Bo Yibo. *Reminiscences of Major Policy Decisions and Events,* vol. 1. Beijing: Central Party School Press, 1991.

Boadway, Robin W. "The Role of Government in a Market Economy." In *Fundamentals of the Economic Role of Government,* ed. Warren J. Samuels, pp. 25–31. New York: Greenwood Press, 1989.

Boltho, Andrea. "European and United States Regional Differentials: A Note." *Oxford Review of Economic Policy* 2 (1989): 105–15.

Bookman, Milica Zarkovic. *The Political Economy of Discontinuous Development: Regional Disparities and Inter-Regional Conflict.* New York: Praeger, 1991.

Booth, Douglas E. *Regional Long Waves, Uneven Growth, and the Cooperative Alternative.* New York: Praeger, 1987.

Borensztein, Eduardo, and Han Hong. "Regional Growth Differentials in Post-Reform China: A Preliminary Assessment." Manuscript, IMF, 1995.

————, and Jonathan D. Ostry. "Accounting for China's Growth Performance." *American Economic Review* 86, no. 2 (1996): 225–27.

————, Jong-Wha Lee, and Jose De Gregorio. "How Does Foreign Direct Investment Affect Economic Growth?" NBER Working Paper, no. 5057. Cambridge: National Bureau of Economic Research, 1993.

Borjas, George J. *Friends or Strangers: The Impact of Immigrants on the U.S. Economy.* New York: Basic Books, 1990.

Borts, George H. "The Equalization of Returns and Regional Economic Growth." *American Economic Review* 50, no. 3 (June 1960): 319–47.

————, and J. L. Stein. *Economic Growth in a Free Market.* New York: Columbia University Press, 1964.

Bowen, Alex, and Ken Mayhew, eds. *Reducing Regional Inequalities.* London: Kogan Page, 1991.

Bowles, Samuel, and Herbert Gintis. "Efficient Redistribution: New Rules for Markets, States, and Communities." *Politics and Society* 24, no. 4 (December 1996): 307–42.

Broadman, Harry G., and Xiaolun Sun. "The Distribution of Foreign Direct Investment in China." *Policy Research Working Paper,* no. 1720. Washington, DC: World Bank, 1997.

Brown, Arthur J., and E. M. Burrows. *Regional Economic Problems: Comparative Experiences of Some Market Economies.* London: George Allen & Unwin, 1977.

Cai, Fang. "An Economic Analysis of Labor Migration and Mobility in China." *Chinese Social Science Quarterly* 14 (Spring 1996): 120–35.

Chang, Roberto. "Income Inequality and Economic Growth: Evidence and Recent Theories." *Economic Review* (Federal Reserve Bank of Atlanta) 79 (July/August 1994): 1–10.

Chen Huai. "Zhongguo 80 niandai yilai quyu jingji fazhan zhanlue de huigu yu qianzhan" [China's Regional Development Strategies in Retrospect and Prospects]. *Jingji gongzuozhe xuexi ziliao* [Research Materials for Economists], no. 52 (1996): 3–12.

Chen, Kuan, Gary H. Jefferson, Thomas G. Rawski, Hongchang Wang, and Yuxin Zheng. "New Estimates of Fixed Investment and Capital Stock for Chinese State Industry." *China Quarterly,* no. 114 (June 1988): 243–66.

Chen Wen et al. "Zhongguo jingji diqu chayi de tedian jiqi yanbian qushi" [The Characteristics and Evolution of China's Regional Economic Disparities]. *Jingji dili* [Economic Geography] 13, no. 1 (1993): 16–21.

Chenery, Hollis B. "Development Policies for Southern Italy." *Quarterly Journal of Economics* 76 (1962): 515–47.

———. *Structural Change and Development Policy.* Washington DC: World Bank, 1979.

Cheng, Tiejun, and Mark Selden. "The Origins and Social Consequences of China's *Hukou* System." *China Quarterly,* no. 139 (Sept 1994): 644–68.

Chow, Gregory C. "Capital Formation and Economic Growth in China." *Quarterly Journal of Economics* 108 (August 1993): 809–42.

Clarke, George R. G. "More Evidence on Income Distribution and Growth." *Journal of Development Economics* 47 (1995): 403–27.

Collins, Susan M., and Barry P. Bosworth. "Economic Growth in East Asia: Accumulation versus Assimilation." *Brookings Papers on Economic Activity,* no. 2 (1996): 135–91, 198–203.

Dai Leping. "Dui woguo dongzhongxibu quyu jingji fazhan wenti de sikao" [Reflections on Regional Development Patterns of East, Central, and West China]. *Jingji yanjiu cankao* [Reference for Economic Research], no. 745 (September 1995): 20–28.

De Long, J. Bradford, and Lawrence H. Summers. "Equipment Investment and Economic Growth." *Quarterly Journal of Economics* 106 (May 1991): 445–502.

Deng Xiaoping. *Selected Works of Deng Xiaoping,* vol. 3. Beijing: People's Press, 1993.

Denison, Edward F. *The Sources of Economic Growth in the United States and the Alternatives Before Us.* New York: Committee for Economic Development, 1962.

———. *Trends in American Economic Growth, 1929–1982.* Washington, DC: Brookings Institution, 1985.

———. *Why Growth Rates Differ.* Washington, DC: Brookings Institution, 1967.

Denny, David. "Regional Economic Differences During the Decade of Reform." In Congress of the United States, Joint Economic Committee, *Dilemmas in the 1990s: The Problems of Reforms: Modernization and Interdependence.* Washington, DC: Government Printing Office, 1991.

Dholakia, Bakul H. *The Sources of Economic Growth in India.* Baroda: Good Companions, 1974.

Document Research Office of the CPC Central Committee. *Selected Important Documents Since the 13th Party Congress,* vol. 2. Beijing: People's Press, 1991.

Domar, Evsey. "Expansion and Employment." *American Economic Review* 37 (1947): 34–55.

Donnithorne, Audrey. "China's Cellular Economy: Some Economic Trends since the Cultural Revolution." *China Quarterly,* no. 52 (1972): 605–19.

Dowrick, Steve, and Duc-Tho Nguyen. "OECD Comparative Economic Growth 1950–85: Catch-Up and Convergence." *American Economic Review* 79, no. 5 (December 1989): 1010–30.

Dubravcic, Dinko. "Economic Causes and Political Context of the Dissolution of a Multinational Federal State: The Case of Yugoslavia." *Communist Economies & Economic Transformation* 5, no. 3 (1993): 259–72.

Dunford, Mick. "Regional Disparities in the European Community: Evidence from the REGIO Databank." *Regional Studies* 27, no. 8 (1995): 727–43.

Easterlin, R. A. "Long Term Regional Income Changes: Some Suggested Factors." *Papers and Proceedings of the Regional Science Association* 4 (1958): 313–25.

Easterly, William, and Sergio Rebelo. "Fiscal Policy and Economic Growth: An Empirical Investigation." *Journal of Monetary Economics* 32, no. 3 (December 1993): 417–58.

Elias, Victor J. *Sources of Growth: A Study of Seven Latin American Economies.* San Francisco: ICS Press, 1992.

Endres, W. T. "Regional Disparities in Industrial Growth in Brazil." *Economic Geography* 56 (1980): 300–310.

Englander, Steven A., and Andrew Gurney. "OECD Productivity Growth: Medium-Term Trends." *OECD Economic Studies,* no. 22 (1994): 111–29.

Ernste, Huib, and Verena Meier, eds. *Regional Development and Contemporary Response: Extending Flexible Specialization.* London: Belhaven Press, 1992.

Estall, R. C. "Economic Geography and Regional Geography." *Geography* 62 (1977): 297–310.

Falaris, E.M. "The Determinants of Internal Migration in Peru: Economic Analysis." *Economic Development and Cultural Change* 27 (1979): 231–54.

Falkenheim, V. C. "Spatial Inequality in China's Modernization Program: Some Political-Administrative Determinants." In *Development and Distribution in China,* ed. C. K. Leung and C. H. Chai. Hong Kong: University of Hong Kong Press, 1985.

Fan, C. Cindy. "Regional Impacts of Foreign Trade in China, 1984–1989." *Growth and Change,* Spring 1992, pp. 129–59.

Fields, Gary S. *Poverty, Inequality, and Development.* Cambridge: Cambridge University Press, 1980.

————, and T. P. Schultz. "Regional Inequality and Other Sources of Income Variation in Colombia." *Economic Development and Cultural Change* 28 (1980): 447–68.

Findlay, Ronald. "Relative Backwardness, Direct Foreign Investment, and the Transfer of Technology: A Simple Dynamic Model." *Quarterly Journal of Economics* 92 (1978): 1–16.

Fischer, Claude S., Michael Hout, Martin Sanchez Jankowski, Samuel R. Lucas, Ann Swidler, and Kim Voss. *Inequality by Design: Cracking the Bell Curve Myth.* Princeton: Princeton University Press, 1996.

Ginneken, Wouter V. *Rural and Urban Income Inequalities in Indonesia, Mexico, Pakistan, Tanzania and Tunisia.* Geneva: ILO Publication, 1976.

Goldsmith, Raymond W. "A Perpetual Inventory of National Wealth." *Studies in Income and Wealth* 14. New York: National Bureau of Economic Research, 1951.

Goodman, David S. G., and Gerald Segal, eds. *China Deconstructs: Politics, Trade and Regionalism.* London: Routledge, 1994.

Gore, Charles G. *Regions in Question: Space Development Theory and Regional Policy.* London: Methuen, 1984.

Gradus, Yehuda. "The Role of Politics in Regional Inequality: The Israeli Case." *Annals of the Association of American Geographers* 73, no. 3 (1983): 388–403.

Griffin, Keith, and Zhao Renwei, eds. *The Distribution of Income in China.* New York: St. Martin's Press, 1993.

Grossman, Gene, and Elhanan Helpman. *Innovation and Growth in the Global Economy.* Cambridge: MIT Press, 1991.

Guo Kesha, and Li Haijian. "Zhongguo diqu duiwai kaifang geju fenxi" [An Analysis of China's Opening Patterns]. *Jingji gongzuozhe xuexi ziliao* [Research Materials for Economists], no. 25 (1995): 20–24.

Gupta, Dipak. *The Economics of Political Violence.* New York: Praeger, 1990.

Hadjimichalis, Costis. *Uneven Development and Regionalism: State, Territory and Class in Southern Europe.* London: Croom Helm, 1987.

Haggett, Peter. *Locational Analysis in Human Geography.* London: Edward Arnold, 1965.

Hansen, Niles M. "An Evaluation of Growth-Centre Theory and Practice." *Environment and Planning* 7 (1975).

Haq, Mahbub ul. *Reflections on Human Development.* New York: Oxford University Press, 1995.

Harrod, Roy F. *Towards a Dynamic Economics.* London: Macmillan, 1948.

Hayami, Yujiro. *Development Economics: From the Poverty to the Wealth of Nations.* Oxford: Oxford University Press, 1997.

He Weixian. "Woguo xibu diqu shixian liangge zhuanbian de nandian yu duice" [Difficulties in Dual Transition in West China and Policy Solution]. *Jingji gaige yu fazhan* [Economic Reform and Development], no. 7 (1996): 51–54.

Hechter, Michael. *Internal Colonialism.* Berkeley: University of California Press, 1975.

Hibbs, Douglas. *Mass Political Violence: A Cross-Sectional Analysis.* New York: John Wiley, 1973.

Hicks, John R. "The Foundations of Welfare Economics." *Economic Journal* 49 (1939): 696–712.

———. *The Theory of Wages.* London: Macmillan, 1932.

Higgins, Benjamin. "Economic Development and Regional Disparities: A Comparative Study of Four Federations." In *Regional Disparities and Economic*

Development, ed. Russell L. Mathews. Canberra: Australian National University, 1981.

————, and Donald J. Savoie, eds. *Regional Economic Development: Essays in Honor of Francois Perroux.* Boston: Unwin Hyman, 1988.

Hill, Hal, ed. *Unity and Diversity: Regional Economic Development in Indonesia Since 1970.* Singapore: Oxford University Press, 1989.

Hirschman, Albert O. *The Strategy of Economic Development.* New Haven: Yale University Press, 1958.

Holland, Stuart. *Capital versus the Region.* London: Macmillan, 1976.

————. *The Regional Problem.* London: Macmillan, 1976.

Hou Yongzhi, and Hu Changshun. "Dongzhongxibu de xietiao fazhan" [Coordinated Development for East, Central, and West China]. *Jingji gongzuozhe xuexi ziliao* [Research Materials for Economists], no. 73 (1995): 13–29.

Howell, Jude. *China Opens Its Doors: The Politics of Economic Transition.* Boulder: Lynne Rienner, 1993.

Hu Angang, Shaoguang Wang, and Xiaoguang Kang. *Zhongguo diqu chaju baogao* [Regional Disparities in China]. Shenyang: Liaoning People's Press, 1995.

Hu Dayuan. "Zhuangui jingji zhong de diqu chaju" [Regional Disparities in a Transition Economy]. *Zhanlue yu guanli* [Strategy and Management], no. 1 (1998): 35–41.

Huang, Yasheng. *Inflation and Investment Controls in China: The Political Economy of Central-Local Relations During the Reform Era.* New York: Cambridge University Press, 1996.

————. "Why China Will Not Collapse." *Foreign Policy,* no. 99 (Summer 1995): 54–68.

Institute of Japan Studies and Chinese Academy of Social Sciences. *Problems, Solutions, and Mechanisms: Experience and Lessons of Japan's Economic Development.* Beijing: Economic Science Press, 1994.

Isard, Walter. *Methods of Regional Analysis: An Introduction to Regional Science.* Cambridge: MIT Press, 1960.

Jia, Liqun, and Clem Tisdell. "Resource Redistribution and Regional Income Inequality in China." *Asian Economies* 24, no. 2 (1995): 48–72.

Jian, Tianlun. "Inequality in Regional Economic Development and Tax Reforms in China." Unpublished manuscript, August 1996.

————, Jeffrey D. Sachs, and Andrew M. Warner. "Trends in Regional Inequality in China." *China Economic Review* 7, no. 1 (1996): 1–21.

Kaldor, Nicholas. "Welfare Propositions of Economics and Interpersonal Comparisons of Utility." *Economic Journal* 49 (1939).

Kato, Hiroyuki. "Regional Development in the Reform Period." In *Economic Reform and Internationalization: China and the Pacific Region,* ed. Ross Garnaut and Liu Guoguang. Sydney: Allen & Unwin, 1992.

Keidel, Albert. "China: Regional Disparities." Unpublished paper, World Bank, June 30, 1995.

Kendrick, John W. "How Much Does Capital Explain?" In Szirmai, Van Ark, and Pilat, eds., *Explaining Economic Growth.*

Keynes, John M. *The General Theory of Employment, Interest and Money.* New York: Harcourt, Brace, 1936.

Khan, Azizur Rahman, and Carl Riskin. "Income and Inequality in China: Composition, Distribution and Growth of Household Income, 1988 to 1995." *China Quarterly,* no. 154 (June 1998): 221–53.

Khan, Azizur Rahman, Keith Griffin, Carl Riskin, and Zhao Renwei. "Household Income and Its Distribution in China." *China Quarterly,* no. 132 (December 1992): 1029–61.

Kim, Jong-il, and Lawrence J. Lau. "The Sources of Economic Growth of the East Asian Newly Industrialized Countries." *Journal of the Japanese and International Economies* 8, no. 3 (September 1994): 235–71.

Kim, Kyung-hwan, and Edwin S. Mills. "Urbanization and Regional Development in Korea." In *Korean Economic Development,* ed. Jene K. Kwon. New York: Greenwood Press, 1990.

Kleinberg, Robert. *China's "Opening" to the Outside World: The Experiment with Foreign Capitalism.* Boulder: Westview Press, 1990.

Kleinman, Anne Simone. "Across China: Regional Pluralism and Developmental Imbalance." Unpublished paper, Center for Strategic and International Studies, Washington, DC, 1995.

Krugman, Paul. *Geography and Trade.* Cambridge: MIT Press, 1991.

Kugler, Jacek, and Marina Arbetman. "Relative Political Capacity: Political Extraction and Political Reach." In Arbetman and Kugler, eds. *Political Capacity and Economic Behavior,* pp. 11–45.

Kuznets, Simon. "Economic Growth and Income Equality." *American Economic Review,* 45, no. 1 (1955): 1–28.

———. *Economic Growth of Nations: Total Output and Production Structure.* Cambridge: Harvard University Press, 1971.

———. "Modern Economic Growth: Findings and Reflections." *American Economic Review* 63, no. 3 (June 1973): 247–58.

———. "Modern Economic Growth and the Less Developed Countries." Paper read at conference on Experiences and Lessons of Economic Development in Taiwan. Taipei, Institute of Economics, Academia Sinica, 1981.

———, A. R. Miller, and R. A. Easterlin. *Population Redistribution and Economic Growth, United States, 1870–1950.* Philadelphia: American Philosophical Society, 1960.

La Croix, Sumner J., and Richard F. Garbaccio. "Convergence in Income and Consumption in China During the Maoist and Reform Regimes." Unpublished manuscript, University of Hawaii, 1996.

Lakshmanan, T. R., and I.H. Chang. "Regional Disparities in China." *International Regional Science Review* 11, no. 1 (1991): 97–103.

Land Planning Institute of the State Planning Commission. "Study of the Coordinated Development of the Regional Economies in China." *Materials for Studying Land Planning and Coordinated Regional Economic Development,* no. 68 (December 1994).

Lardy, Nicholas R. "Consumption and Living Standards in China: 1978–1983." *China Quarterly,* no. 100 (December 1984): 849–65.

———. *Economic Growth and Distribution in China.* Cambridge: Cambridge University Press, 1978.

———. "Regional Growth and Income Distribution in China." In *China's Development Experience in Comparative Perspective,* ed. Robert F. Dernberger. Cambridge: Harvard University Press, 1980.

Lasuen, J. R. "Regional Income Inequalities and the Problem of Growth in Spain." *Regional Science Association,* 8 (1962): 69–88.

Lau, Lawrence J. "The Sources of Long-Term Economic Growth: Observations from the Experience of Developed and Developing Countries." In *The Mosaic of Economic Growth,* ed. Ralph Landau, Timothy Taylor, and Gavin Wright, pp. 63–91. Stanford: Stanford University Press, 1996.

Levi, Margaret. *Of Rule and Revenue.* Berkeley: University of California Press, 1988.

Levine, Ross, and David Renelt. "A Sensitivity Analysis of Cross-Country Growth Regression." *American Economic Review* 82, no. 4 (1992): 942–63.

Lewis, Arthur. "Economic Development with Unlimited Supplies of Labor." *Manchester School* 22 (1958): 131–91.

———. *The Theory of Economic Growth.* London: Allen & Unwin, 1955.

Li Boxi, ed. *Diqu zhengce yu xietiao fazhan* [Regional Policy and Coordinated Development]. Beijing: Zhongguo caizheng jingji chubanshe [China Financial Economics Press], 1995.

Li, Jingwen. "Productivity and China's Economic Growth." *Economic Studies Quarterly* 43, no. 2 (1992): 337–50.

Li Xiangqi. "Guanyu jiakuai xibu gaige yu fazhan ruogan wenti de sikao" [Reflections on How to Speed Up Reform and Development in West China]. *Jingji gongzuozhe xuexi ziliao* [Research Materials for Economists], no. 65 (1995): 37–44.

Li Zhou and Cai Fang. "Shouru chaju lada: nongcun fazhan bupingheng de shizheng fenxi yu zhanlue sikao" [Growing Income Gaps: An Empirical Analysis of Uneven Development of Rural China and Reflections on Strategy]. *Jingji gongzuozhe xuexi ziliao* [Research Materials for Economists], no. 42 (1995): 14–16.

Lim, David. *Explaining Economic Growth: A New Analytical Framework.* Cheltenham, UK: Edward Elgar, 1996.

Lin Lin. "Dongxibu chaju kuoda wenti fenxi" [An Analysis of the Widening Gaps between East and West China]. *Jingji yanjiu* [Economic Studies], no. 7 (1996): 46–53.

Lin Yifu et al. *Zhongguo de qiji: fazhan zhanlue yu jingji gaige* [China's Miracle: Development Strategy and Economic Reform]. Shanghai: Shanghai People's Press, 1994.

Lipshitz, Gabriel. "Divergence or Convergence in Regional Inequality—Consumption Variables versus Policy Variables: The Israeli Case." *Geografiska Annaler* 68 (1986): 13–20.

Liu Suinian, and Wu Qungan. *China's Socialist Economy: An Outline History (1949–1984).* Beijing: Beijing Review, 1986.

Lo, Chor Pang. "The Geography of Rural Regional Inequality in Mainland China." *Transactions of Institute of British Geographers* 15, no. 4 (1990): 446–86.

———. "The Pattern of Urban Settlements in the Zhujiang Delta, South China: A Spatial Analysis." In Veeck, ed. *The Uneven Landscape,* pp. 171–205.

Lou Jiwei, and Li Keping. "Guanyu jianli woguo caizheng zhuanyi zhifu xin zhidu de ruogan wenti" [Issues Concerning the Construction of a New Fiscal Transfer System in China]. *Jingji gaige yu fazhan* [Economic Reform and Development], no. 10 (1995): 68–72.

Lu Dadao. *Quyu fazhan jiqi kongjian jiegou* [Regional Development and Spatial Structure]. Beijing: Kexue chubanshe [Science Press], 1995.

——— et al. *Zhongguo gongye buju de lilun yu shijian* [The Theory and Practice of China's Industrial Distribution]. Beijing: Science Press, 1990.

Lucas, Robert E. "On the Mechanics of Economic Development." *Journal of Monetary Economics* 22 (1988): 3–42.

Lyons, Thomas P. "Interprovincial Disparities in China: Output and Consumption, 1952–1987." *Economic Development and Cultural Change* 39 (1991): 471–506.

Ma, Guonan. "Income Distribution in the 1980s." In *China's Quiet Revolution: New Interactions Between State and Society*, ed. David S.G. Goodman and Beverley Hooper. New York: St. Martin's Press, 1994.

Ma, Jun, and Yong Li. "China's Regional Economic Policy: Effects and Alternatives." *Asian Economic Journal* 8, no. 1 (1994): 39–58.

McKinley, Terry. *The Distribution of Wealth in Rural China*. Armonk, NY: M.E. Sharpe, 1996.

Maddison, Angus. *Economic Progress and Policy in Developing Countries*. New York: Norton, 1970.

———. "Growth and Slowdown in Advanced Capitalist Economies: Techniques of Quantitative Assessment." *Journal of Economic Literature* 25, no. 2 (1987): 649–98.

Malecki, Edward J. "Technological Innovation and Paths to Regional Economic Growth." In *Growth Policy in An Age of High Technology*, ed. J. Schmandt and R. W. Wilson. London: Unwin Hyman, 1990.

———. *Technology and Economic Development*. Harlow: Longman, 1991.

———. "Technology and Regional Development: A Survey." *International Regional Science Review* 8, no. 2 (1983): 89–125.

Mao Huihui. "Suoxiao dongxi chaju bixu jiada zhongxibu de touru lidu" [To Narrow the Gaps between East and West China, It Is Essential to Increase Investment in Central and West China]. *Jingji yu guanli yanjiu* [Studies in Economics and Management], no. 2 (1996): 6–8.

Mao Zedong. *Selected Works,* vol. 5. Beijing: People's Press, 1977.

Marglin, Stephen, and Juliet B. Schor, eds. *The Golden Age of Capitalism: Reinterpreting the Postwar Experience.* Oxford: Clarendon Press, 1990.

Mathews, R. L., ed. *Regional Disparities and Economic Development.* Canberra: Centre for Research on Federal Financial Relations, 1981.

Mera, Koichi. *Income Distribution and Regional Development.* Tokyo: University of Tokyo Press, 1975.

Milanovic, Branko. "Patterns of Regional Growth in Yugoslavia, 1952–83." *Journal of Development Economics* 25 (1987): 1–19.

Ministry of Finance. *Zhongguo caizheng tongji* [China Financial Statistics, 1950–1985]. Beijing: China Financial Economics Press, 1987.

Moudoud, Ezzeddine. *Modernization: The State and Regional Disparity in Developing Countries: Tunisia in Historical Perspective, 1881–1982.* Boulder: Westview Press, 1989.

Myrdal, Gunnar. *Economic Theory and Under-Developed Regions.* London: Gerald Duckworth, 1957.

Nair, K. R. G. "Inter-State Income Differentials in India, 1970–71 to 1979–80." In

Regional Structure of Development and Growth in India, ed. G. P. Mishra. New Delhi: Ashish Publishing House, 1985.

Naughton, Barry. "The Third Front: Defense Industrialization in the Chinese Interior." *China Quarterly,* no. 115 (1988): 351–86.

Nee, Victor, and Raymond V. Liedka. "Markets and Inequality in the Transition from State Socialism." In *Inequality, Democracy, and Economic Development,* ed. Manus I. Midlarsky, pp. 204–24. Cambridge: Cambridge University Press, 1997.

Nolan, Peter, and John Sender. "Death Rates, Life Expectancy and China's Economic Reforms: A Critique of A. K. Sen." *World Development* 20, no. 9 (1992): 1279–1303.

Ohlin, Bertil G. *Interregional and International Trade.* Cambridge: Harvard University Press, 1933.

Okun, Arthur M. *Equality and Efficiency: The Big Trade-off.* Washington, DC: Brookings Institution, 1975.

Ottolenghi, Daniel, and Alfred Steinherr. "Yugoslavia: Was It a Winner's Curse?" *Economics of Transition* 1, no. 2 (1993).

Peng, Yusheng. "Geographical Variations in China's Rural Industrial Output and Employment." Unpublished manuscript. Chinese University of Hong Kong, October 1996.

Perloff, Harvey S., E. S. Dunn, Jr., E. E. Lampard, and R. F. Muth. *Regions, Resources and Economic Growth.* Baltimore: Johns Hopkins University Press, 1960.

Perotti, Roberto. "Growth, Income Distribution, and Democracy: What the Data Say." *Journal of Economic Growth* 1 (June 1996): 149–87.

Persson, Torsten, and Guido Tabellini. "Is Inequality Harmful for Growth?" *American Economic Review* 84 (1994): 600–21.

Pilat, Dirk. *The Economics of Rapid Growth: The Experience of Japan and Korea.* Brookfield, VT: Edward Elgar, 1994.

Plestina, Dijana. *Regional Development in Communist Yugoslavia: Success, Failure and Consequences.* Boulder: Westview Press, 1992.

Prime, Penelope B. "China's Economic Reforms in Regional Perspective." In Veeck, ed., *The Uneven Landscape,* pp. 9–27.

Pritchett, Lant. "Divergence, Big Time." *Journal of Economic Perspectives* 11, no. 3 (1997): 3–17.

Prud'homme, Remy. "On the Dangers of Decentralization." *Policy Research Working Paper,* no. 1252. Washington, DC: World Bank, 1994.

Qi Jingmei. "Diqu guding zichan tongji zhuangkuang de fenxi ji 1997 nian zhanwang" [The Patterns of Regional Fixed Investment and the Forecast for 1997]. *Jingji gongzuozhe xuexi ziliao* [Research Materials for Economists], no. 13 (1997): 3–14.

Rae, Douglas. *Equalities.* Cambridge: Harvard University Press, 1981.

Rawski, Thomas. "The Simple Arithmetic Of Chinese Income Distribution." *Keizai Kenkyu* 33, no. 1 (1984): 21–36.

Richardson, Harry W. *Regional and Urban Economics.* Harmondsworth: Penguin, 1978.

———. *Regional Economics.* Urbana: University of Illinois Press, 1979.

———. *Regional Growth Theory.* New York: John Wiley, 1973.

Riskin, Carl. "Chinese Rural Poverty: Marginalized or Dispersed?" *American Economic Association Papers and Proceedings,* May 1994, pp. 281–84.

Romer, Paul M. "Endogenous Technological Change." *Journal of Political Economy* 98 (1990): 71–102.

———. "Increasing Returns and Long-Run Growth." *Journal of Political Economy* 94, no. 5 (October 1986): 1002–37.

———. "The Origins of Endogenous Growth." *Journal of Economic Perspectives* 8, no. 1 (1994): 3–22.

Rostow, W. W. *The Stages of Economic Growth.* Cambridge: Cambridge University Press, 1960.

Rousseau, Mark O., and Raphael Zariski. *Regionalism and Regional Devolution in Comparative Perspective.* New York: Praeger, 1987.

Rozelle, Scott. "Rural Industrialization and Increasing Inequality: Emerging Patterns in China's Reforming Economy." *Journal of Comparative Economics* 19, no. 4 (December 1994): 300–24.

———. "Stagnation Without Equity: Patterns of Growth and Inequality in China's Rural Economy." *China Journal,* no. 35 (January 1996): 63–92.

Savoie, Donald J. *Regional Economic Development: Canada's Search for Solutions,* 2d ed. Toronto: University of Toronto Press, 1992.

Scott, Maurice F. *A New View of Economic Growth.* Oxford: Oxford University Press, 1989.

Segal, Gerald. "China Changes Shape: Regionalism and Foreign Policy." *Adelphi Paper,* no. 287 (March 1994).

Selden, Mark. "China's Rural Welfare System: Crisis and Transformation." Paper read at the conference on PRC Political Economy: Prospects under the Ninth Five-Year Plan, National Cheng Kung University, Tainan, Taiwan, June 7–10, 1997.

Sen, Amartya. "Food and Freedom." *World Development* 17, no. 6 (1989): 769–81.

———. *On Ethics and Economics.* Oxford: Blackwell, 1987.

———. "Social Commitment and Democracy: The Demands of Equity and Financial Conservatism." In *Living as Equals,* ed. Paul Barker. Oxford: Oxford University Press, 1996.

Sheng Bin and Feng Lun, eds. *Report on Chinese National Conditions.* Shenyang: Liaoning People's Press, 1991.

Shleifer, Andrei. "Externalities and Economic Growth: Lessons from Recent Work." Background Paper 3 to *World Development Report, 1991.* Washington, DC: World Bank, 1990.

Skinner, G. William. "Differential Development in Lingnan." In *The Economic Transformation of South China,* ed. Thomas P. Lyons and Victor Nee. Ithaca: East Asia Program, Cornell University, 1994.

Smith, David. *North and South: Britain's Economic, Social and Political Divide.* London: Penguin Books, 1989.

Smith, David Marshall. *Geography, Inequality and Society.* Cambridge: Cambridge University Press, 1987.

Solow, Robert M. "A Contribution to the Theory of Economic Growth." *Quarterly Journal of Economics* 70 (1956): 65–94.

Song Xueming. "Zhongguo quyu jingji fazhan jiqi shoulianxing" [China's Economic Development and Convergence], *Jingji yanjiu* [Economic Studies], no. 9 (1996): 38–44.

State Council Development Research Center Group. *Zhongguo quyu xietiao fazhan zhanlue* [China's Strategy of Coordinated Regional Development]. Beijing: China Economics Press, 1994.

State Statistical Bureau. *A Statistical Survey of China 1996.* Beijing: China Statistical Press, 1996.

State Statistical Bureau. *Zhongguo tongji nianjian 1996 (ZGTJNJ)* [China Statistical Yearbook, 1996]. Beijing: Zhongguo tongji chubanshe [China Statistical Press], 1996.

Stiglitz, Joseph. "Distribution, Efficiency and Voice: Designing the Second Generation of Reforms." Unpublished manuscript, World Bank, 1998.

Stokey, Nancy L. "Comments on Barro and Lee." *Carnegie-Rochester Conference Series on Public Policy,* no. 40 (1994).

Szirmai, Adam, Bart Van Ark, and Dirk Pilat, eds. *Explaining Economic Growth: Essays in Honour of Angus Maddison.* New York: North-Holland, 1993.

Tan, Kok Chiang. "Small Towns and Regional Development in Wenzhou." In Veeck, ed., *The Uneven Landscape,* pp. 207–34.

Todaro, Michael P. *Economic Development,* 5th ed. New York: Longman, 1994.

Tsai, Diana Hwei-An. "Regional Inequality and Financial Decentralization in Mainland China." *Issues and Studies* 32, no. 5 (May 1996): 40–71.

Tsui, Kai-yuen. "China's Regional Inequality, 1952–1985." *Journal of Comparative Economics* 15 (March 1991): 1–21.

———. "Decomposition of China's Regional Inequalities." *Journal of Comparative Economics* 17 (1993): 600–627.

———. "The Measurement of China's Regional Inequalities: Some Issues and Problems." In *China's Regional Economic Development,* ed. Roger C.K. Chan, Tientung Hsueh, and Chiu-ming Luk, pp. 413–30. Hong Kong: Hong Kong Institute of Asia-Pacific Studies, Chinese University of Hong Kong, 1996.

United Nations Conference on Trade and Development. "Income Distribution, Capital Accumulation, and Growth." *Challenge* 41, no. 2 (March/April 1998): 61–80.

United Nations Development Programme (UNDP). *Human Development Report, 1994.* New York: Oxford University Press, 1994.

———. *Human Development Report, 1995.* New York: Oxford University Press, 1995.

———. *Human Development Report, 1996.* New York: Oxford University Press, 1996.

———. *Human Development Report, 1997.* New York: Oxford University Press, 1997.

Veeck, Gregory, ed. *The Uneven Landscape: Geographical Studies in Post-Reform China.* Baton Rouge: Louisiana State University, 1991.

Venieris, Yannis, and Dipak Gupta. "Income Distribution and Socio-Political Instability as Determinants of Savings: A Cross-Sectional Model." *Journal of Political Economy* 96 (1986): 873–83.

Walter-Busch, E. "Subjective and Objective Indicators of Regional Quality of Life in Switzerland." *Social Indicators Research* 12 (1983): 337–91.

Wang, Shaoguang. "China's 1994 Fiscal Reform: An Initial Assessment." *Asian Survey* 37, no. 9 (Sept. 1997): 801–17.

———. "Deng Xiaoping's Economic Reform and the Chinese Workers' Participation in the Protest Movement of 1989." *Research in Political Economy* 13 (1992).

———. *Fenquan de dixian* [The Limits of Decentralization]. Beijing: Planning Press, 1997.

———. "From a Pillar of Continuity to a Force for Change: Chinese Workers in the Protest Movement of 1989." In *China: The Crisis of 1989*, ed. Roger V. DesForges. Albany: State University of New York Press, 1992.

———. "The Institutional Roots of Central-Local Rivalry: China, 1980–1996." Paper read at the international conference on PRC Tomorrow. National Sun Yat-sen University, Kaohsiung, Taiwan, June 8–9, 1996.

———. "The Institutional Sources of Central-Local Rivalry: 1980–1993." Unpublished manuscript, Yale University, 1997.

———. "The Rise of the Regions: Fiscal Reform and the Decline of Central State Capacity in China." In *The Waning of the Communist State: Economic Origins of Political Decline in China and Hungary*, ed. Andrew G. Walder, pp. 87–113. Berkeley: University of California Press, 1995.

———. "The Roles of the State in the Transition to Market Economy." *Strategy and Management* (Beijing), no. 2 (May 1994).

———, and Angang Hu. *Zhongguo guojia nengli baogao* [A Report on China's State Capacity]. Shenyang: Liaoning People's Press, 1993; Hong Kong: Oxford University Press, 1994. English translation: "Strengthening Central Government's Leading Role Amid China's Transition to a Market Economy." *Chinese Economic Studies* 28, no. 3 (May/June 1995) and no. 4 (July/August 1995).

Wei Houkai. "Lun woguo quji shouru chayi de biandong geju" [The Pattern of Changes in the Regional Income Disparities in China], *Jingji yanjiu* [Economic Research], no. 4 (1992).

———. "Woguo diqi fazhan chaju de xingcheng, yingxiang jiqi xietiao tujing" [The Causes and Influences of Regional Disparities and How to Achieve Coordinated Development]. *Jingji yanjiu cankao* [References for Economic Research], no. 104 (1997): 2–13.

Wei Wei. *Zhongguo jingji fazhan zhong de quyu chayi yu quyu xietiao* [Regional Disparities and Regional Cooperation in China's Economic Development]. Hefei: Anhui People's Press, 1995.

West, Loraine A., and Christine P.W. Wong. "Fiscal Decentralization and Growing Regional Disparities in Rural China: Some Evidence in the Provision of Social Services." *Oxford Review of Economic Policy* 11, no. 4 (1995): 69–83.

Whyte, Martin King. "City Versus Countryside in China's Development." *Problems of Post-Communism* 43 (January/February 1996): 9–22.

Williamson, Jeffrey G. "Regional Inequality and the Process of National Development: A Description of the Patterns." *Economic Development and Cultural Change* 13, no. 4 (1965): 3–45.

Woo Tun-oy, and Hsueh Tien-tung. *Regional Disparities in the Sectoral Structure of Labor Productivity 1985–1989*. Hong Kong: Chinese University Press, 1992.

Woo, Wing Thye. "Chinese Economic Growth: Sources and Prospects." Unpublished manuscript, UCSD, 1995.

World Bank. *China: Regional Disparities.* Washington. DC: World Bank, 1995.
———. *China: Revenue Mobilization and Tax Policy.* Washington, DC: World Bank, 1990.
———. *China 2020: Development Challenges in the New Century.* Washington, DC: World Bank, 1997.
———. *The Chinese Economy: Fighting Inflation, Deepening Reforms.* Washington, DC: World Bank, 1996.
———. *Sharing Rising Incomes: Disparities in China.* Washington DC: World Bank, 1997.
———. *World Development Report, 1991.* Washington, DC: World Bank, 1991.
———. *World Development Report, 1995: Workers in an Integrating World.* New York: Oxford University Press, 1995.
Xinhua News Agency, Beijing, October 4, 1995.
Xu Fengxian, et al. "Diqu jingji fazhan chaju yu weilai duice xuanze" [Regional Development Disparities and Future Policy Options], *Jingji gongzuozhe xuexi ziliao,* no. 47 (1997): 2–26.
Xu Lin. "Gaige kaifang yilai woguo diqu jian jingji fazhan chaju de fenxi" [An Analysis of China's Regional Disparities in Economic Development since the Introduction of Reform]. *Jingji yanjiu cankao* [Reference for Economic Research], no. 414 (January 1994): 18–39.
Yabuki, Sasunne. *A Great Country, Where Is China Going? Nation, Society, and Economy.* Tokyo: Toyu Publisher, 1995.
Yang, Dali. "Patterns of China's Regional Development Strategy." *China Quarterly,* no. 122 (June 1990): 230–57.
Yang Jingchu. "1995–1996 nian minzu diqu jingji shehui xingshi" [Economic and Social Situation in Minority Regions, 1995–1996], In *1995–1996 nian Zhongguo shehui xingshi fenxi yu yuce* [China in 1995–1996: Analysis and Forecast of Social Situation], ed. Jiang Liu, Lu Xueyi, and Jian Tianlun, pp. 212–20. Beijing: Chinese Social Science Press, 1996.
Yang Kaizhong. *Zhongguo quyu fazhan yanjiu* [Study of Regional Development in China]. Beijing: Oceanography Press, 1989.
Yang Qingzhen. "Narrowing the East-West Gaps and Developing the Western Minority-Concentrated Regions." Paper read at International Conference on Coordinated Development Among Regions in China's Economic Reform and Social Development, City University of Hong Kong, December 11–12, 1996.
Yang Weimin. "Diqu jian shouru chaju biandong de shizheng fenxi" [Analysis of the Changes in Regional Income Gaps]. *Jingji yanjiu* [Economic Research], no. 1 (1992): 70–74.
Young, Alwyn. "A Tale of Two Cities: Factor Accumulation and Technical Change in Hong Kong and Singapore." In *NBER Macroeconomics Annual 1992,* ed. Olivier J. Blanchard and Stanley Fischer, pp. 13–54. Cambridge: MIT Press, 1992.
———. "The Tyranny of Numbers: Confronting the Statistical Realities of the East Asian Growth Experience." *Quarterly Journal of Economics* 110 (August 1995): 641–79.
Yuan Gangming. "Diqu jingji chayi yu hongguan jingji bodong" [Regional Disparities and Macroeconomic Instability]. *Jingji yanjiu* [Economic Research], no. 10 (1996): 53.

Zhao, Songqiao. *Geography of China: Environment, Resources, Population and Development.* New York: John Wiley, 1994.

Zhao, Xiaobin. "Spatial Disparities and Economic Development in China, 1953–92: A Comparative Study." *Development and Change* 27, no. 1 (1996).

Zhao, Xiaobin Simon, and Tong S. P. Christopher. "Inequality, Inflation, and Their Impact on China's Investment Environment in the 1990s and Beyond." *Asia Pacific Business Review* 2, no. 3 (1996): 66–100.

Zhu Fengqi et al. *Zhongguo fenpinkun yanjiu* [Research on Poverty in China]. Beijing: China Planning Press, 1996.

Zhu, Min. "The Mechanics and Consequences of China's Revenue Contract System." Unpublished manuscript, World Bank, 1994.

Index

Agriculture
  arable land, 84-85
  employment and, 98-99
  irrigation, 84-85
  mountainous topography, 82-85
  precipitation and, 82-85
  production and, 93
  provincial comparison, 83*t*
  temperature and, 82-84
Anhui
  education, 119
  foreign investment zones, 177
  poverty, 118
Arable land, 84-85

Beijing
  agriculture, 93
  birth rate, 128
  disposable income, 110
  education, 119
  employment, 99
  exports, 105
  foreign investment, 106
  GDP per capita, 46-47, 56-60
  health care provision, 124
  industry, 93-94
  infant mortality, 125
  investment rate, 87
  labor force, 89
  local savings, 86

Beijing *(continued)*
  newspaper readership, 115
  poverty, 116
  service sector, 93-94
  technology, 122
  transportation, 90, 92
  urbanization, 110
  youth dependency, 128
Birth rate, 126*t*, 127-28
Brazil, 7, 28
Budgetary funds, 137-39

Canada
  disparity comparison, 7
  political consequences, 10
Capital accumulation, 154-64
  foreign investment, 155-62, 165
    economic growth rate and, 157-58
    human capital and, 158, 168n.39
    infrastructure and, 158
    market size and, 157
    preferential policy for, 158-62
  GDP per capita and, 86-88
  interregional movement of, 162-64,
    168n.43
  local savings, 86-88, 154-55,
    164-65
Central extractive capacity
  Mao Zedong era, 172-74, 196n.9
  reform era, 183-91

Chinese Communist Party (CCP)
  Deng Xiaoping, 178, 182, 183, 205
  economic inheritance of, 3-4, 171-74
  First Five-Year Plan, 3-4
  Fourth Five-Year Plan, 4
  Fifth Five-Year Plan, 178
  Sixth Five-Year Plan, 178
  Seventh Five-Year Plan, 179
  Eighth Five-Year Plan, 66, 182
  Ninth Five-Year Plan, 5, 182
  Mao Zedong
    coastal/interior relations, 3-4
    economic development, 3-4, 17n.8
    economic policy, 171-74
  See also Political causation
Closed-economy model, 22
Coastal Economic Open Zones
    (CEOZ), 177
Coastal Open Cities (COC), 177
Coastal provinces
  exports, 105-6
  foreign investment, 106-7
  geography, 85, 140n.16
  industry, 3-4, 17n.1, 95, 97-98
  ownership, 103
  policy recommendation, 212-13
  reform era, 174-83, 196n.18
  transportation, 92
  See also specific provinces
Comparative countries, 7
  convergence hypothesis, 27-28
  factor mobility model, 27-28
  GDP per capita, 67-69
Consumption
  private, 112-13, 114f
  public, 136-37
Convergence hypothesis, 5-6, 21-28,
    53, 56
  challenges to, 27-28
  closed-economy model, 22
  comparative countries, 27-28
  export-base model, 22-23
  factor mobility model, 22-28, 38n.6,
    39n.20
  government intervention, 23
  labor migration, 25, 26-27
  neoclassical models, 21-28, 53, 56
  technology, 25-26, 27

Convergence hypothesis (continued)
  vs. political economy hypothesis,
    35-38
Cultural Revolution (1966-76), 172
Customs-Free Zones (CFZ), 177-78

Decentralization policy, 172-74,
    183-91
Deng Xiaoping, 178, 182, 183, 205
Disposable income, 110-12, 141n.42

Economic and Technological
    Development Zones (ETDZ),
    177
Economic causation
  capital accumulation, 154-64
    foreign investment, 155-62, 165
    interregional movement of, 162-64,
      168n.43
    local savings, 154-55, 164-65
  foreign investment, 155-62, 165
    economic growth rate and, 157-58
    human capital and, 158, 168n.39
    infrastructure and, 158
    market size and, 157
    preferential policy for, 158-62
  growth accounting data
    capital input, 145-46, 165n.5,
      232-35
    factor shares, 147, 166n.8, 236-38
    human capital, 146-47
    labor input, 146
    output, 145
  growth accounting method, 144-45,
    165n.2, 228-31
  growth accounting results, 147-53
    capital stock, 147-49, 150t, 151t
    GDP growth, 147-48, 149t, 150t
    human capital, 147, 148t, 149t,
      150-51
    labor capital, 147, 148t, 149-50,
      151t
    other growth sources, 152-53
    technology, 151-52, 153, 167n.30
  overview, 143-44, 164-65
  See also Gross domestic product
    (GDP) per capita; Political
    causation

Economic structure, 92-107, 135-39
  budgetary funds, 137-39
  employment, 94*t*, 98-101
    agriculture, 98-99
    industry, 99
    provincial comparison, 100*t*
    rural, 99-101
  extrabudgetary funds, 137-39
  open-door policy, 105-7
    exports, 105-6, 107*t*
    foreign investment, 106-7
  ownership, 101-5
    non-state sector, 101, 103, 105
    private sector, 101
    state sector, 101, 103-5
  production, 93-98
    agriculture, 93
    industry, 93-98
    provincial comparison tables, 94,
      96, 97
    rural industry, 95, 97
    service sector, 93-94
Education, 118-21
Eighth Five-Year Plan, 66, 182
Employment structure, 94*t*, 98-101
  agriculture, 98-99
  industry, 99
  provincial comparison, 100*t*
  rural, 99-101
Ethics
  Kaldor-Hicks criterion, 8-9
  Pareto criterion, 8-9
  Rawls criterion, 9
  regional development and, 9,
    20n.32
  Verkhovensky criterion, 9
Ethnicity
  GDP per capita, 63-67
  Haixi Mongolian, 64
  Han, 63, 64, 85-86
  Miao Autonomous Prefecture of
    Yunnan, 64
  minority nationality areas, 63-67,
    85-86
  as resource, 85-86
  Tibetan Autonomous Prefecture of
    Qinghai, 64
  Wenshan Zhuang, 64

Exports
  coastal provinces, 105-6
  export-base model, 22-23
  open-door policy, 105-6, 107*t*
Extrabudgetary funds, 137-39

Factor mobility model, 22-28, 38n.6,
    39n.20
  comparative countries, 27-28
  government intervention, 23
  labor migration, 25, 26-27
  policy recommendation, 215-16
  technology, 25-26, 27
Fifth Five-Year Plan, 178
First Five-Year Plan, 3-4
Foreign investment
  economic causation and, 155-62, 165
    economic growth rate, 157-58
    human capital, 158, 168n.39
    infrastructure, 158
    market size, 157
    preferential policy, 158-62
  open-door policy, 106-7
  zones
    Coastal Economic Open Zones
      (CEOZ), 177
    Coastal Open Cities (COC), 177
    Customs-Free Zones (CFZ), 177-78
    Economic and Technological
      Development Zones (ETDZ),
      177
    Special Economic Zones (SEZ),
      177
Fourth Five-Year Plan, 4
France, 7
Fujian
  disposable income, 112
  education, 119
  employment, 98
  exports, 105
  foreign investment, 106
  foreign investment zones, 177
  GDP per capita, 47, 50, 53
  health care provision, 124
  industry, 93, 95, 98
  ownership, 101, 103
  technology, 122
  transportation, 92

Fujian *(continued)*
   youth dependency, 128

Gansu
   disposable income, 112
   education, 119
   employment, 99
   foreign investment, 106
   GDP per capita, 53
   geography, 83, 84
   industry, 93, 95, 97-98
   minority nationalities, 64, 67
   ownership, 103
   poverty, 116
   transportation, 90
GDP per capita. *See* Gross domestic
      product (GDP) per capita
Geography, 81-85, 140n.16
   arable land, 84-85
   coastal vs. interior, 85, 140n.16
   Gansu, 83, 84
   Guangdong, 82
   Guizhou, 84
   Hainan, 82
   Heilongjiang, 82, 84-85
   Inner Mongolia, 83
   irrigation, 84-85
   mountainous topography, 82-85
   Ningxia, 84
   precipitation and, 82-85
   provincial comparison, 83*t*
   Qinghai, 82, 84
   Shaanxi, 84
   Shanghai, 84
   temperature and, 82-84
   Xinjiang, 84
   Zhejiang, 82
Government intervention. *See* Political
      causation
Gradient theory, 175, 179, 212
Great Britain
   disparity comparison, 7
   political consequences, 10
Great Leap Forward (1958-60), 172
Gross domestic product (GDP) per
      capita
   Beijing, 46-47, 56-60
   capital accumulation and, 86-88

Gross domestic product (GDP) per
      capita *(continued)*
   comparative countries, 67-69
   comparative tables, 48, 49, 51, 52,
      54, 55, 57, 59, 61, 62, 63, 65, 68
   Fujian, 47, 50, 53
   Gansu, 53
   Guangdong, 50, 53, 60-63
   Guizhou, 47-50, 58, 60-63
   Hebei, 50
   Jiangsu, 50, 53
   Liaoning, 47, 50
   as measurement indicator, 42-43, 45,
      74n.1, 75n.2, 78-80
   minority nationality areas, 63-67
   1978, 47-50
   1978-1994, 50-60
   1994, 47-50
   Ningxia, 53
   Qinghai, 52, 53
   Shandong, 53
   Shanghai, 46-47, 48-49, 50, 56-60
   Sichuan, 50
   Tianjin, 46-47, 56-60
   Xinjiang, 50
   Zhejiang, 50, 53
   See also Economic causation;
      Multidimensional facets
Growth accounting
   data
      capital input, 145-46, 165n.5,
         232-35
      factor shares, 147, 166n.8, 236-38
      human capital, 146-47
      labor input, 146
      output, 145
   method of, 144-45, 165n.2, 228-31
   results, 147-53
      capital stock and, 147-49, 150*t*,
         151*t*
      GDP growth, 147-48, 149*t*, 150*t*
      human capital and, 147, 148*t*, 149*t*,
         150-51
      labor capital and, 147, 148*t*,
         149-50, 151*t*
      other growth sources, 152-53
      technology and, 151-52, 153,
         167n.30

Guangdong
  disposable income, 110
  education, 119
  employment, 99-100
  exports, 105, 106
  foreign investment, 106
  foreign investment zones, 177, 178
  GDP per capita, 50, 53, 60-63
  geography, 82
  health care provision, 124
  industry, 93, 95, 97
  infant mortality, 125
  labor force, 89
  ownership, 101, 103
  poverty, 116, 214
  technology, 122, 123
  transportation, 90, 92
  youth dependency, 128
Guangxi
  disposable income, 112
  employment, 100
  health care provision, 124
  industry, 93, 97-98
  minority nationalities, 64, 85
  ownership, 103
  technology, 122
  transportation, 92
  youth dependency, 128
Guizhou
  birth rate, 128
  disposable income, 110, 112
  education, 119
  employment, 100
  foreign investment, 106
  GDP per capita, 47-50, 58, 60-63
  geography, 84
  health care provision, 124, 125
  industry, 93, 97-98
  investment rate, 87, 88
  labor force, 89
  local savings, 86
  minority nationalities, 64, 66-67
  newspaper readership, 116
  ownership, 103
  poverty, 116
  technology, 122
  telephone ownership, 116
  television ownership, 113

Guizhou *(continued)*
  transportation, 90
  youth dependency, 128

Hainan
  education, 119
  employment, 98, 99
  foreign investment, 106
  foreign investment zones, 178
  geography, 82
  industry, 95, 97, 98
  labor force, 89
  ownership, 101, 103
  poverty, 214
  service sector, 93
  technology, 123
  television ownership, 113
  transportation, 90, 92
  youth dependency, 128
Health, 124-28
  birth rate, 126t, 127-28
  care provision, 124-25, 126t
  infant mortality, 125-27
  life expectancy, 126-27
  youth dependency, 126t, 128
Hebei
  education, 119
  employment, 98
  GDP per capita, 50
  infant mortality, 125
  ownership, 103
  poverty, 118, 214
  telephone ownership, 116
  transportation, 90, 92
Heilongjiang
  disposable income, 110
  education, 119
  employment, 99, 100
  foreign investment zones, 177
  geography, 82, 84-85
  industry, 95
  investment rate, 88
  ownership, 103
  youth dependency, 128
Henan
  ownership, 103
  poverty, 116, 118
  transportation, 90, 92

Hirschman, Albert, 28-35
Hubei
  foreign investment zones, 177
  industry, 93
  minority nationalities, 64, 67
  transportation, 90, 92
Human welfare, 107-28
  disposable income, 110-12,
      141n.42
  education, 118-21
  health, 124-28
    birth rate, 126t, 127-28
    care provision, 124-25, 126t
    infant mortality, 125-27
    life expectancy, 126-27
    youth dependency, 126t, 128
  information access, 113, 115-16
    newspaper readership, 115-16
    telephone ownership, 115t, 116
    television ownership, 113, 115
  poverty, 116-18, 141n.43
  private consumption, 112-13, 114f
  technology, 121-24
  urbanization, 108-10
Hunan
  education, 119
  industry, 93
  infant mortality, 125
  minority nationalities, 64
  transportation, 90, 92

India
  disparity comparison, 7
  political consequences, 10
Indonesia, 7
Industry
  coastal/interior comparison, 3-4,
      17n.1
  employment and, 99
  production and, 93-98
  rural, 95, 97
Infant mortality, 125-27
Information
  access to, 113, 115-16
    newspaper readership, 115-16
    telephone ownership, 115t, 116
    television ownership, 113, 115
  labor force migration, 25

Infrastructure
  foreign investment and, 158
  policy recommendations, 215
  transportation
    provincial comparison, 91t
    railroads, 90-92
    roads, 90-92
    waterways, 89-92
Inner Mongolia
  disposable income, 110
  education, 119
  employment, 100
  foreign investment, 106
  geography, 83
  health care provision, 124
  industry, 93, 97-98
  minority nationalities, 64, 85
  ownership, 103
  poverty, 116
  transportation, 90
Inverted U-curve hypothesis, 28-35
  challenges to, 32-35
  government intervention, 31-32,
      34-35
  labor migration, 30
  market forces, 33-35
  spread/backwash effects, 29-35,
      39n.28, 40n.44
  trickle down/polarization effects, 29
  vs. political economy hypothesis,
      35-38
  Williamson law, 32-35
Investment
  foreign, 155-62, 165
    economic growth rate and, 157-58
    human capital and, 158, 168n.39
    infrastructure and, 158
    market size and, 157
    open-door policy, 106-7
    preferential policy for, 158-62
  local savings, 86-88, 154-55, 164-65
Irrigation, 84-85
Italy
  disparity comparison, 7
  political consequences, 10

Jiangsu
  birth rate, 128

Jiangsu *(continued)*
  disposable income, 112
  education, 119
  employment, 99-100
  exports, 105
  foreign investment zones, 178
  GDP per capita, 50, 53
  health care provision, 124
  industry, 93, 95, 97
  infant mortality, 125
  ownership, 101, 103
  poverty, 214
  technology, 122, 123
  transportation, 90, 92
Jiangxi
  industry, 93
  infant mortality, 125
  ownership, 103
  transportation, 92
Jilin
  disposable income, 110
  education, 119
  employment, 99, 100
  foreign investment zones, 177
  minority nationalities, 64
  ownership, 103
  transportation, 90
  youth dependency, 128

Kaldor-Hicks criterion, 8-9

Labor force migration
  convergence hypothesis, 25, 26-27
  factor mobility model, 25, 26-27
    information costs, 25
    psychic costs, 25
    retraining costs, 25
    transportation costs, 25
  inverted U-curve hypothesis, 30
Labor force resource, 88-89
Liaoning
  agriculture, 93
  disposable income, 110
  employment, 99
  exports, 105
  foreign investment zones, 177, 178
  GDP per capita, 47, 50
  industry, 93, 95

Liaoning *(continued)*
  infant mortality, 125
  transportation, 90, 92
  youth dependency, 128
Life expectancy, 126-27
Local savings, 86-88, 154-55, 164-65

Manchuria, 3
Mao Zedong
  coastal/interior relations, 3-4
  economic development, 3-4, 17n.8
  economic policy, 171-74
Market forces
  government relations and, 209-10
  inverted U-curve hypothesis, 33-35
  political economy hypothesis, 35
  spread/backwash effects, 33-35
Measurement, regional disparity, 41-47
  absolute vs. relative, 43-44, 56-60,
    62, 76n.21, 129
  coefficient of variation (CV), 43-44,
    56-58, 75n.4
  dimensions, 42
  diversity, 41-42
  indicators, 42-43, 74n.1, 75n.2
  methods, 43-44, 75n.4
  price index, 45
  provincial unit analysis, 45-47,
    76n.10
  standard deviation (SD), 43, 58-60,
    75n.4, 129
Mexico
  disparity comparison, 7
  political consequences, 10-11
Minority nationality areas, 63-67,
    85-86
  See also Ethnicity
Mountainous topography, 82-85
Mrydal, Gunnar, 28-35
Multidimensional facets
  economic structure, 92-107, 135-39
    budgetary funds, 137-39
    employment, 94*t*, 98-101
    exports, 105-6, 107*t*
    extrabudgetary funds, 137-39
    foreign investment, 106-7
    open-door policy, 105-7
    ownership, 101-5

Multidimensional facets
  economic structure *(continued)*
    production, 93-98
  human welfare, 107-28
    disposable income, 110-12, 141n.42
    education, 118-21
    health, 124-28
    information access, 113, 115-16
    poverty, 116-18, 141n.43
    private consumption, 112-13, 114*f*
    technology, 121-24
    urbanization, 108-10
  measurement and, 43, 79, 129
  overview, 128-39
    table, 130-32
  resources, 81-92, 134-35
    capital accumulation, 86-88
    ethnicity, 85-86
    geography, 81-85, 140n.16
    infrastructure, 89-92
    labor force, 88-89
  See also Economic causation; Gross
      domestic product (GDP) per
      capita; Policy
      recommendations; Political
      causation

Neoclassical models, 21-28, 53, 56
  closed-economy model, 22
  export-base model, 22-23
  factor mobility model, 22-28, 38n.6,
    39n.20
    comparative countries, 27-28
    government intervention, 23
    labor migration, 25, 26-27
    technology, 25-26, 27
Newspaper readership, 115-16
Nigeria, 10
Ningxia
  employment, 100
  foreign investment, 106
  GDP per capita, 53
  geography, 84
  health care provision, 124
  industry, 93, 95, 97-98
  minority nationalities, 64, 85
  ownership, 103
  poverty, 116

Ningxia *(continued)*
  technology, 122, 123
  transportation, 90
Ninth Five-Year Plan, 5, 182

Open-door policy, 105-7
  exports, 105-6, 107*t*
  foreign investment, 106-7
Ownership structure, 101-5
  non-state sector, 101, 103, 105
  private sector, 101
  state sector, 101, 103-5

Papua New Guinea, 10
Pareto criterion, 8-9
Policy recommendations
  actions
    coastal bias removal, 212-13
    factor mobility facilitation, 215-16
    infrastructure improvement, 215
    interregional fiscal transfer, 213
    poverty eradication, 213-14
    public service improvement, 214-15
  disparity challenges, 199-202
    gap increase, 199
    gap size, 199
    income, 200-201
    multidimensionality facet, 199-200
    political consequences, 202
    urban/rural, 200-201, 217n.5
  empowerment, 216-17
  equity/efficiency goal, 207-9
    least-difference criterion, 208-9
    maximin criterion, 207, 208
    minimax criterion, 207, 208
    ratio criterion, 207, 208
  inequality inevitability dispute, 203-7
  relationship issues
    central/provincial government,
      210-11
    market/government, 209-10
    policy/institutional change, 211-12
Political causation
  central extractive capacity
    Mao Zedong era, 172-74, 196n.9
    reform era, 183-91
  decentralization policy, 172-74,
    183-91

Political causation *(continued)*
  foreign investment zones
    Coastal Economic Open Zones
      (CEOZ), 177
    Coastal Open Cities (COC), 177
    Customs-Free Zones (CFZ), 177-78
    Economic and Technological
      Development Zones (ETDZ),
      177
    Special Economic Zones (SEZ),
      177
  Mao Zedong era, 171-74
    central extractive capacity, 172-74,
      196n.9
    decentralization policy, 172-74
  overview, 5, 6-7, 9-11, 19n.22,
    169-71, 193-95
  reform era, 174-83
    capital construction, 175-77,
      196n.16
    central extractive capacity, 183-91
    coastal provinces, 174-83, 196n.18
    foreign investment zones, 177-78,
      180-81*t*
    gradient theory, 175, 179, 212
    trickle-down theory, 170, 174,
      212-13
  resource disparities, 191-93, 198n.41
  theory
    convergence hypothesis, 23
    factor mobility model, 23
    gradient, 175, 179, 212
    inverted U-curve hypothesis,
      31-32, 34-35
    political economy hypothesis, 35-38
    trickle-down, 170, 174, 212-13
  See also Economic causation
Political economy hypothesis, 35-38
  government intervention, 35-37
  market forces, 35
Poverty, 116-18, 141n.43, 213-14
Precipitation, 82-85
Production structure, 93-98
  agriculture, 93
  industry, 93-98
  provincial comparison tables, 94, 96,
    97
  rural industry, 95, 97

Production structure *(continued)*
  service sector, 93-94
Provisions for the Encouragement of
  Foreign Investment (1986), 156

Qinghai
  birth rate, 128
  education, 119
  employment, 100
  foreign investment, 106
  GDP per capita, 52, 53
  geography, 82, 84
  industry, 93, 95, 97-98
  minority nationalities, 64, 66-67
  ownership, 101, 103
  technology, 122, 123
  transportation, 90
  urbanization, 110

Railroads, 90-92
Rawls criterion, 9
Regional disparity, overview
  comparative countries, 7
  debate of, 5-7
    causation factors, 5, 6
    convergence vs. divergence, 5-6
    government intervention, 5, 6-7,
      19n.22
    tolerability vs. excessiveness, 5, 6
  economic development, 3-5,
    17n.8
  industry, 3-4
  issue defined, 3-5
  significance of, 7-11
    economic growth, 8, 11, 19n.25
    ethical, 8-9, 11
    political, 9-11
  See also Economic causation;
    Multidimensional facets; Policy
    recommendations; Political
    causation; Theoretical
    framework
Regional disparity, post-1978 trends
  data, 223-26
  GDP per capita
    Beijing, 46-47, 56-60
    capital accumulation, 86-88
    comparative countries, 67-69

Regional disparity, post-1978 trends
   data *(continued)*
      comparative tables, 48, 49, 51, 52,
         54, 55, 57, 59, 61, 62, 63, 65,
         68
      Fujian, 47, 50, 53
      Gansu, 53
      Guangdong, 50, 53, 60-63
      Guizhou, 47-50, 58, 60-63
      Hebei, 50
      Jiangsu, 50, 53
      Liaoning, 47, 50
      as measurement indicator, 42-43,
         45, 74n.1, 75n.2, 78-80
      minority nationality areas, 63-67
      1978, 47-50
      1978-1994, 50-60
      1994, 47-50
      Ningxia, 53
      Qinghai, 52, 53
      Shandong, 53
      Shanghai, 46-47, 48-49, 50, 56-60
      Sichuan, 50
      Tianjin, 46-47, 56-60
      Xinjiang, 50
      Zhejiang, 50, 53
   measurement, 41-47
      absolute vs. relative, 43-44, 56-60,
         62, 76n.21, 129
      coefficient of variation (CV),
         43-44, 56-58, 75n.4
      dimensions, 42
      diversity, 41-42
      GDP per capita, 42-43, 45, 74n.1,
         75n.2
      indicators, 42-43, 74n.1, 75n.2
      methods, 43-44, 75n.4
      as multidimensional, 43, 79, 129
      price index, 45
      provincial unit analysis, 45-47,
         76n.10
      standard deviation (SD), 43, 58-60,
         75n.4, 129
   subjective indicators, 69-74
Resources, 81-92, 134-35
   capital accumulation, 154-64
      foreign investment, 106-7, 155-62,
         165

Resources *(continued)*
      GDP per capita and, 86-88
      interregional movement of, 162-64,
         168n.43
      local savings, 86-88, 154-55,
         164-65
   ethnicity, 85-86
   geography, 81-85, 140n.16
      arable land, 84-85
      coastal vs. interior, 85, 140n.16
      Gansu, 83, 84
      Guangdong, 82
      Guizhou, 84
      Hainan, 82
      Heilongjiang, 82, 84-85
      Inner Mongolia, 83
      irrigation, 84-85
      mountainous topography, 82-85
      Ningxia, 84
      precipitation and, 82-85
      provincial comparison, 83*t*
      Qinghai, 82, 84
      Shaanxi, 84
      Shanghai, 84
      temperature and, 82-84
      Xinjiang, 84
      Zhejiang, 82
   infrastructure, 89-92, 158, 215
   labor force, 88-89
   transportation
      provincial comparison, 91*t*
      railroads, 90-92
      roads, 90-92
      waterways, 89-92
Roads, 90-92
Rural areas
   disposable income, 110-12
   employment, 99-101
   industry, 95, 97
   policy recommendation, 200-201,
      217n.5
Rwanda, 10

Savings, local, 86-88, 154-55, 164-65
Service sector
   employment and, 99
   production and, 93-94
Seventh Five-Year Plan, 179

Shaanxi
  employment, 100
  foreign investment, 106
  geography, 84
  industry, 93, 97-98
  infant mortality, 125
  ownership, 103
  technology, 122
Shandong
  birth rate, 128
  disposable income, 112
  employment, 98
  exports, 105
  foreign investment zones, 178
  GDP per capita, 53
  health care provision, 124
  industry, 93, 95, 97
  infant mortality, 125
  ownership, 103
  poverty, 118, 214
  technology, 122, 123
  telephone ownership, 116
  transportation, 90, 92
Shanghai
  agriculture, 93
  birth rate, 128
  disposable income, 110, 112
  economic development, 4
  education, 120
  employment, 98, 99
  exports, 105
  foreign investment, 106
  foreign investment zones, 177, 178
  GDP per capita, 46-47, 48-49, 50,
    56-60
  geography, 84
  health care provision, 124
  industry, 93-94
  infant mortality, 125
  investment rate, 88
  newspaper readership, 116
  ownership, 101, 103
  poverty, 116
  service sector, 93
  technology, 122
  telephone ownership, 116
  television ownership, 113
  transportation, 90, 92

Shanghai (continued)
  urbanization, 110
  youth dependency, 128
Shanxi
  education, 119
  employment, 99
  foreign investment, 106
  industry, 95, 97-98
  ownership, 103
  poverty, 116
  transportation, 90, 92
Sichuan
  foreign investment zones, 177
  GDP per capita, 50
  industry, 93, 97-98
  minority nationalities, 64, 67
  poverty, 118
Sixth Five-Year Plan, 178
Soviet Union, 10
Special Economic Zones (SEZ), 177
Spread/backwash effects, 29-35,
    39n.28, 40n.44
  challenges to, 32-35
  government intervention, 31-32, 34-35
  labor migration, 30
  market forces, 33-35
  Williamson law, 32-35

Technology
  convergence hypothesis, 25-26, 27
  factor mobility model, 25-26, 27
  growth accounting and, 151-52, 153,
    167n.30
  human welfare and, 121-24
Telephone ownership, 115t, 116
Television ownership, 113, 115
Temperature, 82-84
Theoretical framework
  convergence hypothesis, 5-6, 21-28,
    53, 56
    challenges to, 27-28
    closed-economy model, 22
    comparative countries, 27-28
    export-base model, 22-23
    factor mobility model, 22-28,
      38n.6, 39n.20
    government intervention, 23
    labor migration, 25, 26-27

Theoretical framework *(continued)*
  neoclassical models, 21-28, 53, 56
  technology, 25-26, 27
 inverted U-curve hypothesis, 28-35
  challenges to, 32-35
  government intervention, 31-32,
   34-35
  labor migration, 30
  market forces, 33-35
  spread/backwash effects, 29-35,
   39n.28, 40n.44
  trickle down/polarization effects, 29
  Williamson law, 32-35
 political economy hypothesis, 35-38
  government intervention, 35-37
  market forces, 35
Third Front, 4, 17n.6
Tianjin
 agriculture, 93
 birth rate, 128
 disposable income, 110, 112
 employment, 99
 exports, 105
 foreign investment, 106
 foreign investment zones, 178
 GDP per capita, 46-47, 56-60
 industry, 93
 infant mortality, 125
 newspaper readership, 116
 ownership, 103
 poverty, 116
 service sector, 93
 technology, 122
 transportation, 90, 92
 urbanization, 110
Tibet
 agriculture, 93
 birth rate, 128
 disposable income, 110
 education, 119, 120
 employment, 98, 99, 100
 foreign investment, 106
 health care provision, 124
 industry, 93, 97-98
 infant mortality, 125, 128
 labor force, 89
 life expectancy, 126
 minority nationalities, 64, 85-86

Tibet *(continued)*
 ownership, 103
 technology, 122
 television ownership, 113
 transportation, 90
 youth dependency, 128
Transportation
 labor force migration, 25
 provincial comparison, 91*t*
 railroads, 90-92
 roads, 90-92
 waterways, 89-92
Trickle down/polarization effects, 29
Trickle-down theory, 170, 174, 212-13

UNDP Human Development Report,
 10-11
United States, disparity comparison, 7,
 27-28
Urbanization, 108-10

Verkhovensky criterion, 9

Waterways, 89-92
Williamson, Jeffrey, 32-35
World Bank, 147, 150, 201

Xinjiang
 birth rate, 128
 employment, 99, 100
 foreign investment, 106
 GDP per capita, 50
 geography, 84
 health care provision, 124
 industry, 93, 97-98
 labor force, 89
 minority nationalities, 64, 85
 ownership, 103
 technology, 122, 123
 transportation, 90
 urbanization, 110

Youth dependency, 126*t*, 128
Yugoslavia, 10
Yunnan
 birth rate, 128
 disposable income, 110, 112
 education, 119
 employment, 98, 99, 100

Yunnan *(continued)*
  foreign investment, 106
  health care provision, 125
  industry, 93, 95, 97-98
  minority nationalities, 64, 66-67
  ownership, 103
  poverty, 116
  technology, 122
  television ownership, 113
  transportation, 90
  urbanization, 110
  youth dependency, 128

Zaire, 10
Zhejiang
  birth rate, 128

Zhejiang *(continued)*
  education, 119
  employment, 99-100
  exports, 105
  foreign investment zones, 178
  GDP per capita, 50, 53
  geography, 82
  health care provision, 124
  industry, 93, 95, 97
  infant mortality, 125
  ownership, 101, 103
  poverty, 214
  technology, 122, 123
  transportation, 90, 92
  urbanization, 110
  youth dependency, 128

Wang Shaoguang, associate professor of political science at Yale University, has authored three books: *Failure of Charisma: The Cultural Revolution in Wuhan* (Oxford, 1995), *Rationality and Madness: The Mass in the Chinese Cultural Revolution* (in Chinese, Oxford, 1993), and *Challenging the Market Myth: The Role of the State in Economic Transition* (in Chinese, Oxford, 1997), and numerous articles both in English and Chinese. He has also co-authored three books: *A Study of China's State Capacity* (in Chinese, Oxford, 1994), *Regional Disparities in China* (in Chinese, Liaoning People's Press, 1996), and *Challenges Faced by Jiang Zemin* (in Chinese, Mirror, 1996).

Hu Angang, a senior fellow at the Chinese Academy of Science, has authored and co-authored sixteen books and countless articles. One of the most influential economists in contemporary China, he has advised the Chinese government on such issues as fiscal policy, regional policy, policy on special economic zones, and the like.

WIDENER UNIVERSITY
WOLFGRAM
LIBRARY
CHESTER, PA